# Traditional

# Chinese

# Humor

## A STUDY IN

## Art and

## Literature

# Traditional Chinese Humor

## A STUDY IN

## Art and Literature

---

## Henry W. Wells

*Indiana University Press*

**BLOOMINGTON**

**LONDON**

Library of Congress catalog card number: 78-143248
ISBN: 253-18920-9

Manufactured in the United States of America

Published in Canada by Fitzhenry & Whiteside Limited,
Don Mills, Ontario

# Contents

---

# Illustrations

---

# Preface

---

I<small>N A BOOK ON SO ELUSIVE A SUBJECT AS THE SENSE OF</small> humor some short comment or even apology may be desired as preface or foreword. In the present instance the prime factor is that the book deals with the Chinese, a people undeniably possessing a deep-seated humor. They smile in their own way yet without too great an effort the world smiles with them. We should recall that much of their most admired poetry has strong humorous properties, even when present in overtones. For centuries their theatre has been marked by a peculiar gusto and gaiety. Their fiction incorporates to an exceptional degree a wide range of comedy, from blithe fantasy to dry and insinuating observations on life. Their art abounds in the fantastic or even in the bizarre. Their religious and philosophical visions of life have been distinctly favorable to humor. The Taoist or Buddhist was disciplined to retire from the world, or at least from the heat of its contentions, nevertheless placing himself in a position from which he might smile at what appeared to him the human comedy. The complacent Confucian possessed singularly firm guidelines for good conduct and good manners, finding deviations in many cases amusing. Whoever makes even the most casual approach to traditional Chinese civilization must be struck by these pervasive qualities. Surely, humor is one of its finest flowers.

It is not, of course, to be presumed that all pages of Chinese literature are intended to evoke smiles or that all Chinese works of art are in any reasonable sense of the word humorous. Excessive claims in this regard should be avoided. Yet the vein unquestionably runs through a surprisingly large part of Chinese imaginative productions. These conditions have, doubtless, been observed but it will, I think, be admitted that they have too seldom been closely examined. This book proposes at least an introduction to the subject.

Acknowledgment must be made of help and advice given me by many scholars not only in Chinese fields themselves but in the closely related Japanese and Indian as well. It would have been a rather grim experience to have laughed alone. My dependence on friends and predecessors in this area has been all the greater in that I myself have concentrated my thoughts on Asian matters only after retirement from a considerable period of teaching and writing on the ample fields of British, American, and comparative literatures, with attention to both the medieval and the modern. The half-dozen books which I have written on Asian topics have all appeared since the termination of my conventional teaching career. I can only hope that my too belated concentration on these topics and a consequent deficiency in linguistic study are in some respects offset by these relatively extended perspectives. As this book shows, I have given special attention to making translations of my own into English verse. I have leaned heavily on the works of Osvald Siren, Bernhard Karlgren, Arthur Waley, and, occasionally, even on the much earlier researches of Herbert Giles. Grateful acknowledgment is made to Alfred A. Knopf for permission to quote from *Translations from the Chinese* by Arthur Waley (1941). For cordial assistance from William Hung, Wu-chi Liu, Shih Shun Liu, Friedrich Bischoff, James Crump, C. T. Hsia, and far too many scholars to mention here I am most grateful. To museums, both here and abroad, I am also thankful for substantial aid, especially in the preparation of my chapter dealing with the fine arts. Perhaps I may appreciate such assistance all the more, since for many years I have myself served as a museum curator. Finally, I am especially indebted to the University of South Carolina Press for use in this book of my verse translations that appeared in my anthology, *Ancient Poetry from China, India, and Japan.* Sources of translations other than my own are indicated in the notes.

All such comments must be brief. Just as a long introduction to a jest is especially odious, an extended or formal preface to a book on humor would be signally misplaced. Some preface is required, for humor is a singularly personal commodity, but required also to be brief. I trust the reader will wish to hasten into what I take to be the unusually attractive fields that comprise the subject-matter of this introductory study.

HENRY W. WELLS

*September, 1970*

*Traditional*

*Chinese*

*Humor*

A STUDY IN

*Art and*

*Literature*

*1*

———

## HUMOR IN

## ART

\*

IN COMMENTING ON THE SENSE OF HUMOR REVEALED in Chinese art the meaning of the word art is less elusive than that of humor. One term is more concrete, the other more abstract. To begin with, in the following pages certain arts will be considered and others dismissed. There will be little or no reference to music or architecture, though music is unquestionably capable of a singularly delightful expression of humor and Chinese architecture in particular is rich in caprice and fantasy. Attention will be virtually confined to the representational arts of painting and figure sculpture. If the representation of dragons is included, this, too, may be regarded as legitimate matter, since there is unquestionably a sense in which the ancient Chinese believed in the existence of dragons, though they might not dogmatize as to just what a dragon's physiognomy need be.

Humor, to repeat, is the more elusive term. Though no rigid definition will be insisted on, a reasonable understanding of the word as used here is obviously required, especially since it is popularly used with so many different connotations. For example, the present meaning differs radically from that employed by George Kao in his anthology, *Chinese Wit and Humor*. This editor offers no distinctions between wit and humor. Perhaps the many brief annecdotes that he selects, as a rule having a didactic flavor, he considers wit. Few persons will care to quarrel with this use of the term. But the anthology contains long selections that would naturally be described as satire or invective and others that seem a species of realism or of a merely pleasant fantasy. Possibly no more than a tenth of the book has the quality here understood as humor.

Of course no one should be so humorless as to propose a rigid definition of humor. A reasonably cogent description is all that is required. Humor, then, is the quality of thought that imagines a pleasing incongruity. It is better defined by physical manifestations than in strictly intellectual terms. A smile or a laugh provides a better sign than any pedantic definition. Yet here, particularly where traditional Chinese culture is considered, it may be remarked that some degree of sophistication is presumed. Humor may indeed at times be childlike but never childish. Children smile or laugh when something pleases them. Their laughter may have little to do with what the mature person regards as understanding or intelligence. Again, the cruder forms of hilarity, the exuberant expressions of coarse or excessively simple-minded people, do not constitute humor in the present sense. The word has had an eventful history. Humor is today generally understood as more imaginative than eccentric. By the Elizabethans, on the contrary, the word was often employed to mean mere eccentricity or a purposeless overflow of misdirected spirit, an irrationality akin to intoxication. This is not intended now, though strong liquor was consumed and praised by many of the illustrious humorists considered in these pages. Humor as outlined here ranges from the macabre to the highly refined, from burly outspokenness with freedom from inhibition to subtle and delicate understatement, from extravagance to intimation. It may be tart but never quite acidulous. It flourishes in the arts but extends beyond them, a mood readily superimposed upon the aesthetic experience. It presumes a moment of happiness and a sense of well-being. A clown may have a sorry fall but the audience takes pleasure in it. As will in due time be observed, the Chinese, like other people, occasionally exhibit a distinctly cruel humor. But this is not as a rule present in the items about to be considered. The comic spirit as here understood does not descend to mere farce any more than it rises to righteous indignation or nurses hate in any form. Its incongruities are not conceived in strictly moral terms. It floats serenely above the storm clouds of downright propaganda. It takes positive pleasure in contemplating life's unreasonableness. Perhaps at another time and place faults detected by the humorist may be severely rebuked and amended but humor as here conceived observes fallibility and reacts with amusement.

So much for the more general point of view. More narrowly, the inquiry is into the particular flavor of traditional Chinese humor. Presumably this differs in some respects from that of other lands and times, presumably even from whatever sense of humor exists even in China today under Communism. Here some questions of a virtually metaphysical nature arise. There is no safe presumption that any man today recaptures the total sensibility of any Chinese artist or writer of early times. Above all, in so elusive a pursuit as that now proposed our thought, no matter how scrupulously pursued, is a compromise between the ancients and ourselves. The scholar is not the dilettante. The latter reports only his own spontaneous reactions to works created in a distant past; the former, if true to his profession, will on the one hand admit that he must see all things to some degree through his own eyes but on the other hand will make every effort possible to arrive at the point of view of the creators from whose hands the classical works have sprung. There is no doubt that much that has seemed comic to one age may seem tragic to another and that the converse of this holds equally true. A statue of a green-faced god of the underworld, which may appear thoroughly comic to an intelligent person today, nevertheless suggested only terror or high dignity to the Chinese artist who created it. Time on the whole relaxes tensions. Animal statuary that seems primitive, awkward, naive, comic to a modern may have been viewed in a thoroughly serious light when made. Again, many Chinese of earlier times unquestionably laughed at spectacles that would be revolting and even horrifying to most moderns. Conventions give symbolic meanings that change radically and are not readily construed from a psychological point of view. How does the modern viewer distinguish, for example, between a benign and a malign dragon? What are the meanings of certain gestures in a dance? Will not one viewer find a figure truly noble which another finds absurdly pompous? Who can thread his way without occasionally stumbling in these twilights of the spirit? Everyone is aware that especially when joking or humor is concerned even the most sensitive persons may in social life find themselves wholly mistaken and sadly embarrassed. A remark that is facetiously intended may be taken as an offense or an observation that is meant seriously construed as humorous. Some works present so great a complexity that a virtual allegory is created, one level to be taken as serious, another as comic. One of the greatest Chinese novels, *Monkey*, at least approaches this condition.

These are treacherous paths, leading through forests quite as dangerous for the interpreter as they are delightful. The attempt is made here to see through the eyes of the ancients. Yet choices are made. Attention is given more often to works that have retained undoubted forcefulness as humor than those where the smile has faded. The conclusion is that Chinese humor has lasted surprisingly well, possibly at times even seasoned to richer meanings with the years.

Some further generalizations have importance where humor in the fine arts is seen beside that contained in words. Small justification exists for the view that strictly the same attitudes are expressed in any two media of expression. Within the realm of literature itself, for example, traditional Chinese poetry is singularly chaste when placed beside the often erotic quality of Chinese story-telling. One might almost presume the two genres to proceed from two distinct cultures. Nevertheless by and large, a general accord in any culture may be presumed between two arts when viewed with sufficient breadth. This statement holds especially valid for China when attention is restricted to the expression of the upper class as distinguished from that of the humble. Relatively little folk art survives from earlier centuries. Only a comparatively small and favored minority, of course, were literate. Painting as preserved to us remained largely in the hands of gentlemen or a sophisticated class of professionals. Sculpture, though less of an aristocratic art, was still primarily for the privileged. Even lyric poetry, as represented above all by *The Book of Songs*, though no doubt heard more often than read, became, especially as time advanced, the prized possession of the scholar class. Here what was born as folk poetry became the treasured possession of the literati. There seems to have been a well-marked distinction between folk-music and art-music. Both forms of music have now largely disappeared through the attrition of time. The poems, narratives, paintings, and the sculpture at least to a far more substantial degree remain with us. Hence it is to them that the cultural historian and the philosopher turn with some confidence of reward. It is here assumed that at least in broad and general terms the sentiments and ideas expressed in the fine arts accord with those voiced in literature.

Whether these are more clearly expressed to us in one or in another medium is a question presumed unanswerable, though some profit may be gained from brief reflections and comparisons in this general field. The fine arts enjoy an advantage that may or may not be misleading. Although colors fade and silk disintegrates, stone chips and wood decays, work in the fine arts enjoys a peculiar power of survival. Words notoriously shift their meanings as generations pass. Most intellectuals throughout the world who are at all cognizant of ancient China unfortunately know its literature chiefly or wholly through translation. This is inevitably to see through a glass darkly. Our sensuous apprehensions would seem to encourage us to consider the fine arts as providing the safest testimony.

But what, more seriously, are the facts of the case? A picture may in reality be quite as elusive as a poem. Art critics swarm about the flowers of art like bees, buzz as loudly as those of literature, and differ quite as widely from one another. They presume that they correct misapprehensions and reveal realities. Let us trust that they do so. Nevertheless, these conditions discourage the naive assumption that the picture is in some sense clearer in communication than the poem. If one could assume a thorough knowledge of medieval or classical Chinese among interested Westerners in the areas mentioned thus far one might possibly presume an equal accessibility to literature and to the arts. Inasmuch as the contrary holds true, it may be well to begin an inquiry into classical Chinese humor with reference to the arts. Hence as a prolegomenon to a study of humor in writers of poetry, drama and fiction some examination of the arts should provide a useful and strategic introduction.

It must be initially recognized that only portions of these vast fields are relevant. The world over, it has been conceded that life is in general serious, even if not earnest. Even in Asia the laughing philosophers constitute a minority. Naturally, only a minor proportion of Chinese art and literature reveals a sense of comedy. Nevertheless, it may reasonably be held that no part of China's legacy to civilization is more unusual or precious than its singular gift of humor. As all persons acquainted with Chinese statuary are well aware, the Chinese, unlike most peoples, actually created for themselves a god of humor and of laughter. Many of the very finest poems in *The Book of Songs* as well as in the works of Li Po, Tu Fu, and Po Chü-i are in the present sense of the word humorous. It is generally acknowledged that the finest Chinese play is *The West Chamber*, peculiarly rich in the most sophisticated form of humor. The greater number of the plays by the chief Yüan dramatist, Kuan Han-ch'ing, are certainly comedies. Few, if any, works of Chinese fiction surpass the novel which Arthur Waley has brilliantly translated under the title *Monkey*. Most Chinese stories of the supernatural, as the short tales contained in the collection which Herbert Giles renders under the title *Strange Stories from a Chinese Studio*, are essentially humorous. Similarly, in painting and statuary many of the most memorable works exhibit the most refined sense of humor. China's cultural legacy has too seldom been examined from this point of view.

Chinese thinkers have seldom if ever shown a condescending or deprecatory attitude toward humor, such as occasionally appears in the West, where tragedy has at times been rated above comedy and a fashion in literary criticism has even regarded comedy as trivia, all humorous verse as light verse, and the older Samuel Butler vastly less a poet than John Milton. Deprecation of the role of humor became conspicuous in Renaissance criticism, possibly from fear that truth-sayers would strip baroque rhetoric to its nakedness. Poor Chaucer knew nothing of all this.

Conditions in Chinese thought were much more favorable. The Taoists and the sect of Ch'an Buddhists made virtually a religion of humor, performing ceremonial dances about a sacred toad. Even the Confucian scholar-statesmen devised a scheme of values cordial to humor, to say the least. Their outlook tended more to the comedy of manners than to the comedy of the spheres, as envisaged by the Taoists. Furthermore, they cherished an attitude of detachment that invited a relaxed view. Conspicuous among their ideals was the amused sentiment of the retired statesman who from his quiet retreat in the country looked back upon the bustle of the great Court and smiled. To such men the whole theatre of the world seemed more or less a comedy.

It must be confessed that with these thoughts in mind one approaches the world of pictures with a legitimate doubt. Admittedly, the most prominent types of Chinese painting deal with landscapes, flower and bamboo subjects, or with a pious Buddhist subject matter. A casual examination, especially through Western eyes, invites the conclusion that these domains are almost devoid of humor. Broadly speaking, the view has considerable cogency, yet it should be held with important reservations. Indeed, the reservations may be as stimulating as the affirmations.

Landscape painters were unquestionably inspired with a sense of cosmology. They painted not so much the landscape as the universe, conscious of the forces whereby, as they understood, the universe was upheld. Behind the seen was the unseen, the *yang* and *yin* of the cosmos. But the habitual Chinese sense of the universals themselves was by no means wholly without humor. Insofar as I am aware, only one Judeo-Christian angel in three thousand years is reported to have smiled and he (or she) was more French than Christian, the celebrated Angel of the Annunciation at Rheims. Consider in contrast the Chinese mythology for the moon and stars and the celestial beings inhabiting them. Dante's heaven blushed crimson with anger as it gazed earthward. The Chinese heaven smiled. This bears directly upon landscape painting, where a considerable number of the scenes are nocturnes. Moon and moonlight might suggest to the original viewers the distinctly amusing legends associated with them, such as the stories of the rabbit and the cassia tree. The delectable legends of the cowherd and the spinning maid were present in all starlight.

Such a popular play as *The Mating at Heaven's Gate*, with its story of the Oxherd and the Golden Star, brought the heavens themselves into the domain of humorously fortuitous human living. Although the ancient Greeks and countless other peoples read diverting legends in the stars, few peoples, if any, read them more eagerly and more often than the Chinese. India's myths of the creation are certainly more diverting than those of the Jews and Christians and the Chinese are considerably more diverting than the Indian. Traditional Chinese thought not only humanized the heavens but brought them within range of laughter and smiles. Such a philosophy inevitably affects the spirit of landscape painting and all painting with subjects from nature.

Humor has its roots in animal vitality, which, when joined with the nature of man, reveals itself in the physical manifestations of smiling and laughter. It is at the same time one of man's most primitive and most sophisticated attributes. The more life has developed, the more humor has developed. Inanimate nature may to some persons seem unproductive of humor but no one who sees beneath the surface of the animal world can fail to detect its germinal presence. Many of the higher animals unmistakably show a sense of fun and play. Apes in particular seem in this regard close to man. It is by no means surprising, then, that throughout the world even from the most primitive societies comes evidence that artists have found a rich source for humor in the depicting of animals. The classical Chinese not only lived close to animals, successfully domesticating many species, but showed an unusual fondness for animals and birds as pets. Their artists exhibit more humor in picturing these creatures than almost any other group of artists in the world. Laughing at or with animals seems a portal by which they enter into the more spacious domain of the *comédie humaine*. Of this in some detail later. But it should by no means be unrewarding to note how the foundations of a humorous attitude are laid by

Chinese artists even in representation of nature outside the animal kingdom, with its worlds of beast, bird, fish, crustaceans, insects. Humor becomes pervasive.

This appears conspicuously in an early development of the notion of the fantastic. Much of the rock-formation of China appears to a foreigner fantastic and almost incredible. This condition the artists at an early date embraced with enthusiasm, even outdoing nature itself with their extravagance. The result may be described as humor already in the stage of the bizarre or grotesque. The national taste ran to the extravagant. Thus that representative poet, Tu Fu, especially enjoyed fantastic scenes in nature, seeking out ravines, gorges, caves, irregular cliffs, and rugged mountain walls. The Chinese had an eye for bats, clearly a mark of eccentricity. With much effort and expense they dragged curious, irregular rocks into their gardens and, as sculptors, fashioned stone with still more irregularity than nature. They proved themselves not only disciples of Confucian law and order, regimentation and stability, but lovers of the extremes of aesthetic eccentricity. One of the most famous of early poems, Ch'ü Yüan's *Li Sao*, or *Encountering Sorrow*, is one of the most fantastic poems ever written. Its imagery is for the most part a vast panorama of earth and sky, a cosmic landscape and starscape. Sculptors delight in carving miniature mountains out of rocks, large or small, with trees, animals, and men shown in relief against the convoluted stone. A typical instance of such art is a relatively small piece of carved stone entitled "Mountain," belonging to the Avery Brundage Collection, San Francisco. The notably sensitive curator, René-Yvon Lefebvre d'Argencé, remarks in the catalogue (1968) "A boulder carved in high relief shows Buddhist scenes in landscape settings. ["Boulder" is perhaps an exaggeration, since the jade itself is only six and three-quarters inches high and nine inches wide.] The whole scene is permeated with a slightly humoristic touch." [1] Incidentally, as a companion piece the Avery Brundage exhibit presents a very similar piece, carved by the same artist, of only slightly larger dimensions but of lapis lazuli with Taoist instead of Buddhist symbolism. The two are equally "humoristic." Each stone contains the representation of a temple. This is significant for the humanization of a Chinese landscape. Both religion and landscape are humanistic. The landscape is explicitly to be seen through human eyes. Hence man's most precious infirmity, his sense of humor, has a place even in landscape painting. Only a few eccentrics, such as Ni Tsan, favored landscapes without at least one figure and as a rule with more; even Ni Tsan frequently admitted a pavilion for serious meditation, though, with metaphysical instinct, he preferred to have his philosopher invisible, like the empty niche symbolizing Buddha.

The botanical world marked an advance over the inanimate. Here, again, emphasis often fell on the incongruous and asymmetrical. Thus we have such pictures as Wen Cheng-ming's famous juniper trees, with their amazing convolutions. Artists show the freedom of the humorist by favoring eccentric angles of vision, as Wu Chen's album leaf known as "Fisherman." One looks downward from high in air at a cliffside, a river, and a small boat. Again, the very hostility of nature may be turned into a kindly but somewhat perverse humor. An anonymous painting now in the National Museum at Taiwan, entitled "Fishing on a Snowy Day," depicts an indefatigable enthusiast for fishing in the act of sneezing as result of the inclement weather. The picture is more landscape than figure painting but the figure gives to the whole a humorous aspect.

Obviously more rewarding in the examination of humor are the representations of animals and birds. Here it becomes clear at once that Chinese artists are in general disinclined to be either confirmed realists or idealists but instead are disposed to emphasize certain special characteristics. This results on the one hand in humor close to caricature and on the other in exhilarating fantasy. Though occasionally the figures seem naturalistic, this is by no means their primary quality. Here it must be acknowledged that the viewer should proceed with caution. The Western tradition is on the whole to idealize animals, much as it has been to idealize the human form. The Chinese prefer a more diversified representation, using bodies to express a great variety of conceptions. Degas as sculptor represented the female figure in an amazing number of postures but the figure itself was almost always that of a shapely dancer. The Chinese were, of course, singularly disinterested in the nude and peculiarly attracted to an amazing variety of costumes and postures. Their imagination preferred freedom and scope to conventional grace. In this respect, too, they escaped the fashion-plate manner so popular in the declining period of Japanese art. When depicting animals, also, they preferred to explore a vast range of posture and at the same time to use the natural form as base for departure in terms of art. They caught their animals in the most surprising attitudes, which, however, need not have been impossible. Indeed, their explorations up to a certain point present extremely faithful observations. Yet surprising the spectator with ever new observations, they shake off conventionalized notions and stimulate his sense of humor. They go still further, almost always taking their cue from nature, and press forward to meaningful exaggeration. Thus special moods are established. Chinese artists created a positively enormous vocabulary for the bird and animal worlds. The incongruity of their art not only reflects the incongruities in nature itself but presses beyond them into meaningful and imaginative creation that is at once observation and discovery. Their water buffaloes, dogs, pigs, cows, horses, sheep, bears, toads are at once derived from intimate observation and emphatically are more than nature. They are at once at home in nature and inhabitants of a world beyond it that is both natural and essentially human.

From one point of view the Chinese have much more the attitude of the naturalist than do the artists and writers in India and the West. The age-old tradition in lands to the west and south is to retell beast stories that are moral allegories. The animal story is an *exemplum*, a parable for man. So Aesop taught wisdom and so La Fontaine affected to instruct children. Although the Chinese are one of the most moralistic of people, traditionally finding in Confucius their ultimate master, when turning to nature they customarily become pure artists. Their departure from mere unimaginative naturalism leads by easy gradations into humor. Art's peculiar contribution creates an incongruity when placed against the unimaginative reportage of nature. Here lie the seeds of humor. Frequently the seed burgeons into unmistakable humor. This conspicuously proves the case where animals or birds are depicted.

Doubtless the strong social and ethical bias of the Chinese to some degree sobered their representation of man's social world in art. Good evidence exists that they took special pleasure on turning to animals as a domain where relaxation from ethical restrictions was found. At least the birds and buffaloes did not have to accord with Confucian precept! What a welcome relief man finds everywhere in turning to the animals, at least to such as are not dangerous beasts of prey! They become simply and naively lovable. Also the affinity commonly existing between animals and children is to be noted. The urban man of the modern world, especially in the West, too easily overlooks this. He loses what is in reality a substantial therapeutic asset. Animals may in this respect be better friends and guardians for man than angels. The Chinese somehow contrived to retain and to profit from this childlike propensity even when they also, with an inspired freedom from logical consistency, developed strong ethical and intellectual faculties. The birds and beasts became to at least a perceptible degree man's liberators from his own self-wrought confinements. To live imaginatively with animals was to live in a world without walls. While Western thinking penned animals up within man-wrought fences, Chinese thought liberated man by giving him an infinitely varied and multitudinous society of comrades. Let us never underestimate the basic meaning of animals in Chinese painting and sculpture!

Religious concepts are important even in so specialized an

area as the attitude toward animals and their representation in art and literature. If, as some Christian thought argues, the physical world is inherently evil and man's own physical or animal being suspect, animals, as representing the physical side of man's nature, will themselves be suspect. If, on the contrary, a prevalent belief exists in the transmigration of souls, even though animals are graded from high to low and man is regarded as the highest form of earthly life, the view of animals will be relatively cordial. The latter view, existing for many centuries in China, assisted in bringing man into a comparatively cordial relation to the animal world. He had something to learn from animals. Never in China could an epithet such as "beastly" have acquired a derogatory meaning.

It will be well to begin a systematic survey with the domestic animals not only because these are the most prevalent in the humorous images of art but because it was unquestionably through them that the Chinese people acquired the greater part of their singularly felicitous relation with the animal kingdom. The path from the farmyard led outward through an open gate to the very limits of the universe.

Perhaps not all animals and birds are viewed with a sense of humor but most of them are so treated. That most useful creature, the water buffalo, affords a good example and is probably the most often seen in a humorous aspect. Of course the representation differs on different occasions. Close-ups, where the physiognomy is revealed in considerable detail, are more likely to be humorous than distant views. The Metropolitan Museum of Art possesses a picture attributed to Chiang Ts'an, a river scene with a hundred buffaloes. The scroll is diverting rather than humorous. Here as in a large number of pictures the gaiety of the scene is enhanced by the presence of innumerable small boys to whom the care of the bulky animals is assigned. The Chinese early discovered that such boys could ride on the backs of these powerful, clumsy creatures and lead them about where adult men encountered considerable resistance. The youths herded and tamed the unruly beasts. A humorous incongruity with an optimistic conclusion arose from the spectacle of children represented in the pictures as singularly small and agile while the vast animals beneath them reluctantly but surely followed their guidance. These conditions exist in Chiang Ts'an's scroll but the breadth of the landscape dwarfs the humorous intention. The river and its shores diminish the importance of the living figures. A closer position is required to bring the humorous meaning to full fruition. As a matter of fact, most Chinese pictures with animals are close-ups or, so to speak, animal portraits. This holds especially true in the drawings of buffaloes. Animals as grotesque as water buffalo call for relatively little distortion from the artist's hand to produce a humorous effect. If seen in zoological gardens, especially through the eye of a child, they will appear at least amusing. The artists are untiring in emphasizing and exaggerating their smile-inducing quality. In sculptural form the animal is frequently represented cut from a small piece of jade. In such cases he is generally curled up into a compact ball, asleep, his head resting on his thigh. This is the buffalo happily tamed. No attendant is required. In pictures he is usually accompanied by the herdboy, the latter a tiny figure quite out of proportion to the crude beast, who invariably appears humorously awkward. Sometimes the boy has a staff in hand; in one delightful picture, now in the Cleveland Museum, we see both mother and calf while the boy, confident of controlling his charges, turns his back to them, leans against a gnarled tree trunk and plays with a bird in hand. The mother buffalo shows humorous solicitude for her lively offspring. In these pictures the animals occupy the center of attention. Sometimes, however, the buffalo shares this almost equally with one or more humans. Thus in a much loved picture in the Boston Museum of Art we see a buffalo staggering forward beneath a peasant returning from a village feast, while the attendant boy struggles to support the drunken man precariously perched on the animal's rugged back.

In general the evidence of art suggests that the Chinese

found dogs more amusing than useful. Yet from the earliest times the dog is depicted, especially in sculpture. Well does the discerning Sherman Lee observe of one of the earliest representations: "The seated mastiff in the Musée Cernuschi is one of the appealing animals in the Han ceramic menagerie—one of thousands of tomb figurines." [2] Such images were placed in the tombs not only to protect but to divert the worthy men and women who had passed into the nether darkness. They represent the road by which entities pass from what we call real life into art's immortality. The domestic pet becomes a heathen guardian angel.

A delightful creature who seems to be a puppy is found in the Avery Brundage collection. René-Yvon d'Argencé's description for a catalogue of the Brundage treasures gives without any peculiar bias or intention a faithful indication of its humorous quality: "This seated watchdog barks as his tail wags. His large head tops a long, pillar-like neck; his face is square, with flat forehead and eyes in relief; the moustache is incised. The dog's ears are leaf-like and the legs stumpy. A thick, brown glaze covers the red pottery." [3] The figure is dated as Han (206 B.C. to A.D. 221). It is inconceivable that it should not have been viewed with a sense of humor. Incidentally, the creature is totally unlike the compact aforementioned mastiff. They are similar only in being dogs and humorous. Another no less amusing representation of a dog, totally different from either of the preceding, is a bronze statuette now in Czechoslovakia. Dispensing altogether with curves, this deals only in angles, rendering the image all the more artificial. The dog, which seems also to be a puppy, looks upward while its tail, almost completely erect, attains a considerably greater height than its head. The effect is of extreme eagerness, vitality, humor. One longs to throw it an offering of dog biscuit.

The common pig, by nature a well-compacted animal, lent itself especially to three-dimensional representation. Again, from the earliest times known to us this animal played a conspicuous part in the Chinese art-menagerie; again the Brundage collection presents an interesting early specimen well described by the curator, who writes: "The animal rests on its voluminous belly but its head is raised and alert. The rounded contours are barely disturbed by the sketchy surface details which indicate ears, limbs and tail. The eyes are carved in relief, the nostrils perforated." [4] Incidentally, this jade figure is less than four inches long. The Indiana University Museum possesses a rude pig with a prodigiously long snout and tail conveniently curved to serve as handle. The impression made by these figures is incontestably diverting.

That the Chinese lived intimately and happily with their domestic animals is indicated by a pig from the T'ang period in form of a headrest. Although the snout, eyes, and ears are almost alarmingly realistic, the whole is designed to lie solidly on a couch, the sleeper's neck resting in the slight indentation between the animal's head and haunches. There are virtually no indications of legs. It is certainly a humorous conception. One wonders what carnal dreams the sleeper may have had with head reposing on such an image.

The cow was never as prevalent or highly regarded in China as in India. In their art the Chinese made only minor distinctions between cow and buffalo. This has even resulted in some questionable nomenclature. Thus in William Cohn's generally excellent book, *Chinese Art*, a picture is said to represent a milch cow when presumably it represents a buffalo followed by its calf. Similar as the representations of the two animals are, two jade figurines depicted in H. F. E. Visser's valuable book, *Asiatic Art*, are, on the contrary, rightly designated cows. These have singularly humorous, bovine features with the artist's attention chiefly on the facial expression. There is none of the rugged, restless sentiment exuding even from the representation of the sleeping buffalo. A humorous docility is well expressed as typical of the bovine character.

Whereas the Indians worshipped the cow, the Chinese at least gave extreme honor to the horse, which had a valuable part in both their domestic and military life. It was even more important in Court life than on the farm, the use of horses, especially in the hunt, bringing high prestige. Breeding of horses received great attention. At first the animals were employed conspicuously with chariots; at a later date they were commonly used as mounts. Fine horses were welcomed as tribute to the Chinese Court from the tribes living to the north and west of China's borders. A vigorous school of horse-painting developed where far more than in most provinces of Chinese art idealization prevailed. It would be preposterous to say, of course, that in the minds of the Chinese the unadorned horse held a place comparable to the nude human figure in Western art, yet the statement would have at least some element of truth. Under these circumstances the humorous factor so conspicuous in much Chinese animal painting and sculpture found in horse-painting much less scope and play. Landscape and flower painting excepted, few areas of their art won as great favor as the painting and sculpture of horses. This held true for several centuries. By and large, the horse was not a subject for humor. Yet there are occasional exceptions which are of considerable interest.

For much of the most cheerful work in Chinese art one goes to the tomb figurines. Occasionally, there can be no doubt, such figures appear ridiculous simply on account of the amateurishness in the technique or the unpretentious spirit of the folk craftsmen. These clay images were hardly regarded by the Chinese themselves as objects of aesthetic distinction. They were for use and diversion in the future life. Specimens of horse-figures with a mildly humorous connotation are found in almost all museums specializing in Oriental art. As an instance may be mentioned one in the Metropolitan Museum described as "T'ang or earlier." Here emphasis falls most heavily on two heads, those of horse and rider. Each has a threatening air; the horse has its mouth opened wide, revealing its menacing teeth; the rider is apparently a soldier, possibly a barbarian, with a singularly grim countenance. The whole is remarkably compact, almost like conventional figures for chess.

The over-all effect even to its first viewers must have appeared risible. The fierceness of the animal is matched only by its rider. A tomb horse giving entirely the opposite impression but almost equally risible is depicted in Lubor Hajek's *Chinese Art*. Here emphasis falls on the horse's docility. There is no rider but an extremely commodious saddle and ample saddle-cloth. The head is large, suggesting a stupid but thoroughly well-meaning and amiable creature. This horse looks more like a chair than a charger. Many T'ang horses, on the contrary, admirably express speed and grace. The animal in question is a proletarian or middle-class animal, for comfort of the rider and practical farm use. It would be ridiculous to use it for hunting.

The lower the animal descends on the social scale for horses, the more likely the artist is to take liberties with it and suggest a humorous attitude. George Kao, in his anthology of Chinese humor, relates a striking scene with Chinese farmers whom he once saw by the roadside laughing uproariously at the vain efforts of a team of horses to drag a heavily loaded wagon up a steep hill.[5] This attitude in one form or another may be traced far back in Chinese history. As work-horses depart from the ideal form of horses in the service of the aristocracy they may well appear in the native eyes to take on humorous qualities. There is a discrepancy between the practical and the ideal. It is a view with which we are familiar today. We think of the race-horse as an ideal object of pure beauty, to be viewed seriously and with admiration. The common donkey or mule, whether laboring in Asia Minor or in the American Southwest, is at the same time an object for ridicule and affection. These are precisely the conditions agreeable to humor. There is neither satire nor pure admiration but only the necessary distortions of real life. So in the National Palace Museum, now in Taiwan, is a picture by Ma Yüan, a Sung artist, entitled "Through Snowy Mountains at Dawn." Two heavily laden donkeys, or possibly horses, with long, outstretched ears, are stepping with utmost care along a snowy pass over the mountains. They are the central features of the picture, although the inevitable custodian trudges behind his animals, carrying a staff to urge them on and warming his hands by holding them within reach of his breath. The animals are at once noble and absurd, patiently plodding onward upon their assigned task. One appears to be carrying eatables, the other possibly a load of firewood. They also carry with them the singularly Chinese sense of the ridiculous.

The camel is at best an ungainly animal, almost invariably exposing himself to the brush of the humorous artist. Naturally, the Chinese, who not infrequently encountered these animals, driven in caravans across the western deserts, took full advantage of their opportunity to exploit the subject. From the south, also, though more rarely, came the elephant, likewise an animal of eccentric features by no means overlooked by the artists. Whereas the Indians, who were on the whole much more familiar with elephants, treated them with a striking realism that left small place for humor, the Chinese almost invariably represent the elephant in humorous disproportion, rather as a mythical than as a real being. (Similarly, of course, they romanticized the lion, which was generally unfamiliar to them.) Elephants of a decorative character are frequently found in the later or decadent stages of Chinese art. The subject especially attracted makers of decorated, painted porcelain, where brilliant coloring replaced the creature's sober gray and added to the gay, humorous effect of the already fantastic form. But like most themes in Chinese art, this was ancient as well as relatively modern. For example, a bronze elephant survives from the fifth century. It has a humorously upturned trunk and face, a huge shield hanging down beside its stubby legs, a large tortoise upon its back, and, ascending to more than twice the elephant's own height, an elaborately decorated pagoda. The impression is still and doubtless originally was inescapably amusing. No elephant has ever presented less of a menace. The lifted trunk serves to balance the otherwise overpowering pagoda, signaling a friendly greeting to all observers.

Last among the domesticated animals to be presented in a humorous light is the sheep. This subject was likewise occasion for much caprice and fantasy. Staffs were often decorated with jade sheep, thought symbolical of good fortune. The Imperial collection possesses a black jade ram with a highly heroic and imperious expression on its face. Perching on top of its rear haunches and looking backward is a diminutive shepherd only a quarter the size of the animal itself. The human is completely dwarfed by this absurdly arrogant beast, which is obviously created in the spirit of fun and humor, even though a pastoral sheep-deity may be invoked.

Such were the chief animals of use to man, the creatures which he knew best and which served artists and craftsmen best for purposes of an uninhibited and entertaining art. But imagination soared far beyond the obvious province of utility, endowing most creatures known to mankind with some peculiar power and fascination. Mythology got to work where utility left off. Later in this study, after real animals have been considered, we shall turn to the purely mythological creatures, the chimeras of the human mind, such as dragons, which were lineally descended from actual lizards. But, not unnaturally, the toad, to which Shakespeare ascribed supernatural qualities, proves especially fascinating and significant. Both by virtue of its form and habits the toad is, clearly, one of the most extraordinary of creatures. It became a leading stage-property in the rituals of Taoism, associated with legends of immortality. Its grotesque form is seen in countless small ornaments. The toad, nature's ideal monster, is found also in many paintings dedicated to a mystic subject-matter. Sages or immortals are seen to contemplate it. The Metropolitan Museum has a scroll on this subject. Sometimes, as in a painting by Liu Chun, in the Boston Museum of Art, the sages are presented in wild, drunken antics performed in veneration of the toad. This picture is entitled "Three Sennin Dancing Around a Toad." The celebrants are mad with glee in contemplation of this absurd-looking creature.

Most explicitly comic and amusing of all animals is, presumably, the monkey. Chinese artists soon developed a special relish for its proverbial antics. Best of all creatures this mimics and seemingly ridicules the antics of man. So the leading figure in the most humorous of all Chinese narratives, already referred to, the novel well known to English readers by way of Arthur Waley's translation under the title *Monkey*, has for its hero the pilgrim called Monkey, whose habits of thought and action lend meaning to the name. His closest friend, it will be recalled, is likewise half-animal and half-man, Pigsy. One of these figures exercises ingenuity and agility, the other pursues purely physical pleasures and the luxury of idleness. The monkey had once been turned to stone but seldom in art appeared in that material. The free-moving, spontaneous Chinese brush-stroke served best to depict him. Consequently, he is found in countless paintings. Many of these are works of the Ch'an artists, impelled by mystical inspiration. Quite notably these monks even executed pictures of themselves where they approach the uncouth appearance of monkeys. The Chinese government possesses a remarkable painting by an unknown artist entitled "Monkeys at Play in a Loquat Tree." Some of the best monkey pictures are by the inspired Ch'an artist, the monk Mu Ch'i. Several of these reached Japan, where the subject won great popularity, especially for screen painting. Among Mu Ch'i's works now in Japan is a delectable scroll, "Mother Monkey and Child." The drawing is especially inspired from the humorous point of view. The mother's face is virtually a circle wholly bright with a tiny, dark nose and mouth for its center. The legs are fantastically outstretched to right and left along the limb of a tree. The child clings desperately to its parent, who, though all but eyeless, appears to be staring at the viewer. The pair is perched upon the limb of an aged pine. Clearly, the painters and their public derived endless fun from the representation of these erratic creatures.

To proceed with other beasts, the bear is almost always treated disrespectfully in a palpably humorous manner. He sometimes dances on his hind legs. More often he crouches in the manner of a singularly absurd dog, with, however, an odd facial expression peculiar to himself. A remarkably amusing bear in gilt bronze, with an infectious smile, deriving from the Chou Dynasty, was at one time in the Oppenheim collection. A figure of a slightly different but equally humorous sort is now in the Indiana University Museum. The former is comically pathetic, the latter appears humorously affectionate, the type of creature that a child would long to embrace.

The frog, quite often seen, is for artists little more than another toad, although to the original viewers the latter enjoyed more supernatural properties. Yet there is enough realism to make the two readily distinguishable. Thus there can be no doubt that the creature depicted in H. F. E. Visser's aforementioned book, *Asiatic Art* (page 145), is a frog and not a toad. This bronze object was evidently a receptacle for some liquid. The streamlining of the figure immediately suggests its watery home. Especially the mouth and eyes emphatically belong to a frog. The figure is perspicuously amusing. By far the most diverting Chinese frog, so far as I am aware, to be seen in the United States is in the Detroit Museum, on a scroll by Ch'ien Hsuan, also depicting insects and water-plants. The frog supplies its most humorous figure.

Tigers were generally found too much of a menace to be treated lightly, as were lions; the latter were less often actually known and existed for most Chinese artists only in a world of their own convention or fantasy. That both were ranked high by virtue of their pride of place in the world of animals tended to divorce them from a sense of levity. But where there was a will there was a way and the Chinese even found occasion at times to treat both within the area of comedy. The tiger in particular offered a decorative motif which, though not humorous, was at least a source of pleasure. At times the distortions of a figure raise the question whether or not humor is intended. Certainly for a modern and quite possibly for an ancient, the bronze tiger of the Chou Dynasty in the Schoenlicht Collection has a humorous intention. It lies poised on the middle of its back, its rear feet firmly on the ground, its front shoulders lifted, its massive head turned completely around and also, like its fore paws, raised high in air. The distortion is surely comic. Again, nothing is impossible in religion. There is a tenth-century picture, now in Japan, by Shih K'o, of a Ch'an monk in meditation with his head resting on the shoulder of a tiger which has been cast by magic spells into profound slumber. Both saint and tiger are asleep to this world, though the sage's spirit is presumably in a supernal sphere. No conceivable religious or mystical conviction can deny the picture a high degree of humor. The sage in his capacity as magician has performed his masterpiece in magic.

Partly from their invaders from the north and west the Chinese, when they so desired, acquired an heroic style in representation of tigers. Their lions, viewed by modern eyes strictly as lions, are less convincing as representations of known animals, though several of the colossal guardian figures of lions with wings are noble and impressive. As early as the T'ang period lions were treated facetiously. Thus in the collection of Baron Koyata Iwasaki, in Japan, is a pair of ceramic lions shown in undignified attitudes, one yawning and obviously sleepy, scratching his neck with his paw, the other, a blasé expression on his face, also scratching his neck. In Brussels is still another T'ang lion, made of iron inlaid with silver and gold, whose muscles are so fantastically distended that it must have been all but impossible to take his show of force seriously. The king of beasts in the role of braggart is unquestionably reduced to ridicule. Nevertheless, in some instances, whatever may be the impression on a man in the twentieth century, the original intention remains, to say the least, unclear. How far are the guardian lions to be taken seriously? The presumption is that to begin with such figures were erected in full earnestness. But views seem to have altered. Many brightly painted china lions of comparatively recent times presumably stand much closer to being comic than to being serious. Instead of glowering with anger they appear to be smiling with a sense of security. With the centuries the lion image became increasingly baroque. It also became decreasingly significant when considered from the aesthetic point of view. In time the lion more resembles a fantastic distortion of a dog than a lord of beasts. Whatever humor these figures may once have had is dissipated in frivolity.

That diminutive lion, the household cat, is well known in Chinese art. It is more often met in the softer medium of painting than in sculpture. The intrinsic beauty so commonly found in the real animals of this species may have somewhat discouraged the Chinese humorists. At least the cat is never demoted as is the lordly lion. When he is shown he is usually treated respectfully and endowed with the sophistication that cats possess at their best. But the subject may be seen from still another angle. Cats embody humor as elusive as the smile of the famous Cheshire cat. They are often shown as adjuncts to refined, courtly life, in company of ladies of the household and their children. They constitute a vital part of a picture that is amusing as a whole. An unforgettable and delightful painting in the Boston Museum shows ladies, children, and a cat all in an elegant setting. The entire scene is conceived in an atmosphere of high comedy but this comedy lies rather in an emanation of the cat than in the actual depiction of the animal itself, which is both gracious and idealistic. The mood represented in the cat-pictures is often appropriately subtle, reticent, rarely if ever hilarious. Thus the gifted eighteenth-century painter, Chin Nung, gives us a cat turned away from the observer, intently watching some object beyond the picture's border and forever unknown. This indirection impinges on humor though it may not actually cross into its territory.

Another of the lesser animals occasionally provoking the artist's smile is the rabbit, found in both sculpture and painting. Timidity is, quite naturally, its leading quality to attract attention. This as a rule is accentuated by the rabbit's peculiarly long, sensitive ears. Like many frightened animals in Asian art, he habitually looks backward over his shoulder at an imagined pursuer. It is in this position that he appears, for example, on a thirteenth-century vase now in the British Museum.

Actually, there is virtually no animal which the Chinese artist saw or even heard of that he was not inclined to depict with a sympathetic sense of humor. Man was, on the whole, safely master. He could afford to smile at the endlessly variegated forms of life existing by his side. The artist does not stop short of the hideous or the bizarre. He finds himself at home among insects and vermin. Take, for example, the rat, subject of one of the most deftly written lyrics in the Confucian *Book of Songs*. There are many sly and clever pictures of this rodent, almost always, like the verses in the *Book of Songs*, instinct with humor. The rat is first of all a bold but sly scavenger. Very well, then, the inspired artist, Ch'ien Hsuan (A.D. 1235– c. 1290), gives us a picture, now in Japan, of a family of rats in process of eating a melon already half consumed. It is an idyl out of garbage. The mother rat has already eaten her way through the heart of the fruit so that her extremely long, thin tail protrudes from one end while her head peeks forth from the other. She is scuffling out small pieces of the melon on which her eager brood, three diminutive rats, are feeding. The picture is a bizarre idyl of decadence. It unquestionably has wry humor, quite unlike the idealized still-life paintings of ripe and perfect melons or the exquisite images of those super-rats that have won elegance and respectability, the always graceful squirrels. The treatment of still life is aesthetic without humor; that of the pert squirrel is as a rule half-way between the idealization of fruit and the slightly sardonic view of the rat. Ch'ien also has a delightful picture, now in the National Gallery at

Taiwan, of a squirrel whose tail is ampler than its singularly agile body. It would be impossible here to overpraise the delicate drawing of feet and toes but such art remains for the most part innocent of open and overt humor.

As already indicated, the freedom of play for the imagination afforded by subject-matter drawn from the less familiar animals encouraged the insatiable thirst of the Chinese for humorous representation that reached its peak in their creation of strange or wholly fabulous and imaginary beings. Especially diverting are the representations of animals as exotic from the Chinese point of view as the rhinoceros. A bronze image of this creature in the form of a *tsun* vessel presumed to be from approximately the eleventh century B.C. is in the Avery Brundage Collection. An amusing feature here is the relation of body to bowl. This major portion of the figure is actually more bowl than body, though four extremely short, stumpy legs, with naturalistically shaped hoofs, support it. The protruding element, as in all such vessels, is the oversized head, wearing a curiously sombre and humorless expression that conversely stimulates the sense of the ludicrous.

The artists found bizarre fascination in the almost incredible world of insects, such creatures as the praying mantis gaining their special favor. There can be no question that they saw these creatures with a dash of humor, though their humor has a slightly sharper spice and more acidity than most humor in the West. Their imagination was as much at home in air and sea as on the surface of the earth. Among the marine life such beings as the crab commanded their curious interest. To Fan An-jun, for example, is ascribed a large hanging scroll, now in Japan, containing images of fish (carp) and, in the extreme foreground, a meticulously drawn crab. Never has this crustacean seemed more diverting or "out of this world," as the familiar idiom expresses it.

Some fish evoke so pure and innocent an aesthetic experience that in their representation humor takes small part or none at all. Yet occasionally fish are as bizarre as any insect.

This is often suggested in representations on ceramic objects. Chinese art was not only a menagerie but an aquarium. The Minneapolis Museum of Art has a dish, possibly at one time a wedding gift, where two completely grotesque fish are molded in relief on the inside. They are singularly gay and powerful little creatures. Occasionally a dish or bowl reveals fish true to the general nature of fish but presumably such as never were, with vastly protruding goggle eyes and flower-like fins and tail. They are truly monsters, half way to becoming dragons.

The dragon encountered on land, in air and in the water and, from the modern point of view, essentially a fabulous being, is the last subject, save birds, that calls for consideration here. The scholar who today approaches it must, of course, make careful adjustments in his thinking, since for Westerners dragons are not only fabulous but an extinct species. Not over five hundred years ago all Europeans believed in their existence, although in the West they never played as large a role as in China, homeland of dragons. There can be no end to the lore and history of Chinese dragons. They are both less sinister and more eclectic than dragons in the West. The Emperor or any powerful man might through symbol or metaphor be represented as a dragon. The conception was, then, half spiritual and half materialistic. Any great natural force might be conceived as a dragon. When boating on rough waters or sailing over a deep lake one might see real, corporeal dragons emerging from the waves. In general these monsters implied a force either for good or ill so potent as on no account to be viewed lightly. The spirit of humor was not in them. But here again there were important exceptions. A dragon might preside over a festival and enhance the general gaiety; even in itself it might be a creature to regard humorously.

Given these almost bewildering inconsistencies, the dragon in art does not always explain itself in the sense that it exists in a known context or reveals explicit characteristics of a symbolic nature. It stands freely by itself or crawls on the surface of a plate or bowl. Interpretation of whatever symbolic meaning it has, if any, becomes somewhat perplexing. Dragons live in labyrinths. Threading one's way toward them must always be something of an intuitive experience, possibly a mysterious or even mystical adventure. As composite creatures, fashioned of reptile, bird, and beast, their incongruity suggests the very heart of humor.

The Chinese lived as naturally with dragons as with birds and beasts. Their common-sense, useful lives, following the dictates of Confucian thought and discipline, were relieved, as the sage himself presumed, by the boldest flights of creative imagination. This emphatically included the privileges and risks of consorting with dragons. Miniature dragons disported themselves on the surface of early sacred ritual bowls of bronze. Humor provided part of this free play of poetic fancy which was the very air wherein the dragon lived and moved. This compact between utility and fancy is well symbolized in those porcelain bowls or vases whose handles are either fully developed or incipient dragons. The useful vase which itself may be entirely plain or devoid of ornament may stand for prosaic, down-to-earth experience; the gay little handles, with their dragon scales, attest a play of unrestrained imagination that almost inevitably includes pleasure, smiles, and laughter. The little figure may represent either a lizard or the Emperor. The dragons of the ancient Teutonic world, as revealed in *Beowulf*, are unquestionably forces of unmitigated evil, as sinister as the Germanic conception of witchcraft. If possible, they should be stamped under foot. Western conceptions of sin and evil are compacted in them and come to vivid imaginative reality. To that great symbolist, Edmund Spenser, a good dragon was barely thinkable. The Chinese dragon, on the contrary, is far less a creature of a morally conceived universe. On the one hand it is by no means alien to the modern conceptions promulgated by science of natural or even of mental powers; on the other hand it stands as a vivid symbol of freedom of the creative imagination and the sheer joy of far-roam-ing fantasy. As symbol of vitalism in all its phases, this dragon-world must include the joy that resides in humor, the underlying, deep-seated sense of the incongruous within the soul.

Many dragons appear scarcely more terrifying than would a puppy with wings. To be specific, consider a celadon altar jar of the eleventh century from the Brundage Collection, as superbly illustrated in one of the Museum's catalogues (1968). The dragon encircling its neck is certainly a gay, florid creature, no more menacing than the tiny puppy with upturned nose and tail that tops the jar's cover. This is a happy dragon; it can only be imagined as humorous.

Two dragons admirably illustrated in the aforementioned book, *Asiatic Art*, by H. F. E. Visser, contribute to this study, the first (plates 29–31), shown from three distinct postures revealing side, back, and head. The whole is flamboyant in the extreme. The mouth is closed but with a suggestion that it is toothless. The excrescences are so large, the body is so small, that no menace whatsoever is suggested. This figure is from the Chou period. The second dragon, dating from the Six Dynasties (Visser, plate 61), is equally extravagant, though in different ways. Its horns are those of a common snail. They are balanced by a long, slender beard. The pose is angry and alarmed but certainly not terrifying, suggesting an excited puppy playing the watch-dog, whose bark is far worse than its bite. Both are admirable works of art and both are clearly intended not only to give aesthetic pleasure but to arouse awareness of the preposterous and the absurd. No one would, of course, propose that the stupendous dragon-monsters on the world-famous scroll in the Boston Museum of Art are to be conceived in any spirit but that of high seriousness. But dragons are really of almost as many species as birds and beasts.

Unquestionably that legendary bird, the phoenix, belongs as a rule to a world of solemn, pious ceremony where humor is out of the question. As seen, for example, on the richly embroidered mandarin squares with their symbols for the Emperor, the elements of the universe, and the mandarin insignia of office, humor remains unthinkable. Fantastic as the divine bird flying sunward seems to modern eyes, nothing humorous or amusing is intended. Nevertheless, with the habitual ambivalence in Chinese thought and expression, this is by no means at all times the destiny of the phoenix. Especially where the context is genial, the bird may share in the general good humor. A table-dish, for example, not intended for the more solemn rituals, when ornamented by the phoenix may have a smiling aspect. Such is the case with a gold dish now in a private collection in Holland and pictured in H. F. E. Visser's *Asiatic Art* (plate 48). Again the gaiety implicit in almost all representations of the phoenix, suggesting a bird that outdoes even the peacock in splendor, assists the image to pass over into the realm of entertainment. Many times the viewer of an ancient figurine may seriously be at a loss as to whether a colorful domestic cock, a peacock, or a phoenix is intended. Whatever may in fact have been the case, even presuming that a fixed interpretation existed in the artist's mind, there is virtually no doubt that the image carries a considerable element of humor. Sometimes this is indicated by the boldly flourishing tail. This may be seen in the bronze image of a bird now in a Czechoslovakian collection, brilliantly illustrated in *Chinese Art*, by Lubor Hajek. Like so many creations of the Chinese mind, the phoenix is extremely human and hence a creature of many contrasting moods, one of which incontestably is humor.

Let us consider what the Chinese when in quest of comedy achieved in relation to birds that are not legendary, like the phoenix, but familiar species in nature. No species served this purpose better than the duck. As humorists throughout the world have discovered, the duck and especially the duckling commonly provoke our sense of humor. In this regard an American may well recall Walt Disney's Donald Duck. The phrase in American slang, "queer duck," is a further indication. All the Western World knows the tale of the ugly duckling. Similar thoughts by no means escaped the Chinese.

The duck was generally regarded as an auspicious bird; the brilliant mandarin duck, in particular, was conceived as living closely in pairs and hence as symbol of conjugal fidelity. Ducks swam in a whole sea of cheerfulness, living in an atmosphere inevitably conducive to humor. Moreover, like most water-birds, ducks could readily be depicted in peculiarly amusing postures. Graceful in many of their movements when swimming, their forms themselves, especially when seen out of water, are likely to appear ludicrous. Their necks may be bent in an unexpected fashion, equally surprising and amusing. Sculpture affords the ideal medium in which to capture their absurdity. Their bills are curiously shaped, their webbed feet ungainly for walking, their tails superfluous and preposterous. All these features and others of like nature are to be found, for example, in a pair of porcelain ducks admirably photographed by Visser (plate 96). Even when the duck is imagined within the water, the figure may take on an amusing aspect. Merely the turn of the neck of an unglazed model of a duck as illustrated in Basil Gray's *Early Chinese Pottery and Porcelain* has an unmistakably humorous effect. In the same volume is a photograph of a celadon saucer with an incised design of a duck among waves. The image may be described as a transparency, where the entire bird is visible in profile, no distinction being made between the parts above and under the water-line. This method of presentation reveals the feet in process of swimming. An amusing balance is surprisingly disclosed between the large, forward-stretching neck and the backward-bending legs. Every outline of the bird, as in the protruding breast and raised tail, is amusing. This is, surely, the creation of an artist blessed not only with acute observation of nature but with a well developed sense of the ridiculous.

Ducks frequently have a deliciously comic expression in the features of bill, head and eyes. A comic duck perfectly answering this description appears on a bowl of the Sung period belonging to the Detroit Institute of Arts and illustrated by James Cahill in *The Art of Southern Sung China*. The humorous waddle of the duckling is also depicted on a plate photographed in the aforementioned volume by Lubor Hajek.

The duck appears in virtually every medium of Chinese art. It is present with a strong comic effect in a vessel of the Ch'ien-lung period of cloisonné enamel with a copper base, in the Chinese National Collection. This duck carries a pagoda-like structure on its back above which rises a tall handle. The vessel stands on rather tall and extremely stout legs. There is a flowing tail but the most humorous features in the entire bizarre image are the sharply bent but protruding neck and the impertinently outstretched head and bill. Who could possibly see or use such a vessel without a genuine sense of amusement?

The owl is another bird recognized the world over as extremely expressive and possessing decidedly amusing features. So stupid looking is it that it has very generally been thought wise, a politician who only feigns dullness. Its incongruous habits arise partly from the fact that it blinks stupidly by day and flies with extraordinary precision at night. The wise old owl amuses us. In Western iconography it lurks under the dignified robe of Minerva, Goddess of Wisdom, to some degree redeeming her well-deserved reputation for didacticism and prudery. None of these connotations are found in the East, yet the bird there has also become a symbol for the inscrutable, the oracular, and, more often, the amusing. Many examples might be cited; only a few must suffice.

The owl appears to have been one of the earliest bird-symbols to have been established in China, much earlier, for example, than the phoenix or the duck. Thus from the Shang Dynasty, or, roughly speaking, the fourteenth century B.C., comes an owl in marble, now in the Academia Sinica, Formosa. It was a tomb figure but this, as we have seen, is far from excluding a humorous meaning. This owl has two stumpy legs of elephantine thickness, which support it as a tripod by means of an amusingly curved tail. Its body is covered with incised symbolic designs. There is virtually no neck. Feathers are indicated on its head, which is from the standpoint of proportion enormous. The ears are completely human. The eyes are huge and glaring, the prominent beak protruding from a curiously bold angular design like an asymmetrical window conceived by some modern architect. The general effect of this completely stylized figure is, strange to say, astonishingly naturalistic. It expresses precisely that conjunction of absurdity and self-importance found in real owls, especially in the young.

This type of figure is extremely familiar among early bronzes. Examples are seen in virtually every major collection of ancient Chinese art, some of the best being in the Freer Collection, Washington. Naturally, the form, with certain modifications, passed into almost all media. Two extremely amusing specimens are in the collection of the King of Sweden. These figurines, five and a half inches high, so simplified as to appear virtually as owl chicks or even owl embryos, are Chou pottery, described as a pair of containers. The form is chunky; legs are minute; small handles are attached to the wings; heads are detachable; expression is pert. Few images are more diverting.

To the Chinese mind the crane is a peculiarly sacred, symbolic, significant bird. In particular, it signifies longevity and felicity. In all respects it is a good augury. Two features, then, contribute to its possessing a humorous connotation: its generally benign meaning and the obviously fantastic form of this long-legged species. It should, perhaps, be added that the varieties of the crane common in China are themselves, even for cranes, extremely fantastic, having excessively long, slender legs and a similarly long, sinuous neck. The configuration of these birds discourages their representation in certain media, as, for example, ceramics or stone. They are an ideal subject for works in bronze. A fine example of bronze crane-figures is depicted in the previously-mentioned volume, *Chinese Art*, by Lubor Hajek. Here every amusing feature of the birds themselves is represented with artful exaggeration. Each is resting on one foot. The immense feet are meticulously molded. One bird lifts its head high in air; it is clearly emitting its shrill, unearthly cry. The other peers into the rich mud on which the two are standing, its bill as yet closed but the entire spirit of the bird bent on extracting some delectable bit of half-hidden food beside their feet. The pair is clearly a masterpiece of the bronze-caster's art. It is also both fantastic and amusing.

In some respects the shrike as a humorous figure surpasses even the crane, though it is less of a water-bird, and water-fowl are, by and large, well known to be more eccentric than land birds. The shrike is a plebeian, coarse in appearance and still coarser in voice. It has none of the quiet and infinitely patient deportment of the crane, which has aided in giving the latter its reputation for wisdom and meditation. But it, too, is long-billed, long-legged, and of a strangely eerie appearance. It is also the supreme satirist. Not unnaturally, the shrike appealed to artists of the mystic cults whose members had frequently retired with anger from a degenerate world. Hence we are not surprised to find such a picture as Mu-chi's "Shrike Perched on a Pine Tree," now in Japan. The connotation is at once sinister and bizarre, where signs of a dark humor are undeniably present. The decayed pine suggests a disillusioned view of existence. The bird has its back morosely turned to the spectator, his head hidden sullenly beneath his wing.

The amusing distortion of bird forms appears especially in minor figures. A good instance is found in the Brundage Collection. This figure is of a swan carved in jade. It is presumed that it was worn as a head-ornament. The design is eclectic to an extreme degree. This the description by René-Yvon d'Argencé well expresses: "The bird's body is elongated, and arched to the point where one of the tail feathers rests on the flattened crest. Facial features and wing feathers are incised in a fairly realistic manner, but the movement of the large, curving tail feathers is emphasized by purely calligraphic lines. The legs, tucked up against the body, are rendered in relief." [6] As in so much Chinese art, the very incongruity in the relationships between realistic and artificial features becomes in itself a cause of amusement. The figure both is and is not a swan. A discerning eye is sure to be entertained. The sheer ingenuity of the thing is humorous.

Two bird species that purely as birds and irrespective of their appearance in art traditionally carry a humorous connotation are the magpie and the mynah, almost equally eccentric in appearance and behavior. Both are celebrated for their vocal proficiency. The sensitive Chinese painters commencing with the popular view developed it with skill and emphasis found only in their own works. Nature and folklore provided clues followed with peculiar relish. Since the two species are communicative, not surprisingly they led to pictures of their intercourse and interrelationships. These frequently have a comic flavor. Thus in the National Museum in Taiwan is a screen-picture of a pair of noisy magpies chattering angrily at a sufficiently innocuous looking rabbit. Their mouths are wide open; the wings of both are spread to indicate high agitation. Were the figures here translated into humans, the picture would be a lively "conversation piece."

The highly humorous, eccentric Chu Ta (his very name suggests the chatter of birds) has given us a pair of hanging scrolls entitled "Mynah Birds and Rocks." These birds are equally awkward and disparate. As James Cahill in *Fantastics and Eccentrics in Chinese Painting* observes: "A pair of mynah birds perch on a tipsy boulder, beneath a threateningly overhanging bank. . . . The other composition is just as unstable. One of the birds in each picture balances tensely on a single leg, and peers intently upwards, while the other is withdrawn and self-contained." [7] This is the eccentricity of wry humor, where humor's incongruity is at its height, though the temper is much more dark than bright, far more sinister than gay. Every feature of each bird is bizarre and their relation to each other unresolved. Brush strokes are equally capricious and effective. The artist himself is known to history as a mad humorist. He is scarcely less a humorist for being ill-humored or in any case affecting ill humor. Tragic he is not. Cahill is of the opinion that his harsh comments turn inward.[8] Conceding this to be the case, the spirit of these introspective pictures would be more humorous than satiric. Sophisticated Chinese humor has its shadows as well as its highlights.

Other birds celebrated for humorous and vocal attainments include the parrots, with their many varieties. These naturally have strong appeal for the artists. Sometimes the image is to all appearances wholly serious, as in the highly academic bird-painting of the Emperor Hui Tsung. But then, the parrot himself both looks and behaves academically, as humorists the world over have from time to time observed. Other representations of parrots, especially in three dimensions, frankly sustain the familiar image of this bird as an actor in the universal comedy. By and large, it is indisputably true that the makers of figurines, who were common craftsmen, took themselves and their works less seriously than the painters, most of whom were scholars and many high in the ranks of the aristocracy. Presumably all persons acquainted with the Chinese arts are familiar with the amusing parrots and parrakeets so often encountered in porcelain. To be specific in this matter, a pair may be mentioned attractively illustrated in H. F. E. Visser's comprehensive volume (plate 96). These are irritable chatterers with beaks out of all proportion to their diminutive bodies. But they are clearly more of a nuisance than a menace. They are anything but birds of prey. Their shrill colors and eccentric forms can only in the end contribute to the gaiety and relaxation of all who hear and see them imaginatively. Although minor objects in comparison with many figures discussed in these pages, they, too, play their part in the comprehensive and catholic world of Chinese humor. They are as light as Chu Ta's mynah birds are dark. One complements the other. Humor's house has many chambers.

In this respect it may further be noted that the tactile values of Chinese figures have a meaning that enhances their humorous effect. Since objects on public exhibition are not to be touched, such matters need not be referred to public collections. Insofar as I am aware, writers on art seldom comment on the weight or even the texture of an object. Among my own small collection is, on the one hand, for example, a monster humorously terrific, rough in surface, very small, but of metals enormously heavy. It vaguely resembles a rhinoceros though I prefer to regard it as a spectre in a dream. The image has a ponderous meaning; it also has a literal ponderosity truly amazing in proportion to its size. On the other hand are decorative objects in porcelain gracefully humorous, surprisingly light in weight, bland and smooth to the touch. Even a blind man might perceive the humorous connotations of Chinese art.

Finally, as for the humorous representation of the human image itself, the story is far too long even to be summarized here. However, being at home among the birds and animals, man at least merits a paragraph. The paintings of drunken monks or of the religious performing deliberately absurd actions are extremely familiar. The Chinese genius in drawing grotesque figures from all classes in society is at once apparent. Chinese classical artists are the foremost of cartoonists. What caricatures are to be seen in the anonymous scroll, "Yang P'u Moving His Family," in the Art Institute of Chicago! What an amazingly sophisticated image is Lo P'ing's "Portrait of the Artist's Friend I-an," from the Ching Yüan Chai Collection! There are delectable images of scholars rejoicing in their ease; of village peddlers, of common servants, of playful children. The figures on the famous Han tiles in the Boston Museum of Fine Art are among the most perfect of all images of sophisticated and supercilious aristocrats. Liang K'ai ranks among the world's greatest humorists, his imaginary portrait-sketch of Li Po being his masterpiece. As observed in the early pages of this chapter, humor is deep-seated in the heart of ancient China, resting on profound and philosophical foundations. Blessed were the scholars who smiled, for they were good Confucians and were comfortable. Blessed were the sages who laughed, for they were good Taoists and comprehended the universe.

# 2

---

## HUMOR IN

## POETRY

*

## 1 / *The Book of Songs*

To a remarkable degree the essential qualities distinguishing the civilization of the Chinese are expressed in the oldest of their extant works of pure literature, the *Shih Ching,* or *Book of Songs.* Hence whoever wishes to explore the nature of Chinese humor may expect to find in it clues of substantial value. It is a book without close parallel elsewhere in the world, as the Chinese themselves are beyond doubt a most unusual people. As preliminary to a description of the humorous elements in the *Songs* some observations on the general character of the collection are helpful. Such reflections serve to indicate the importance of this earliest chapter in the entire story of Chinese culture. It is a Book of Genesis in the history of cultural, aesthetic, and social life. The end of any investigation largely depends upon the course set from its beginning. A good start goes far toward a successful ending. In such studies as those undertaken here there can be no introduction remotely as auspicious as that provided by the *Shih Ching*. Let us take stock of this at the commencement of our enterprise before entering upon the actual undertaking.

To repeat, *The Book of Songs* is unique, as Chinese history is itself distinctly out of the ordinary. The earliest poetry of a people commonly consists of epics or hymns based upon a theogony, as in India, where the *Rigveda* and the *Mahabharata* answer this description. But, as we are often reminded, China has no epic nor does it possess a theogony in the customary sense of the word. Its first known compositions are ethical, political, historical, and geophysical treatises, accompanied by *The Book of Songs*, the last by far the most important specimen of early imaginative or poetic literature. To be sure, a few of the *Songs*, being dynastic hymns, possess certain properties often found in epic poetry but epics they certainly are not. Insofar as can be ascertained, for long periods of time the *Songs* constituted the firm and established basis for secular, imaginative literature. Though ethically idealistic, they are neither religious nor heroic in the strictest sense of these words. Their confirmed secularity and freedom from theology assist in providing within them a fertile ground for development of one of mankind's most social qualities, namely, a sense of humor. The conjunction of the words with music unquestionably assisted in maintaining within the poems a prevailingly aesthetic attitude. The *Songs* were in this respect clearly set over and against the more voluminous didactic writings. They sustained perforce what longings the people possessed for an aesthetic life where words and music supplied the media for expression. Incidentally, it may be added that a few *Songs* as seen in book form imply not only music as a presentational art but dancing. It is, however, as poetry, not as dance or music, that the work is known and apprehended today. Its leading role or influence has been in literature rather than in the sister arts to which for so long a time it was happily allied.

It is, then, hardly too much to maintain that the *Shih Ching* constitutes the cornerstone or foundation of the spacious and long-lived structure of Chinese verse. Of course other elements, even at an early date, are known to have entered into the picture, among them mystical, shamanistic chants and popular verse narratives. Important types of poetry absent from *The Book of Songs* enlarge the field, with admixture of verse and prose. But the genius and even the forms and rhetorical figures in the *Songs* remained characteristic of Chinese poetic thought and expression for well over two millennia. These odes have set the key for much of the style and spirit of Chinese poetry even to the present day. Communism has revolutionized the theatre, for example, more thoroughly than it has altered the course of Chinese verse.

It has been held that the *Songs* have no parallel in literary history. This does not mean, of course, that there are no other collections where some instructive comparisons or contrasts may be advanced. The only collection of songs whose long life and wide dissemination remotely compares with the Chinese anthology is the Hebrew *Book of Psalms*. Here contrast is more significant than comparison. One collection is primarily religious and devotional, the other humanistic and secular. No people and above all no early or primitive civilization can dispense with nature and with nature, aided by some attractive folklore, the *Songs* maintain a firm relation. Yet the philosophy of the *Songs* accords with that of the primarily social Confucius and, indeed, they have long been associated with his name. It has been widely held that he first determined the canon of the *Songs* and in particular established their orthodox musical setting. The relation of the *Songs* to the other so-called Confucian Books is, of course, both clear and instructive. Whereas the prose works are essentially critical and intellectual, being treatises on moral, historical, and philosophical subjects, providing a system of thought, formulating and clarifying ideas, the *Songs*, on the contrary, reflect the emotions of the people, their experiences and feelings in the course of their daily living. One supplements the other. Deprived of either, Chinese civilization, which implies a synthesis of mind and heart, would be far other than it is.

Although the *Songs* were never forgotten, they experienced a history almost as strange and remarkable as the mystery of their creation, so that today fresh starts must be made to arrive at a satisfactory understanding and appreciation. In their interpretation the attitudes represented in the prose writings associated with the Confucian school lay heavily upon them and often, as the world of thought views the record today, much distorted their meaning. Although the odes have been at times attributed to Confucius himself, however the truth of this matter may be, it is certain that much misinterpretation of them must be ascribed to subsequent Confucianism. Much as the fathers of the Christian Church read new meanings inherent in Christianity into the Psalms of David, scholars for many centuries read allegorical meanings into the Odes which they cannot originally have possessed. This does not signify that symbolism especially of a political nature may not occasionally lie hidden in the *Songs*, but much of the fresh and singularly spontaneous quality of the poems as they were created was lost on the Confucian scholars, who read in them instruction in history and political theory. Although the *Songs* were unquestionably sung at all times by large portions of the Chinese people without thought for allegorical interpretations, the scholar class came to see in them primarily occult and hidden meanings. The *Songs* were, of course, one of the few books which all scholars passing the official examinations for government posts were required to know virtually by heart. Theoretically their prominent position on the required list of readings was justified by the literati through insistence upon these allegorical interpretations. One result was beyond doubt to diminish the original element of humor and even to diminish the total vitality and emotional force of the poems. It is on the whole a sorry story which has to some extent cast its shadow over the *Songs* to the present day. The *Songs*, in other words, passed through Dark Ages of scholastic pedantry. An interpretation of them in modern times is the better for overleaping this episode that persisted through long centuries in order to arrive at the probable meaning entertained even before Confucius bequeathed to them a canonical blessing that was by no means an unqualified asset. The *Songs*, like other true poems, miraculously survive their critics.

The humor in the great Chinese anthology is an adjunct of its predominant quality, an astonishing resilience. Whatever smile or laughter issues from it is characterized by its emergence from a basic condition of extraordinary health, welfare, and confidence in life. No stronger assertion of the positive values of life can be found than *The Book of Songs*. No wonder the civilization that it announced in ringing notes so many centuries ago proved in all records of human history the most enduring! Such a healthy child was destined to remarkable longevity. It is also important, of course, that the *Songs* contain no trace of the false romantic flush of optimism, the feverish high coloring of romantic sensibility. Many of the poems are sharply and bitterly satiric. Others are in their mood deeply tragic. Yet the general view of life remains incontestably affirmative. Even though a considerable proportion of the *Songs* belongs to the category of public protest, presenting images of social and economic oppression, of privation and distress, the spirit itself is not distressed. Man is free to exclaim loudly against his oppressors, honest enough to confess the misery to which not only bad government but conditions inevitable in life subject him. *The Book of Songs* by no means gives life an unqualified cheer. Yet behind the darkened image is incontestably a confidence in mankind's strength to survive even the worst oppression and to emerge into light. Neither poverty, sickness, exile, nor any other evil freely acknowledged undermines the fact of human dignity, which no guardian angel is required to support. Man, if he will, may inhale oxygen to support a wholesome life. There is round about enough fresh air for him to breathe freely. Given this atmosphere in which to live, the sense of humor becomes not only inevitable but one of humanity's peculiar and most precious possessions. Animals may grimace but not actually smile. Humor flourishes in *The Book of Songs* as naturally as vegetation in a temperate zone. To a critical eye it is equally important to observe both the extent and the limits of its provenance. It is an important and necessary ingredient in the book as a whole but it would be erroneous to consider it the predominant quality. For purposes of analysis the part must be carefully assessed in relation to the whole.

Mention has already been made of one quality found in a number of the poems and categorically distinct from the mood of comedy, namely the tragic sense. The collection contains a few poems that may be described as elegies, or threnodies for the dead. All such pieces, though tragic, are in the heroic mood. A reasonable number of poems are strictly focused upon sufferings, expressions in admirable verse of the various miseries that man is heir to. A large number of pieces acknowledge these miseries, become angry or satirical by describing misfortunes or conditions that may or might have been removed. Sometimes the attack is barbed with keen wit. If the arrow is poisoned, the poem is indubitably satire. If it is clean, it at least impinges upon humor. The line here is difficult to draw. The distinction lies to a large degree in the author's motives. If it appears that he has been more angry at his enemy than pleased by his own skill in marksmanship, his work will be pure satire, if the contrary, comedy. The didactic element is conducive to weight and a direct attack, the aesthetic element to lightness and to humor.

The *Songs* contain no specimens of pure wit in poetry, such as are found in the Greek or Latin classical epigrams or in other and later pieces in both Chinese and Japanese poetry. Wit as understood in these terms is foreign to the earliest Chinese poets, who excel in the more genial quality of humor. Yet it must be recalled that the *Songs* are by no means naive, inasmuch as they exhibit great rhetorical ingenuity with much artistry in nuances, understatement and innuendo. A sly quality, peculiarly agreeable to the Chinese, is one of their principal characteristics, which in turn becomes one of their leading assets and especially favors their style in humor.

The critic must take pains to distinguish between the good humor that springs from an exhilarating experience and the humor that belongs to awareness of the human comedy. The distinction might at first seem transparent but is not as lucid as it may seem. A smile is no clear indication, since this arises almost as readily from a sense of well-being as from a sense of comedy. Laughter provides the better criterion, but then laughter is no true guide. The reader in his study may thoroughly enjoy a highly ludicrous experience without laughing, indeed the solitary laugher may be almost as much an object of suspicion as the solitary drinker. All that may be said is that an experience of well-being provides the best and most fertile ground for the sense of humor as exhibited in the *Songs*. Fortified by a confident spirit, the writers of the poems are enabled to view an incongruous incident which quite possibly includes some misfortune with actual amusement. Such humor springs from affirmation and happiness, satire from anger and dissent. The condition of being amused implies a basis of well-being. From the firm take-off of this condition the poets of the *Songs* achieve their flights of comedy and humor. The well-being is not in itself humor but the mother of humor. It provides a state of detachment equally favorable to the detachment of art and of comedy. Moreover, the artist whose spirits are exhilarated by the pure pleasure of his achievement of form enjoys a favorable station to exploit the free fantasies agreeable to humor. Humor must always be oblique; satire or wit is direct. The Chinese mind was destined to excel in the former, the Latin mind in the latter.

Nevertheless, where *The Book of Songs* is concerned, it must be acknowledged that all such truisms need to be observed with some caution. It should not be forgotten that the poems were highly acceptable to Confucians and that Confucius was above all a moralist. He was also a musician who, incidentally, expressed one of the most moralistic theories of music ever devised. The *Songs* are neither amoral nor immoral. Many— perhaps even the majority—are explicitly didactic. But here there is no skepticism, no area of disturbing and corroding doubt. No poem even goes so far as to present an argument, for who wishes to argue in song? Where, on occasion, a poem seems to the modern reader to pose a question which, morally speaking, calls for an answer, the question is never raised in the poem itself. Thus in Song 141 an injured wife declares that she will reform her roving husband by circulating reports of his wild ways. The poet recognizes the claims on both sides of the case, the possibility that the man is profligate and the possibility that the woman is a scold. From the pragmatic point of view it is fairly clear that the wife will not succeed, as she asserts, in taming her man by her complaints. But such is not the moral issue. The poet does not raise this issue and is the better humorist on this account. It would, of course, be unjust to presume that as a man the humorist who fails to raise a moral issue either denies or undermines the claims of morality. He simply does not deal in moral dialectics or moral statements in the particular work in question. Most of the *Songs* imply a world in which ethical values exist and have considerable force. A number are satires making explicit statements. As it happens, all the poems dealing specifically with war, of which there are many, imply that the war policy has been unwise and therefore evil. In the truly humorous poems there is irony but no doubt; an ethical incongruity appears but no answer is for the moment found necessary. That values are known and important is nowhere questioned. The Chinese humorist lives in an ethical world but sets himself to writing only on holidays, when the courts are out of session. The *Songs* provide many holidays for the moralist. They are so much the more artful and the better both as poems and as humor because, at least in many cases, they carry the issues no farther than irony and incongruity. One cannot avoid the conclusion that the more humorous pieces existed in ancient China as a longed-for relief from the excessive pressure put upon the mind and heart by a society on the whole so strictly regimented. Precisely because the values in society were assured, the comic poet found an especially favorable climate. He could presume a large number of standards that in actual experience existed in conflict. At this conflict he could afford to smile because he, at least, was not committed to an answer.

Pure humor, as represented in so many of the *Songs*, resembles mathematics. All such thinking is in this sense an abstraction from real life. Its images are assumptions. These assumptions may or may not have an ethical reference. Because the Chinese have lived so fully in a world ethically conceived, they have enjoyed the advantage of playing with ethical abstractions, as in so many of the *Songs*. With the advent of Buddhism, religious conceptions offered themselves to the humorists and hence one of the most brilliant of all humorous works, the story known as *Monkey*, came into being, a book in which the virtues and limitations of Buddhism are presented but not adjudicated. All is grist to the humorist's mill. The incongruities of the psyche, for example, are especially attractive to the humorous poet. He reflects on the inconsistencies within the soul. Thus many of the *Songs* discover humor by exploring incoherence and inconsistency within the heart. This appears especially in a considerable section of the most admired and popular pieces, those dealing with what is allegedly the wayward and vacillating heart of woman. The humorist does not declare which of two attitudes is "right." Instead, he relishes the perversity of the human spirit.

The *Songs* are, then, from many causes properly associated with Confucius not because he wrote or may even have edited them but because the society of which he became leading spokesman peculiarly invited both satirist and humorist. As Chinese thought is to so great a measure the coexistence of two spiritual ways of thought, Confucianism and Taoism, so Chinese humor is almost equally indebted to the two philosophies of life and to their interaction. Confucianism supplied the substantial materials of which the house was built, Taoism the freedom with which the design was decorated. The works that seem to us pure fantasy are, of course, largely inspired by Taoism, those that contain a realistic and a social content are inspired by Confucianism. The Chinese humorist in particular from the very beginning occupied a favorable position. His freedom of play he owed largely to the mystical sect, his fixed points of reference and his favorite objects of ridicule or grounds for amusement resided in the inveterate tendency of the formalists and moralists to assume rigid and affected postures.

The Chinese humorist acknowledges the value of both outlooks but, like most humorists, leans with favor upon those persons who follow dictates of nature or the heart as opposed to those who side with convention and rule. As centuries advanced the prudish, pedantic Confucian formalist became the favorite butt for the humorist. No true humorist ever condemned Confucianism as a way of life, for no true humorist, insofar as humor is his profession, ever implicitly condemns. But the pedant in thought and the stickler in conduct and manners offer the most fertile fields for his exploitation. These conditions exist only in an incipient form in *The Book of Songs*, although their roots may easily be detected. Chinese society had not as yet crystalized into its most rigid formalism. But the tensions were present in their early stages. Especially in matters of sex, the early humorists, like the later, are generally on the side of desire as against restraint and of youth as against age. This is the natural consequence of a point of view springing, as we have seen, from a sense of cheerful well-being rather than aggressive power. Humor in man is virtually instinctive. Like the visions that Wordsworth imagined in his ode dealing with immortality, it is too readily crushed by pressures of society and the shackles of formalistic education. But in these very shackles and pressures the superior humorist, who is heir to the condition of being an impudent child, finds the richest grist for his mill. The humor of *The Book of Songs*, then, expresses a culture still relatively young, sturdy and, above all, free from disillusionment. Although it lacks the ultimate subtleties attained in such masterpieces of the comic spirit as *The West Chamber* and *Monkey*, it has a sure refinement of its own. For all humor when examined from the rationalist's standpoint must seem complex, as life itself is complex. It has the perfume and intricacy of a flower. Irony, insinuation, indirection, and nuance are of its essence. Although in some respects abstract as mathematics, it wholly avoids the conclusiveness of mathematics. It would be a gross humbug to assert that there are answers at the back of the book. The humor of *The Book of Songs* is as delicious as may anywhere be found; it lacks only the involvements of more intricately concocted draughts of humor.

With the foregoing comments as introduction, several of the more striking poems inspired with humor may be examined. The first song in the collection I take to be a sly comment on the unsuccessful attempts of a lord to seduce a peasant girl. This is but one of many instances in which the *Songs* express the point of view of the less powerful in contrast to the demands of the more powerful. It is part of the very essence of humor that it surprises us by showing the weaker in reality the stronger and to this extent, at least, sides with the underdog. The point of view is taken, however, not so much from moral grounds as from the humorist's quest for surprise. David defeats Goliath. So in a large number of the *Songs* the common people seem superior to their masters and weak women stronger than strong men. Children are favored above their parents.

The poem, when put into its English dress, reads as follows:

> On an island in the river
> A bird proclaims, "ki, ki";
> A girl, fit for a lover,
> Is beautiful to see.
>
> On tendrils long and short
> The water-mallows sway;
> The lord sighs for the loved one
> Dreaming night and day.
>
> To left and right we gather
> The mallow-plants that grow
> By streams, while the lord tosses
> Restlessly to and fro.
>
> But not awake or sleeping
> Can he catch hold of her,
> Though soul and limbs are reeling
> Stormily astir.
>
> Sweet are those varied branches
> We pluck from water-wells;
> The girl, so fair and lovely,
> Is hailed by drums and bells.
>
> Water-plants are swarming
> Above the river-bars,
> The lovely girl saluted
> By flutes and by guitars.

The second song shows much the same qualities but is more humorous than Song One and more readily elucidated by the modern critic. A young girl, presumably still a child, takes part in the family business of making and maintaining the clothes. She has gone to the irrigated valley to fetch the materials for cloth and to do the necessary washing. A maid has been sent to watch over her. But the child has ideas of her own. She is mistress of both the maid and the situation. As befits the poem's organic form, its main point, which is its humor, appears primarily in the last stanza:

> I tell the watchful matron
> That I shall shortly cease,
> Quit scrubbing, rinse the garments,
> (I'll wash what clothes I please)
> And then, returning homeward,
> Wish both my parents peace.

Clearly, the child has sound ideas of her own and succeeds against any possible opposition in putting them into effect. As in many of the *Songs*, the opening stanza may at first seem irrelevant but is not so. It reads:

> Into the deepest valley
> The vines extend and cling;
> Yellow birds assemble
> Fluttering on the wing,
> Alight on the dense foliage
> And resolutely sing.

The poetic meaning, left, as it should be, to implication, is that the young girl is herself a happy spirit completely at home and free to do as her naturally healthy will dictates. In short, she is partner with the yellow birds. Like the poet, she is a singer.

Most of the humorous lyrics in the first half of the collection were originally conceived as love songs and of these a large proportion are decidedly humorous. The times were not ripe for solemn eroticism. A few specimens of these beguiling songs may be examined in the order in which they are customarily given. By far the greater number imagine the woman speaking. Number Twenty is unusually simple and direct but nonetheless humor appears in the discrepancy between the girl's expectation and experience. She is urged to be more receptive:

The plum-tree drops its fruits;
By summer seven are left:
Several lads are wooers;
I shall not be bereft.

The plum-tree drops its fruits;
Autumn leaves only three:
Fewer men are wooers;
May one soon turn to me!

The plum-tree drops its fruits;
In later fall I carry
My harvest basket out,
Hoping I still shall marry.

The next poem in the sequence is a song imagined to be sung by the members of the royal harem. The astronomical imagery in which the harem girls are likened to the multitude of minor stars and the queen to the moon in whose brilliance they are eclipsed is clearly humorous. They are indeed lesser stars or rather less than stars. The undignified language of the second and final stanza adds to the amusing imagery the certainty of a light, humorous touch. The poem follows:

Pale are those minor stars,
Triad and Pleiades;
We hasten through the night
Early or late to please,
A harem of small lights
Who sparkle and then cease.

Pale are we, minor stars,
Who with the wife have striven,
Who hurry through the dark
From our lord-master riven,
With blanket and chemise,
Poor concubines of heaven.

The Court of China was, of course, habitually likened to heaven, the ruler to the sun.

The thirty-ninth song, in four quatrains and possibly over-long to quote, is more advanced in its psychology. It is the soliloquy of a woman who is on the journey to her marriage but has presumably enjoyed some more spontaneous sexual relations and from still other causes is reluctant to place herself beneath a husband's sway. Her words and actions are disingenuous. She does not acknowledge, perhaps even to herself, her true motives but consults with her female attendants how she may prolong her marriage journey. A humorous situation receives exquisite lyrical form.

Number Forty-Three presents a relatively primitive form of humor, although, as always in the *Songs,* with technical skill that is a sheer delight. It mocks a woman who has asked much of love but in the end "drew an ugly toad." Several poems mock romantic and excessive pretensions of various sorts, as for the ultimate in wealth or beauty. Song 138 asks the rhetorical question whether any man should insist on having the most delicate food or the most beautiful woman at his command. Typical of Chinese thought, humor ridicules the pursuit of anything in excess. One of the most familiar of the Confucian texts, it will be remembered, is devoted to the doctrine of the mean.

Song Seventy-Two is an arch smile—no more than that—at the relativity of time as reflected in the lover's heart. Different circumstances, as the lover, who is a farm laborer, finds, make a day pass more or less slowly. In some instances a day seems three months, in others an entire season, in still others a year. The Song which follows is conceived from the woman's point of view; the man is depicted as vain, pretentious, and presuming. He peevishly complains that the woman dare not elope—it should be recalled that the Confucians were great sticklers in behalf of arranged and highly formal marriages. The humor is enhanced by a suspension of the comic intention. Not, perhaps, until the extravagance implied in the last lines, when the lover offers to provide his wife with a separate chamber and a splendid gravestone and swears endless fidelity by invoking the sun, is this intention clear. This is the humor of insinuation, an advanced phase of comedy in which the Chinese achieved virtual perfection.

The seventy-sixth lyric is a peculiarly winsome affair. A young girl advises her lover to be cautious and wait. It is his impatience that introduces the note of humorous, kindly ridicule. The girl in turn advises him (there are three stanzas) in the course of his secret visits not to break the willows by the street, the mulberries by the fence, nor the flowers by the garden gate. The immediately following poem is even more amusing in its mockery of passion that so clearly causes the lover to view the loved one in a light out of all proportion to reality. There is no satire here, for the song is wholly kind, sympathetic, and humorous. It has a rollicking mood. I have chosen to render it in limericks:

> Shu has gone to the hunt; in the street
> There is not one person to meet—
> Of course they are there
> But cannot compare
> With Shu, who is fair and discreet.
>
> Shu has gone to the hunt and no sign
> In the street of the drinkers of wine—
> Of course they are there
> But cannot compare
> With Shu, who is handsome and fine.
>
> Shu has gone to the hunt, but, of course,
> No one in our street rides a horse—
> Of course they are there
> But cannot compare
> With Shu, who has beauty and force.

Timidity is well known as passion's worst enemy. It is also singularly susceptible to ridicule, especially when appearing in the male, who is generally presumed to make the chief advances. The woman is presumed to be reticent but much humor is universally found in illustrating the truth that in sex she is commonly bolder than the man. A very short, succinct lyric, number eighty-seven, clearly humorous, is founded on these observations. The lady, if lady she be, with an impetuous gesture throws modesty aside:

> If you love me truly
> I will lift my skirt and wade,
> But if you do not love me
> My love for you shall fade—
> Why were such cowards made!
>
> If you love me truly
> I will wade the river Wei,
> But if you do not love me
> No such fool am I—
> So great a fool should die!

This is certainly frank enough and by way of frankness lies the humor, since this is no common virtue. Another piece from this section of the *Songs*, number ninety-five, depends for its humorous effect upon overtones. Like several of the *Songs*, it contains barely concealed sexual allusions. The form, which is rather unusual in Chinese, suggests a duet. The lovers, specified to be of the aristocracy, are on a spring outing beside the confluence of the rivers Wei and Chen. Again, the girl takes the initiative.

> The Chen and the Wei rivers
> Flow past clear banks of sand;
> Each knight and girl holds up
> The first spring flowers in hand.
> The girl says, "Have you looked?"
> The knight, "Indeed have I."
> "Then shall we look again
> Beyond the banks of Wei?"
> Knight and girl are going
> Joking happily;
> One presents the other
> A shining peony.
>
> The Chen and the Wei rivers
> Flow past clear banks of sand;

Knights and girls in crowds
Fill all the shining strand.
The girl says, "Have you looked?"
The knight, "Indeed have I."
"Then shall we look again
Beyond the banks of Wei?"
Knight and girl are going
Joking happily;
One presents the other
A shining peony.

The mood here is especially gay and jaunty. Humor lies largely in the sexual insinuations. Unlike the girl in the earlier lyric, who offered to wade the same river, these lovers are highly bred and prefer to speak with indirection. The *Shih Ching* is a remarkable compilation of folksongs and courtly songs, although such is the universality of the art and such was evidently the character of Chinese society almost three millennia ago that the gap between the classes was much less than it became at a later time and considerably less than it has generally been in the Western world.

A few of the *Songs* having a folklorish quality suggest poems by the German minnesingers; a few of them with a more courtly flavor still more strongly suggest Provençal lyrics, especially the *aubade*. But from causes already stated, the Chinese poets are less romantic and more humorous, less inflated and more succinct. In a word, they appear superior both in art and humor. Poem Ninety-Six imagines the familiar situation of lovers parting at dawn. Here the man is evidently a counselor in the prince's Court. In his love affair he cuts a wholly ridiculous figure:

"The cock has crowed aloud,
The court is summoned. Rise!"
"It was not the cock
But buzzing of green flies."

"The Eastern sky is bright,
The court in full array."

"It was not the dawn
But the clear moon-ray."

"The insects fly in throngs."
"It's sweet to lie reclined."
"The court will soon adjourn
And we shall be maligned!"

Poem One Hundred, in the same sequence, has a similar character but stands closer to burlesque. The woman is speaking:

It is not yet bright in the East
But, called to the Prince's feast,
He behaves like a country clown,
Putting clothes on upside down!

Dawnlight still is dim;
The court has summoned him;
He behaves like a lout,
Putting clothes on inside out!

He breaks the willow fence
Rushing madly hence,
Too early, too late, never right,
He cannot tell day from night.

Chinese writers can, of course, be from the Western point of view heavily didactic, yet it is notable how at times, in the hands of the more artful poets, pure Confucian teachings may be found together with lightness of touch. So here, the favorite doctrine of the mean is given a happily poetic expression.

The song in the Confucian collection immediately to follow the foregoing has a light, bantering tone notwithstanding the poet's barefaced advice-giving addressed to a man who, presumably under the influence of strong emotion, has violated social proprieties. The situation is as follows. The usual family arrangements, quite disregarding the persons chiefly concerned, have been made for the marriage of a young man and woman. A second man, it seems, with something of Peer Gynt's impetuosity, has projected a kidnapping of the lady on her long journey between two cities. The poet simply insists that such things are not done! He speaks mockingly, in the manner of a custodian of manners and morals. Does not the man know how to plant hemp? Does not he know how to split firewood? The planting must be orderly, the ax must strike a clean blow. (There may be sexual references here.) As for marriage, there is as everyone knows only one way of going about it, which is through marriage brokers! Besides, does not the man see that his project is wildly imprudent? The girl has already gone far on her way, along a well-traveled public road, where security is complete. The proper gifts have already been presented. Moreover, the husband is a sly fox. Thus prudence and decorum alike make the plan absurd.

It is true that a modern man, especially a Westerner, is likely to find persons in an old firmly established culture absurdly complacent where their values are concerned. Decisions are difficult. Much that does not seem amusing to the Chinese seems amusing to the West and the reverse of this, of course, holds true. Yet I cannot for a moment believe that the first singers of this song failed to regard it primarily as humorous. The moralist here seems so assured of himself that there is an absurdity in his very confidence, weakness in his assurance. Stranger things have happened in nature, or in China, than the arrest of an itinerant bride. This the poet instinctively knows. One almost hopes that despite the sly fox the bride-hunter disregarded the warnings and was successful. Certainly the metaphor of the fox fails to place the friends of morality in an ingratiating light. Although the Chinese might in general be extremely complacent, their very complacency afforded ideal material for their humorists, much of whose best work is spent in exploiting this subject.

Frustration in the love-quest, as in Aristophanes, is in *The Book of Songs* frequently viewed in a ludicrous light. When seen from the detachment of art and humor, how great may be the discrepancy between the quest and whatever ending there may be! There is ample occasion for humor, either as a defense mechanism for those immediately concerned or as a possible lesson in wisdom for momentarily objective observers. The humor begins in Song 129 with the basic situation. The woman is pursuing the man, who ingeniously avoids her. The scene, as often in Chinese love-poems, is beside a river. It is a winding stream and a circuitous chase. At the close of the first strophe the man is standing in midstream to the north of the point where the chase began; at the close of the second stanza he is in midstream to the south; at the close of the third and last he escapes by comfortably isolating himself on an island. Unquestionably a facetious spirit prevails throughout, although there is nothing in the plot to keep the episode from being a minor tragedy.

Song 125, though more kindly to the woman, is no less humorous. As often, there are three stanzas, each with only slight variations from the others. The focus is on the girl's insistence that on going to Shou-yang hill she has been picking herbs, such as licorice and parsley (suspicious items). Her fellow townsmen simply should spread no more mischievous gossip! Whether she tells the truth or not makes small difference. In any case, the lilting lines certainly have comic value. The girl is evidently witty, never without her excuse. Whether or not she deceives us, she is certainly amusing, an admirable girl who knows her way around this circuitous world. The poem, like most in the collection, remains as fresh as the day it was first sung.

So much for the humorous poems with reference to love, which as a group comprise some of the most admired and most popular works in the anthology though a relatively small part of the whole. For long periods later on in Chinese literature the poets enjoying the highest prestige among the scholar class gave relatively little attention to erotic themes, leaving this for the most part to less esteemed and more popular song writers. By far the greater number of pieces in *The Book of Songs* deal with other aspects of life and many of these pieces also reveal humorous attitudes. Sometimes moral judgment itself takes on such a jaunty air as to be palpably humorous. This appears in a very short poem likening a man without morals to a rat:

> Look at the rat,
> Pale skin and sly,
> A man without morals—
> Why doesn't he die?

> Look at the rat,
> It has teeth to ply.
> A man without morals—
> Why doesn't he die?

> Look at the rat,
> Its limbs are spry.
> A man without worth—
> Why doesn't he die?

The good nature prevailing in so much of *The Book of Songs* often makes such moral or social judgments possible while the sense of humor is still strong. We encounter the highly civilized condition of reproof without anger. Even if the poet is unconvinced, he succeeds in smiling at the plight in which he finds himself, while placing his opponent in a ludicrous rather than infamous position. The following, Song 135, is typical of this phase of Chinese humor:

> Deceptively, the stately house was grand.
> In time scant food was served at any meal.
> The end in no way answered the beginning.
> Great is the disappointment that I feel.

> Ah me! at first at every meal I had
> Four vessels with four courses for my treat.
> Now from each meal I walk away with hunger.
> Great is the disappointment that I meet.

The following song is still more happily humorous. It reproves the vanity and zeal of a musician who plays too loudly, too often, and who too much loves to be heard. It might almost be described as a humorous character-sketch or specimen of caricature in verse. The first line is simple Confucian precept. Prosaic as this, too, may seem, the poem develops on lines rendering it as a whole aesthetically satisfying, warmly imaginative and in no way prosaic or trite. It is Chinese to the core but the Chinese heart is itself surprisingly universal:

> Too much is much too much. In the feasting hall
> You play your music with a zest above
> Discretion. I admire your passionate zeal
> But your extravagance I cannot love.

> Winter and summer you strike your rattling drum;
> Loud through the feasting hall its fierce beats boom.
> Summer or winter by the public road
> You wave aloft your egret's dancing plume.

Several poems begin with questions that are clearly regarded as so preposterous as to be amusing. When to this condition is added the sense of well-being and diffused happiness, humor may well be said to be achieved. This becomes especially clear as the poet's manner takes on a rollicking tone. Poem 190 may be translated as follows, with an effort to convey in English the genial informality of the Chinese lyric:

> Who says you have no sheep? You have three hundred.
> Who says you have no cattle? There are ninety steers,
> All seven feet high. Your sheep have curly horns,
> Your cattle come with stately, flapping ears.

> Some stray down hill to sip the valley pool;
> Some sleep, some walk; your herdsmen's coats are straw;
> They have bamboo hats and spacious carrying bags;
> Your beasts accord with sacrificial law.

> Your workmen bring in wood and forest game;
> Your sheep are strong and handsome to behold;
> When your herdsmen wave to them they come,
> Obsequiously trotting into fold.

> The herdsmen dream of locusts and of fishes,
> Of tortoise-and-snake and falcon banners flying.
> The diviner says: "Locusts and fish mean riches,
> Snake-and-bird banners mean a race undying."

Poem 217 begins with a similar proposition considered so erroneous as to be absurd. Each of the three stanzas uses this formula. The question is, shall the feast of the clan be open to strangers? The answer is, quite obviously, no, for clannishness constituted one of the most cherished forms in ancient Chinese society. The song asserts that the good things at the festival, especially its rich foods and wines, shall be solely for the clan, never for others. It is clear that although the poet accepts the basic social values as he finds them, he recognizes that they can be pressed to ridiculous extremes. Tu Fu's poem, later to be examined, "Given to Cousin Tu Tsi," similarly pokes good-humored fun at the clan system. The institution is approved but the humorist exercises his well-known function of rejecting too much of a good thing, good custom made foolish by excess. "Too much is much too much," as the Confucian poet declares. This is a salutary phase of the comic spirit, so often vocal in behalf of moderation and common sense and against fanaticism and radicalism. The position has been made famous by Aristophanes, first and foremost of humorists in the West, but is even more often exhibited in China.

Unlike pure fantasy, humor may operate under a degree of restraint, indeed it often flourishes with understatement. An out-and-out satirist is likely to be extravagant, his temper manifest by the flush of anger rather than by smiles. Moreover, throughout the world humor has often appeared in one of its most felicitous forms when employing a muted voice, since the heavy hand of an oppressive ruler suppresses all adverse criticism that comes into the open. Understatement flourishes with shrewd and humorous innuendo. It attracts skilled hands where nuances and implications are generally discovered more congenial to the true spirit of poetry than rational statement or moral assertion. To be sure, one of the most striking and surprising aspects of *The Book of Songs* is the free and outspoken character of many of the lyrics. A few of the longer poems in the latter pages of the collection are dynastic hymns in loud praise of the houses of reigning princes. Also many more poems are complaints by the mass of the public against rulers who have thrust them into war and reduced them to poverty while amassing wealth for themselves by the most cruel and ruthless means.

Extending this line of thought, a large part of the voluminous commentaries on the *Songs* has regarded even the lyrics that are apparently love poems as hidden allegories directed by the people against their rulers. In most cases the commentaries are now regarded as misleading, much as beyond any doubt the Scholastic commentaries on the *Psalms* read into the Hebrew works meanings never intended by their composers. Whatever may be the truth in these matters, the disputes have little or no direct bearing on the humor of the poems. Most of the angry poems within the famous collection are astonishingly direct in their approach and in no way concern the analyst of humor. The relatively few pieces clearly rich in innuendo do, however, bear upon this, illustrating one of the most enjoyable and truly typical phases of Chinese humor.

As specimen may be cited Song 225. Here the nature of the poet's praise of the bureaucracy only serves to betray his dislike. He specifically renounces any desire to deal in adverse criticism. Yet with refined imagination he unmistakably expresses his contempt. What he pretends to admire he actually condemns. The poem is a masterpiece in the humor of the oblique, the very opposite of true satire. To give an adequate conception of its sly, ironic method, it is necessary to quote the whole:

> Court officials wear fox-furs of saffron.
> Their bearing is important and refined.
> They come to Chou, the gaze of common people.
> Such noblemen are greatly to my mind.
> Court officials wear broad palm-shaped hats
> Or tall black caps; their ladies wear a pad

Of long thick hairs, most marvelous to see.
When I cannot see them I am sad.

Court officials wear ear-plugs of jade.
Men call their noble ladies fair and good.
When I am absent my poor heart is knit
In knots and sentiments ill understood.

Court officials flourish long thick sashes,
Like gorgeous trains; hair like a diadem
Or scorpion's tail is now the ladies' wear.—
They pass, and I walk swiftly after them.

It is not that the sash is really a train;
It is not that the sashes are so long.
It is not that ladies really curl their hair;
It naturally turns up: my thoughts were wrong!

Even this cursory review indicates how large a role is played by humor in the *Shih Ching*. As befits the poetry of an heroic age, the prevailing spirit of the humor is affirmative. It provides a critique of life but no disillusionment with it. The humor itself is of various sorts, derived from many moods. Into whatever path it turns it bears peculiar evidence of being Chinese, yet the humorous poems have a great sturdiness appearing in their remarkable power to survive the erosion of centuries and in many cases to show a bloom astonishingly fresh even to the present hour.

## 2 / *Poetry* (300 B.C.–1200 A.D.)

ALTHOUGH *The Book of Songs*, WITH ITS MANY ODES of a lusty, indubitably humorous spirit, remained a keynote of Chinese poetry virtually to the dawn of the twentieth century, during the tempestuous periods shortly following the death of Confucius the quality of the poetry began to change materially. Popular verse naturally followed with less radical change from the prevailing styles of the *Shih Ching* than did more sophisticated forms, as the esoteric or mystical lyrics and the eloquent Court poetry. In serious art-poetry a strong vogue developed for personal confessions in a mood of refined melancholy. It is far from a rash statement that for nearly two millennia the finest poetry produced in the Empire was on the whole weighted on the side of sadness and the minor key. At the same time that in general, it may be said, the prevailing sentiment of the people was resilient if not actually optimistic, fashions in verse tended to gravity. More elegance could, apparently, be obtained with melancholy than with mirth. The tragic spirit in poetry, if not in actual life, carried more weight than the comic spirit. More prestige was to be gained by composing a sad song than a gay or humorous one.

In the judgment, at least, of the present writer only one of the lyrics in *The Book of Songs* (number 184) can possibly be considered to reflect wholeheartedly the Taoist strain in Chinese thought, which was, nevertheless, distinctly powerful throughout the entire period actually recorded by historians of literature. As a philosophy, Taoism was at least as potent a force as Confucianism in the development of Chinese art and verse. Its profuse literature and powerful traditions, nursing romantic fantasy and imagination, strongly appealed to the aesthetic mind. Both the popular and the esoteric elements in this great movement encouraged highly fantastic and even eccentric modes of thought and expression. Also, another phase of the movement promoted quietism that encouraged what may be called "the still, small voice" in Chinese poetry, heard at its best from such masters as T'ao Ch'ien and Su Tung-p'o, over a period of nearly a thousand years. In their essential temper, Taoism and Chinese Buddhism had much in common, containing, of course, more powerful elements of mysticism and supernaturalism than does Confucianism. Thus in the arts, the Ch'an Buddhists assimilated much from the native Chinese tradition of Taoism, the Confucians standing apart from the two mystical religions though almost always occupying the center of the arena. Two great poets of the eighth century A.D., Tu Fu and Po Chü-i, presumably owed most to the Confucian tradition: Li Po and Li Ho may well have owed more to the mystical sects. In any case, mystical and romantic tendencies made themselves strongly felt in both poetry and prose shortly after Confucius' death. The rise of Buddhism as a potent factor shortly before the times of T'ao Ch'ien (372–427 A.D.) like a converging river added materially to this force. All the major poets to some degree felt these influences, though no two of them, of course, in quite the same manner. This being so, the full-throated, natural humor and gaiety expressed in so many pieces in *The Book of Songs* was not only never to be equaled but never closely approached.

One persistently asks, what is humor and where are its manifestations in poetry most clearly discerned? Where are the springheads of this spirit in Chinese poetry if, indeed, any such primal sources are discoverable? On the whole, I should maintain, in *The Book of Songs*, but the immediately preceding observations seriously qualify the statement. Occasionally critics have rashly presumed that they have found an answer. So in the Introduction to George Kao's anthology, *Chinese Wit and Humor*, Lin Yutang writes:

> There emerged what seems to my mind the most mature humorous spirit of China. I refer to T'ao Ch'ien, the poet, in whose spirit the last slightly sour note which existed in Changtzu was lost, and humor, joined to an understanding acceptance of life, evoked only a kindly, leisurely smile. Confucianism and Taoism had sufficiently combined to make his appearance possible. T'ao Ch'ien was both responsible and irresponsible, and we see at last neither a crusader nor a cynic, but a family man, one of us, and therefore truly a great human spirit, conscious of the limitations of human existence, but nevertheless achieving his own freedom without abandon, and peace of mind without rebellion. It would be difficult, though possible, to point to some particular piece of T'ao's as showing his humorous spirit; but that is so with the greatest and best

kind of humor when it becomes a pervading view of life. In him, humor becomes perfectly natural. T'ao had come to terms with himself and with his relations with the human world.[9]

This statement appears to the present writer less than half a truth, ascribing too much to T'ao Ch'ien in a general appraisal of the humorous element in Chinese literature. Who will wish to say that the clear, pure voice of humor is anywhere heard more admirably than in certain lyrics of *The Book of Songs?* Wang I and Wang Yen-chou, writing nearly three centuries before T'ao, at least equal him in humor. The great T'ang poets are clearly more powerful than he in this domain. As a humorist he does not remotely approach the writers of plays and novels that appeared considerably later in the stream of Chinese literature. T'ao Ch'ien is obviously a quietist. He may have pronounced a magic charm that stilled alien voices and created a quietness through which the voices of the true humorists were to be heard. As will later be shown, some of his poems certainly present a rather mild, though charming, expression of the humorous spirit. As might be supposed, there is no actual father of humor in Chinese literature. Its growth and evolution were continuous and directed through the collaboration of countless hands. It may be well to pursue the inquiry at a point that will presumably, to some minds, appear capricious and paradoxical. But humor is not to be traced by consulting ruler and compass. Let us examine the famous poem, Ch'ü Yüan's *Encountering Sorrow*, or the *Li Sao*.

This English title frequently given the poem as a rendering of the Chinese certainly does not suggest that research into the secrets of Chinese humor need take the least account of it. One of the most recent scholars to discuss the poem, Burton Watson, would appear to discourage any such thought. He writes: "At one point in particular, after the poet has been refused admittance to Heaven by the surly porter and tells us that 'knotting orchids, I stand in indecision,' there seems a real danger that inadvertent humor may intrude its fatal presence." [10] I suggest that Professor Watson to at least some degree yield to temptation. The result may not be as "fatal" as might be supposed.

Before examining any possible relation of this strange poem to humor a brief account of it and of its critics should be useful. It has been observed that the work, traditionally ascribed to Ch'ü Yüan, was composed in a section of China well to the south of that represented by *The Book of Songs*. There is indeed a tropical luxuriance in its rhetoric. Its style has been accounted for in part by its religious flavor, for it certainly reflects the invocations of the shamans, or magicians, who possessed among their other powers an ability to summon the souls of the dead. Several poems of the same school as *Encountering Sorrow* are almost surely of this nature, in other words, hymns of a magical power, incantations primarily religious and not strictly aesthetic in character, or, in any case, religious in their primary function and aesthetic only in a secondary phase. It may be asked if such poetry can be anything else than wholly serious? The answer depends in part on the meaning of the word "serious." One of the most powerful of the Chinese incantations apparently designed to summon the soul of a dead or dying prince back to its normal consciousness contains a long and very beautiful passage gleaming with gaiety, laughter, and sensual delights.[11] These exhilarating pleasures are promised the soul as inducements for its return from the borders of the world of shadows. Such a poetic landscape cannot be said resolutely to exclude the sense of humor. Not all religion is as grim as that of the Pilgrim Fathers.

*Encountering Sorrow* is a spiritual extravaganza beside which a mass by Charpentier might seem almost prosaic. It far outbaroques the baroque. It is difficult to believe that in the case of writing of such intoxicated imagination as seen in *Encountering Sorrow* the self-praise is without some grains of salt. It is hard to believe that even in the early stages of Chinese poetry a poet could shower himself with flowers without a gleam of amusement or that a man in such a period could have assumed himself to be a woman, his sovereign to be his mistress, and showered her with an extreme erotic imagery without a trace of a smile. It is clear from the profuse rhetoric that the poet is as highly self-conscious in art as his imagined figure is self-conscious and self-pitying in life. With so many mirrors flashing at once, many variations in mood are not only plausible but probable.

It is indeed remarkable that two of the earliest specimens of Chinese poetry to come down to us through the centuries, the *Shih Ching* and the *Li Sao*, should be so drastically opposed to each other in style, the first so patently forthright and direct, the second so elusive and convoluted. But the mystery in literature is surely no greater than that in philosophy, since the same land and age produced Confucius and Lao Tse.

It is at least plausible to hold that an inordinate love of rhetoric gives a tang of humor to some of the first major poets to succeed Ch'ü Yüan. A fantastic view of both language and nature characterizes some of the most striking poems of the Han dynasty, such as Sung Yü's *The Wind*, Wang I's The *Lychee-Tree*, and a master-piece by that poet's son, Wang Yen-shou, *The Wangsun*. The *Lychee-Tree* is a lyrical flight of joy, fantasy, and ingenuity reflecting a distinct phase of humor; *The Wangsun* is a pure grotesque, imaging a quaint, odd little animal that not only smiles but compels those who contemplate it to smile.

The most remarkable poet in the long, troubled period between the Han and T'ang is presumably the before-mentioned T'ao Ch'ien, sometimes called T'ao Yüan-ming. His general position in relation to humor in poetry has already been briefly examined, with indication that the question has received various answers and still merits attention. Inasmuch as he exercised a strong and lasting influence on many aspects of Chinese verse, his work calls for further examination.

T'ao Ch'ien's contribution to the evolution of the sense of humor among his countrymen clearly hangs upon the character of his singularly well-established and confirmed philosophy of life. Virtually all his poems unmistakably express this outlook, fortified by precept and doctrine. He is a quietist in the sense that in his verses he cherishes divorce from all the more strenuous and stirring forces in life and society. He discourages all commitment to both the emotional and the public life. His prescription is simply to let the world drift as it will; all moral idealism and crusading zeal is renounced as fanaticism and illusion. Furthermore, he renounces ascetic fanaticism as conclusively as he rejects political activism. His own ideal, if an ideal it can be called, is retirement to domestic life in the quiet of the countryside. Only the fantasy is free to roam. Rejecting the ethical responsibilities demanded by Confucianism, he admits and even invites the pleasure of wine and drunkenness. Playfulness of the mind is to take the place of exertions of the will. Moreover, he holds small commerce with the world of magic, which so profoundly attracted Ch'ü Yüan and the poets of the Southern school. The roots of his philosophy are clearly in Taoism, although he dismisses the more exuberant and the more popular forms of that faith. He weds the Confucian sense of moderation to the Taoist sense of detachment. Although his position somewhat resembles the "sweet reasonableness" of the English seventeenth-century quietists and the worldly wisdom of the French eighteenth-century rationalists who advised each man to cultivate his private garden, his position is emphatically Chinese. There is enough of the universal in the outlook to render it, broadly speaking, intelligible to all the world, yet the peculiar blend of its constituent elements gives it a unique aroma. The major Chinese poets were for centuries to declare that T'ao Ch'ien's verse was the most exquisite and highly refined in the course of literary history.

This view encouraged a few remarkably satisfying symbols expressing basic ideas. One was the image of the official returning to his home and family in the country. He comes in a boat happily approaching the landing-place. Such was the central image in his most famous poem, *The Return,* used by countless painters as their subject-matter. The spirit of the scene is happy but certainly not ecstatic. The returning official is represented as an elderly man wholly resigned to shaking off the burdens of officialdom and pleased to enjoy the quiet pleasures provided by the play of children and the charms of a hospitable countryside. A skeptic might, of course, remark that the play of children does not always seem quiet to their elders nor does nature at all times appear hospitable. Such reflections seldom find expression in the verses of T'ao Ch'ien and his followers. In both literature and art the proponent of T'ao Ch'ien's school of thought is commonly represented as an elderly man, a retired statesman or gentleman, who has somehow contrived to look smilingly upon existence. Insofar as he wears a smile, he at least shares in the outlook of humor; insofar as he is restrained or even faint, he occupies only a minor province in the humorist's world.

T'ao Ch'ien's view of humor is, then, to a large extent compromising. In some of his poems we are sure that a quiet humor is to be detected; in others all humor appears to have dissipated, refined out of existence. There are no violent tempests. There is only a high degree of humidity. Laughter has given place to smiles and even the smile tends to vanish. In an over-all view it must be acknowledged that the philosophy is conducive to certain forms of humor but actually hostile to a lusty development of humorous expression. What humor does manifest itself is more genteel than forceful. The major humorist smiles at himself, the minor humorist smiles only at the world. Humor and the complacent man cannot live altogether happily together. For this reason Po Chü-i and Tu Fu represent a far more developed form of humor than T'ao Ch'ien and his followers. The quietist's philosophy led to a finely cultivated but, comparatively speaking, overbred and over-tamed mentality. It declined at length into the gracious but relatively tepid world of the Sung poet, Su Tung-p'o, where the voice of comedy is reduced to a whisper. While T'ao Ch'ien's philosophy encouraged a mild variety of humor, it discouraged all stronger manifestation of humorous verse. Comic his vein certainly is not. At its best it may possibly be called humoristic.

Some typical poems by T'ao Ch'ien bearing upon the sense of humor may be noted to clarify the foregoing statements. *Blaming Sons*, for example, shows him mildly vexed that none of his sons exhibits the slightest talent for literature. This state of affairs, he maintains, has driven him to drink. But the entire tone of the piece shows that he is more vexed than desperate. Although his words are a protest and, no doubt, voice sincere disappointment, the archness and wit of the expression indicate that the father is actually reconciled to these deficiencies in his family. It is doubtless a part of the vexing contradictions in nature and destiny that son does not always follow father, that life unhappily abounds in troublesome contradictions. The wise man, insists T'ao Ch'ien, dismisses these with a smile. He does not, in Chaucer's image, break the crock against the wall. In this, as in many of the poems, the poet has searched out and discovered the art of smiling at life's irregularities and inconsistencies. Humor is present with its healing force. But it must further be admitted that the bruises are minor and the therapy itself light and easy. His gauze bandages are for minor wounds.

Such poetry and such humor obviously depend upon a lightness of touch. This is well seen in *Reading the Book of Strange Places and Seas*. The book in question consists of strange and fantastic legends concerning far away places. The poet imagines himself contented with home on a peaceful spring day. After performing the light work demanded by his farm, he retires to the uninterrupted quiet of books and study. Even the lane to his house is so narrow and rough that friends who might come as visitors are discouraged from interrupting his peace of mind. Pulling a book from his shelf, he takes out his carafe of wine. Outside there is a fine rain and a light breeze, no violent downpour. He enjoys the luxurious sense of idleness. His eyes merely roam over the pages that describe the far away and long ago. He experiences perfect happiness.

This highly contrived and artful poem may well be described as humorous. The gesture by which T'ao Ch'ien wraps his soft, protective garments around him causes both him and the reader to smile. He does not, however, even suggest that his indulgence is in any way a defect. He does not laugh at himself; he somehow contrives to smile at his success as he sees it in taming the universe. The well-being of the humorist is here but a well-being under highly contrived and constricted circumstances. Such flowers of humor are blossoms of plants grown indoors. Chinese verse for many centuries provided such ornaments. It also provided more substantial things. It must be confessed that in the greater number of T'ao Ch'ien's poems even the milder forms of humor are absent. Like Su Tung-p'o, the love of wine notwithstanding, he is primarily a sober poet. In a fair number of his pieces there is rather an intimation of humor than the essential quality itself. Most of his successors read him with pleasure, for he is a master of the poetic idiom, but in respect to humor he has negative rather than positive qualities. By easing the mind from the straightjackets of moral and intellectual conformity, T'ao Ch'ien opened the ground for lustier growths of imagination and, above all, for the more powerful creations of the comic spirit. Technically he came close to perfection. In this respect his art resembles the extremely refined style of the chief English laureate of genteel country living and humor in retirement, William Cowper. But greater spirits in China had been before him and were still to come.

The story hastens on to Li Po, flourishing over three hundred years later. Li, a man of the most commanding genius, was essentially a poet of ecstasies, owing more to the followers of Ch'ü Yüan than to those of the quietist, T'ao Ch'ien, though he was to some extent the heir also of the younger man. Many of his poems are erotic and still more are colored by magic, mysticism, and religion. He seemed equally at home when at Court or when in exile. There are at least some parallels with Pushkin. When at court, Li was arrogant and untamable, when in exile he apparently denied himself the quietude of domestic happiness and rural life. Unlike T'ao Ch'ien, he was in no conceivable sense a pastoral poet. Instead, he searched for the elixir of immortality, for inspiration that should lift him above vulgar existence into an ecstatic life. His excess of violence was almost as hostile to the exploiting of humor as T'ao Ch'ien's quietism. But humor is on the whole more robust than peaceful. Hence research into the springs of humor is more profitable in the instance of Li Po than in that of his predecessor. Li's habitual extravagance provided a happier soil for humor than T'ao Ch'ien's studied and habitual understatement.

There even is more of orthodox Taoism, with its element of enthusiasm, and more, paradoxically, of simple quietism, in the following poem by Li Po than in the many more or less analogous pieces from T'ao Ch'ien:

> Life is only a dream. Why all this unrest?
> To me wisdom
> Lies is being drunk perpetually
> And sleeping the rest of the time.
> And that I did one day;
> When I awoke and looked around me,
> I saw a bird chirping among the flowers.
> I asked what day it was. They told me:
> 'It's spring. An oriole is singing.'
> I sighed deeply, for the voice had touched me.
> I helped myself again to a copious draught,
> And sang a cheerful song, while waiting for the moon;
> When I had ended, it was all forgotten.[12]

This is, doubtless, not an especially humorous poem but nevertheless is the work of a humorist. There is a note of humorous illogicality in the discrepancy in the poet's moods. The oriole's cheerful singing at first causes him to sigh. But presently he has recovered his accustomed bright spirits and sings a cheerful song. The poem as a whole is unquestionably ex-hilarating.

Perhaps his most famous poem is also a drinking song. It reveals a much more developed spirit of humor. This is the piece entitled *Drinking Alone under Moonlight*. Li imagines himself dancing, with the moon and his shadow as his companions. The wine-cup affords the center of this ritual inasmuch as the dancer's leading thought is that neither of his comrades knows the joy of drinking as he does. This is a mad, exuberant lyric that can only be understood as humor in its most hilarious mood.

It is creditably reported that Li Po at one period of his life was much of a bravo, flinging himself about with riotous fun at the expense of persons weaker and much more sober than he. His extravagant moods and actions proceeded from an irrational excess of high spirits further impelled by the irrationalist's sense of humor. His very defiance of convention was a humorous extravagance. Such a poem as *The Bravo of Chao* is not only an apology for extravagant and unruly conduct; like much Chinese lyrical poetry it is also self-expression. Its essential meanings will be clear even without quotation. Satire is contained in it but the poem is not properly satire. Two characters are present who are actually symbols. *The Bravo of Chao* clearly reflects the poet himself though in no sense is he literally the poet. The meaning is clarified by certain references in the verses. In the final stanza mention is made of a Confucian scholar, Yang Hsiung, author of a commentary on the classical text, *The Book of Changes*. This worthy had lived in the first century B.C. Tu Fu especially despised him as typical of the pedant in the class of scholar-gentleman. As a modern commentator reports: "He is said to have studied by the window for so long that men had forgotten whether there was any part of him except his white head." [13] The Bravo is declared by Li Po to be vastly more alive and effectual than this notorious pedant. The poem as a whole is more concerned with the high spirits of its hero than with the conformity of the hero's antithesis. Hence it is much more in the spirit of humor than of satire. The school of T'ao Ch'ien looked askance at the busy world and further declared it to be absurd but the alternative which its poets placed over and against the prevailing follies of society was quietism, which actually attracted Li Po far less than vigorous exercise of the will, mind, soul, and body. He was accordingly the stronger humorist.

*The Bravo of Chao* is related to the earlier part of Li's life, when he was chiefly active in Court affairs. It best exhibits his humor as related to society. As a reveler or man of the world he presents analogies to figures familiar in the West, as Benvenuto Cellini and the aforementioned Pushkin. The strong religious and metaphysical aspect of his thinking, chiefly characteristic of his later years, is seen in the half-humorous poem, *To a Monk on the Tai-Pei Mountains.* For Li Po was at heart both bravo and monk and in each capacity a profound humorist. His religion is chiefly derived from Taoism, indeed his friend Tu Fu reports him to have been seeking the elixir of immortality among the hills. His poetry abounds in flights of pure magic. The alchemists of the West seem prosaic beside him. He is visionary, transcendental, at one with the forces of nature and with the soul of the landscape. Through his fondness for this phase of the Chinese mind he becomes also the humorist. He laughs more often and in verse more effectively from sheer joy through oneness with the illogical forces of the universe than from a stooping to satirize either human folly or vice. He cultivates the fantastic images familiarized in Chinese art by the Ch'an Buddhists. To the Taoist monk, subject of the last mentioned poem, he ascribes the properties of the true magician who delights in playing humorous tricks on the mind. These are not to make the observer appear foolish but are above all to give to the performer a sense of power and joy. The aged monk in Li's poem appears and vanishes at will. He floats high in air. Inaccessible mountains are his habitation. His diet is the dew. The nearest villagers have never seen him. The entire universe he envisages as a cosmic caprice.

Li Po's humor unhappily transcends our common vision. He himself cannot give adequate expression to his vision. No man can explain it and perhaps no one fully understands it. But we believe in it nevertheless. His ethereal poetry is one of the most precious achievements of Chinese civilization. The West, to repeat, has nothing quite analogous to it. In English the nearest approach may well be the highly intuitive poetry of Coleridge or Poe. But how limited in comparison appear the visions of these masters of English verse! Their products have a forced and hothouse quality when seen beside the visions of the Chinese poet-sage. In his poetry is epitomized much of the mysterious insight and beauty of Chinese landscape painting at its best. Of all major Chinese poets he seems farthest divorced from Confucianism. Even the visionary Ch'ü Yüan stooped at times to mere satire of corruption. But even in his bitterest poems Li Po rises above this. He soars into heights of an exalted humor, his spirit the epitome of an O *Altitudo*. Humor becomes an essential ingredient even in his supernaturalism.

His great compatriots, Tu Fu and Po Chü'i, brought humor once more down to earth. Like almost all major poets, with the exception of the masters of theatrical comedy, they appear more often in a serious than in a humorous guise. But humor constitutes an important phase of their achievement. By far the greater part of the work of the two men deals with man in his social relationships, no matter whether the poet himself is the chief actor or the vision is purely objective. As the older, more synthetic and possibly more inspired of the two, Tu Fu calls for first consideration. The refinement and subtlety of his art demands considerable quotation to clarify generalizations. The quotations unless otherwise specified are translations by the present writer.

Social humor frequently resides in the successful acting of a role where there is a subtle element of understatement and restraint. The incongruity at the root of virtually all humor lies along these oblique lines. An agreeable bait covers a hidden hook. Such is a special quality of Tu Fu's poem, *On Rejecting a Gift of a Satin Brocade.* A further feature of the humor here is one already mentioned in other connections, the turn of the humorous criticism against the poet himself. Here this strategy, though certainly present, has still a further refinement. The poet's humility is not only a mask to deceive the villain of the piece; it is in fact an affectation on the poet's part. Even while he seems to be demeaning himself he is not really doing so. He does not think meanly of himself, though such is the appearance that he assumes. The truth is that he may even take some pride in his rectitude. Although he assumes that he is too humble and undeserving a man to receive a gift fit only for princes, his deeper thought is that the giver and not the man to whom the gift is offered demeans himself. The obvious impolitic reaction of the moralist would be indignation at the offer of a bribe. Expression would be one of anger. Instead, the poet's response is couched in the irony of humorous indirection. The reader is presumed to take a far different view of the situation from that of the figure to whom the speaker's remarks are addressed. This is the leading formula for high comedy on the stage. Here the actor is the official offering the bribe. The reader takes the place of both audience and poet, seeing the action through radically different eyes from those of the unlucky victim of the jest. The poem is as follows:

> My honored guest from the Northwest has made
> A present to me of this bright brocade.
> Opening the package somewhat gingerly,
> I look on seething waves of a vast sea.
> A whale among them lashes his huge tail;
> Other creatures swim in shining mail
> But at the distance it's too far to see
> What their true identity may be.
> My guest says: "This is for your cushion's seat.
> Take it as a present, I entreat.
> Doing so, your joy will be increased
> When you sit on it at some glorious feast.

Sleep on it, and you will have dreamless rest.
Display it, and bad luck will be suppressed."
My guest's great kindness I appreciate.
But since I am no minister of state,
This could not be auspicious. I decline
To place it in this modest house of mine.
There is a fitting law of long duration
That gifts should be appropriate to one's station.
Since I'm a humble man, precedent shows
I should be satisfied with plainest clothes.
So exquisite an object's only fit
For the Imperial Palace. Surely it
Would never be appropriate in my home
And from it only much bad luck could come.
I am surprised how in these cursed years
Of fighting and disorder it appears
That many leading men in high command
Have snatched advantage of their power in hand
To stock themselves with finest clothes and horse.
Li Ting died in Ch'i-yang since in his course
Of governing he showed excessive pride.
Lai T'ien was forced to commit suicide
Because his arrogance hindered the war.
Both were well known to have amassed a store
Of tainted wealth. It's no surprise at all
They met their sad, inevitable fall.

How can an old and common farmer dare
Accept so sumptuous a gift or wear
Such fabrics? Let me fold this whale-brocade
Which you have with such courtesy displayed
And so return it to you, if you please.
Then only shall I feel myself at ease.
Let me dust off this mat. Please take your seat!
Only thus can my pleasure be complete.
Even so my shy and timid spirits droop
Handing you this thin cup of vegetable soup.

How close this comes to techniques familiar in the comic
theatre appears in the last line, which combines humorous

understatement with theatrical exaggeration. The poet's hand actually trembles as, frightened by the dignity of his illustrious guest, he hands him a cup of thin, unsavory soup.

Another sampling shows the poet's social humor with delicate variations. Here instead of assuming humility he assumes an air of supercilious superiority. In each case there is a figure who clearly gets the worst of it; on one occasion the unscrupulous official offers a bribe, on the other is a foolish and impecunious cousin. In each case are incongruities and contradictions that comprise the chief formula for humor itself. In the second poem is the somewhat improbable assumption that the poor relation does not know that he is placed in a rather absurd light. He should have known enough in his unfortunate condition to economize and take greater care of things about the farm. He must not draw recklessly from a shrinking well; he must not be careless in cutting down his sunflowers; he should not use too much water in cooking rice; he should stop gossiping with neighbors across the fence and, worst of all, with strangers; he should keep within the circle of family and the clan. Such is the advice of the successful relative and official.

The poem is spared the aspersion of being merely didactic and is all the more clearly assured in its humor by some irregular features in the delineation of the speaker. He begins by announcing that he is lazy. He will not, he tells us, attempt to do business with rich and clever men but instead will pursue his duties as overseer by visiting his poor relation. By virtue of his authority and place rather than through any peculiar insight or merit he lords it over his inferior. There is no intimation that he blames himself morally for this. Yet it is evident that he is on both a moral and a physical holiday, riding out into the countryside and dispensing advice which he well knows to be commonplace to a simple soul willing to take all seriously and in the best spirit. The official and the reader smile inwardly. A sophisticated humor is enjoyed at the expense of a countrified relative. A qualifying feature in the apparent stupidity of the farmer is seen in the second of the poem's three parts. The man's impoverishment is not altogether his own fault. He has suffered from frost and other hostilities in nature. This renders the critique more genial and more removed from either satire or a gross type of humor. The humor is all the more refined for being to a great degree kindly.

I am an old man, lazy as can be
And you, my boy, can either walk or run
Beside me, as you choose. It pleases me
To ride my donkey in the morning sun.
My duty is to travel and inspect.
I'll go not to the mighty and the high
Because from them small profit can accrue.
My cousin is a person such as I
And at his cottage I shall win respect;
So this is what this morning I shall do.

You are a simple person, unemployed;
Your homestead stands like a deserted town.
In autumn's frost your tall bamboo were spoiled;
Some of your lily plants have fallen down.
Under such circumstances it is right
That, as an elder in our family,
I should keep your vicissitudes in mind.
I do not come for porridge, as you see,
But to place matters in a lucid light
And to say what is rational and kind.

Too many drawings make a muddy well,
So don't use too much water to wash rice.
When cutting your ripe sunflowers, do not fell
Plants with a broad-axe, or you'll pay the price
By injuring their taproots. Do not be
Lured by idle gossiping that serves
No useful purposes. Carefully scan
The counsel of outsiders; it deserves
Always to be viewed suspiciously;
The Ancients favor a united clan.

Apparently all peoples capable of detecting human vanity regard it as a prime cause of risibility. The discrepancy between reality and presumption and the exaggeration which the individual places upon his own importance and dignity lead to an amused smile. The higher reaches of enlightenment and sophistication are attained when a person is shrewd enough to smile at his own vanity. Such is the case in an amusing and exceptionally well sustained poem, *Drunk, I Fell from Horseback*. The narrative contained in the poem is so circumstantial as to be thoroughly convincing; the story clearly reflects an actual experience. Tu Fu has been feted at a party. Though already elderly, he drinks heavily and rises to perform a lively dance. So successful is this that he aspires to prove to his friends that he has maintained at his advanced age the skill in dashing horsemanship for which he was celebrated in his youth. On riding rapidly down a mountain-side he experiences a sharp fall, encountering minor but by no means negligible injuries. A few days later, to prove their undiminished admiration of him, his good friends arrange a banquet in his honor. At the same time that they fete him they laugh at him. The poet's good humor is unshaken. He receives the ridicule in the best of spirit. In fact, his last remarks in the poem, far from being of a repentant or cautionary nature, recall a scholar who had written a book on the laborious means of guarding health but who himself died at the hands of the public executioner. Although for most of its length the poem promises to be a cautionary tale in behalf of reasonable conduct, its closing lines, where, if anywhere a conventional moral might be expected, actually advance a plea in behalf of daring, risk and even recklessness. They afford a delightfully humorous surprise.

> I was the Governor's old, welcome guest
> Whose warmth and hospitality expressed
> Itself in lavish feasting and strong wine.
> Then, in one of those mad moods of mine,
> I rose hilariously to sing and dance

The lively figure of "the Golden Lance."
Next, suddenly remembering my pride
In youth, I mounted a swift horse to ride.
Outside the K'uei-chou Gate steep highways go
To where the stream and clouds stretch out below.
Precipitously the canyon walls dive down
Nine hundred yards beneath the white-walled town.
Like summer lightning the white fort flashed past
My purple bridle. Faster and more fast
I rushed across the level plain beside
The rustic village at the river's side.
Across the plain and underneath the bluff
The hills are rugged and the pathways rough.
Easing the rein, letting the whiplash trail,
I galloped with the madness of a gale
Over red, dusty land.

                My foolish ends
Were always to surprise my many friends
And garner for a white-haired man the praise
Won by his valor in his early days,
Showing I still can ride and shoot as then.
Though I might gain some favor among men,
I was indeed a fool to think of course
My views of speed congenial to my horse.
The white foam on his lips and the red sweat
Along his streaming body might have let
Me grasp the matter clearly as I ought
And know he could not share my private thought.
A careless stumble left a serious hurt.
To follow impulse so is to pervert
The truth of nature and to court disgrace.
Now I confront my error face to face.
I've much to ponder as I lie in bed
Reflecting on sad follies time has bred.

Kind souls and neighbors come with searching eyes;
I must now shamefacedly arise,
Leaning upon my servants and my cane.
I tell my tale. Good friends cannot refrain

FIG. 1. *Incense Burner. Lao-tzu on a Water-Buffalo. Sung dynasty*, A.D. 960–1280. *Bronze, 8¼ inches high. Courtesy of the Worcester Art Museum.*

FIG. 2. *The Poet Li Po on a Stroll, by Liang K'ai (13th century). Hanging scroll. Courtesy of the Tokyo National Museum.*

FIG. 3. *The Poet Tu Fu on a Donkey's Back, by Sesshū Tōyō, late 15th–early 16th century. Hanging scroll, ink on paper, height 33½ inches. Courtesy the Tokiwayama Foundation, Kamakura.*

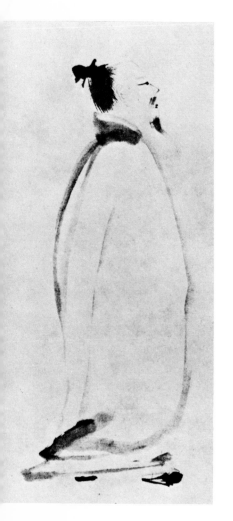

FIG. 4. *Portrait of the Artist's Friend I-an, by Lo P'ing (1733–1799). Hanging scroll, ink and light colors on paper, 47⅛ inches high, 17⅛ inches wide. Courtesy of James Cahill.*

含章每賦風詠已傳橫斜疏影自有年梅花著論真

不貝

吳廉不忍先生大齊癸亥...戊午秋奉歸齊溪長蘆作此奉別

盖隨一綫以傳笑和

兩峯羅聘

FIG. 5. *Two Men in Conversation. Detail of painting on hollow tiles. Late Han–early Six Dynasties, 2nd–4th century* A.D. *Courtesy of the Museum of Fine Arts, Boston.*

FIG. 6. *Chung K'uei, the Demon-queller, on His Travels, by Kung K'ai. Sung, 13th century. Detail from painted scroll. Courtesy of the Freer Gallery of Art.*

FIG. 7. *Mother Monkey and Child, by Mu ch'i (middle of the
13th century). Detail of hanging scroll. Courtesy of the Daito-
kuji, Tokyo.*

FIG. 8. *Boy, Buffalo, and Calf (album leaf). Southern Sung dynasty. Color and ink on silk. Courtesy of the Cleveland Museum of Art, Mr. and Mrs. Severance A. Millikin Collection.*

FIG. 9. *A Quadruped. Late Chou dynasty, 6th–3rd century* B.C. *Bronze. Width 7¼ inches. Courtesy of the Freer Gallery of Art.*

FIG. 10. *Boar. Ordos. Fifth century* B.C. *or later. Bronze. Courtesy of the Indiana University Art Museum.*

FIG. 11. *Bear. Shang dynasty* (1523–1028 B.C.). *Jade. Height 2½ inches. Courtesy of the Fogg Art Museum, Harvard University.*

FIG. 12. *Winged Dragon. Early part of the Huai period* (947–770 B.C.). *Bronze. 7 inches high, 8½ inches long. Courtesy of the Minneapolis Institute of Arts, Alfred F. Pillsbury Bequest, 1950.*

From bursts of laughter. Now they carry me
To fields beside a stream that pleasantly
Purls on and there a mountainous feast is laid
With music that weird strings and flutes have made.
All pointing to the West, profoundly say
Time passes and the sun will not delay.
They shout for everyone to drain his glass,
Sipping the sparkling moments as they pass.
But why, good friends, envoys of gentleness,
Give me this comfort in my late distress?
The author of *Good Health* held prudence high
Until a headsman led him out to die.

The sense of humor as properly understood does not consist
in verbal wit, mirth, satire, or the hilarity that induces loud
laughter and guffaws, though it borders on these and at least
to some extent shares territory with them. It is a branch of
the comic spirit on which grow fruits of various colors, shapes
and sizes, many being hybrids. On one extreme it approaches
a low comedy of mere slapstick, farce, or nonsense, too rude
to be called pure humor. On the other, it borders on archness,
urbanity, and pleasantry. It is neither entirely of the body nor
of the mind but a condition of the spirit expressed by a refined
smile or civilized laughter. Much of the finest Chinese humor
is remarkably sophisticated and cultured, expression proceeding
from a state of mind where delicate shades of thought and feeling are apprehended and amusement derived from incongruities within an advanced stage of society. This condition presumes at most a smiling, certainly not a loudly laughing, audience. It appears at most in overtones. These may even be heard
against bass-notes played in a distinctly minor key. A work of
this kind, actually inspired by highly refined humor, may on
too cursory reading appear altogether serious. The impression
received becomes a matter of sensibility. What was altogether
apparent to the Chinese scholar class in the brighter periods of
their culture is not equally apparent to persons of other times
and places. Yet the finest expressions of this state of mind and

the species of art springing from it will be apprehensible and enjoyable to those of educated sensibilities in any time or place where advanced civilization exists. Some of the most fragrant flowers of humor or the comic spirit undoubtedly flourished in China from an early date and for a long period of time. By the side of the completely robust, uproarious humor of such a prose narrative as *Monkey* flourished humorous works of a much quieter but essentially more refined nature. The culmination of the urbane Chinese humor is found in Tu Fu. Let us examine another of his pieces exhibiting this delicate, muted variety of humor, played, as it were, upon the harpsichord.

*Annoyed!* is a poem not quite in a manner familiar to Western light verse but approaching it. The mood dominating its early lines appears to be a familiar though paradoxical fusion of irritability and boredom. The speaker is clearly one of the masks of the poet himself. There can be no question of the poem's considerable faithfulness to social actuality. The speaker's irritability derives from frustrations that in turn spring from several sources. The weather is bad; transportation in the city is wretched; he cannot be on time at his place of business (the Court); prices are rising; above all, he finds it especially hard to indulge in his greatest pleasure, which is to share with his best friend wine, music, and verses. The irritability amounts almost to peevishness. A distinct suspicion arises that the poet engages to a certain degree in self-mockery. The view of life is anything but heroic. No emotional storms, philosophical or religious doctrines, nor moral values are at stake. To say the least, life is not taken overseriously. Yet is it not an honest reflection of the life of a truly civilized and lovable person? The enlightenment comes, as the best standards of form lead us to expect, in the last few lines. Apart from his friend, obviously one of the comparatively few intelligent persons in town, life tends to become tedious. With his friend all is changed. A desert bursts into bloom. Affection, charm, beauty, wit come abruptly into their own. Ill humors vanish before the force of true humor. This is social comedy, high comedy. Some readers will prefer John Milton, others may prefer Tu Fu.

I am highly annoyed! We live at two ends of a row
So why haven't we seen each other for ten long days?
I gave up the horse that the government loaned me and so
I'm faced with the rough, rugged ground of the public ways.
I'm far too poor to hire a personal chaise,
And, again, if I walked, my superiors wouldn't approve!
So a warm wish to see you suffers vexatious delays.
This is my problem, so please do not question my love!

This morning it rains; spring winds make house-walls tremble.
I was sleeping soundly so didn't hear the bell
And loud drum that summon courtiers to assemble.
To be sure, I have some kindly neighbors who dwell
To the east who would loan me a donkey. That's all very well,
But the mud is so slippery I dare not ride it to Court.
My troubles and trials are more than a man can tell.
I've petitioned to be excused as a last resort!

How can I bear the whole day with a longing heart
To hear your poems that impress me so movingly?
Youth fades as these early magnolia blossoms depart
And the high price of wine is a frightful thing to see!
Inebriate sleep comes seldom to you and me.
Come quickly, please, and release the wine-keg's stoppers!
We'll empty a hearty gallon immediately,
For I happen to have precisely three hundred coppers.

A variation in this fertile vein of high comedy appears in *Poem Sent to Tu Tso*. This piece is less personal than those by Tu Fu so far examined, though the poet is a figure in it. Like *Annoyed!* it is conceived as an epistle. The humor lies in the high degree of inference contained in it and the sharp interplay of two contrasting themes. The address is to a cousin who has recently paid Tu Fu a visit. Their relation unquestionably is friendly and even affectionate. Tu Fu hopes that the man has returned to his house safely and at not too late an hour. Earlier in the season Tu Fu had visited Tu Tso and assisted in some harvesting of grain. The poet himself is relatively poor. With a delicate understatement he declares that "he seems to remember" a promise from his cousin of a gift of millet. Although the time has passed when this grain must have been ground, no gift of it has arrived. Besides, Tu Tso must have harvested some green-mallow and some especially succulent shallots. The poet only hints but the hint is unmistakable. Why has Tu Tso procrastinated and thus failed to send these products of his farm that would contribute so much to the table of his poor and affectionate uncle? This poem is a gentle reminder that begins with an expression of solicitude and concern for his cousin's comfort and ends with a petition for a gift to enhance his own. Tu Fu by no means conceals his desire to have not only the basic food derived from the millet but the delicacies that will add relish to the table of an epicure. He petitions for the one and in addition smacks his lips at thought of the other. This, almost as much as the tactful understatement, relieves the poem from any suspicion of being a harsh or heated complaint and graces the lines with cool, sparkling humor. Inconsequential as the piece may at first appear, it is a masterpiece of light verse according to the peculiar genius of the scholar-poets of the T'ang period. Some persons may well hold that poetic art has attained greater heights; civilization, one presumes, has not.

> Floating clouds must have darkened the afternoon hills
> And I fear that bad roads have caused you some harm
> And birds must have silenced their musical bills
> When at last you re-entered your tree-shaded farm.
> Uncle Tu Fu, who is lazy and calm
> In disaster, stays here with his children and spouse.
> They have traveled rough roads and now long for the balm
> Of your aid to maintain this impoverished house.
>
> The millet we gleaned in early September
> You promised to share when it first should appear.
> It must be ground fine, for I seem to remember

It's been over a month now in reaching me here.
We hardly need wait for the peak of the year,
When the golden chrysanthemums come into flower.
I hold green-mallow soup with fresh millet most dear,
My mouth waters to taste it at this very hour.

What turbulent freshets of spring must have been
In your garden where so many eatables grow!
Those sturdy fall shrubs must by this time be thin;
You'll see more high clouds as the autumn leaves go.
Fragrant plants must be lush where the pond-waters flow
And the dodder vines rich in the neighboring wood.
Your frost-covered shallots are ripe now, I know.
Do send me some, please, if you will be so good!

As already indicated at some length, the word humor, which
has enjoyed so long and checkered a history, is even today
understood with a considerable variety of meanings. One phase
of our understanding of it tends to merge with another. Good
humor is a state of mind, comic humor a factor in the arts.
The two have a brotherly relation. Life or art may be amusing
without being patently comic. There is a tendency in the
poems quoted above to be decreasingly robust or hilarious and
increasingly muted and refined. Along the same line of co-
ordinates but representing approximately the minimum of
assertiveness in humor is a poem, *To Prefect Chang*, where the
humorous point of view is certainly maintained but outright
jesting is reserved for only the last line or two. The poet is
amused throughout but certainly not hilarious. He moralizes
in his final utterance but to the discerning reader his moralizing will certainly be taken with a grain of salt.

Tu Fu, a man with Shakespearean breadth of vision, sym-
pathized with the miseries of the myriad Chinese who were
poor and wretched, suffering above all from the wounds of
civil war. Despite the long continuity of social and political
institutions in China, the continuity of the language and the
Empire, the country has suffered more than most lands from
war, since its wars have been for the most part civil rather than

foreign, fought on its own soil. Tu Fu also had a fellow feeling with the gay and dazzling life of the Court, its outrageous luxury and display. He obviously enjoyed its brilliance. Yet he knew clearly what this lavishness cost the common people. There was a weight of irony here that at times lay heavily on his heart. All this appears in his poems. Some are almost entirely gay and epicurean, others almost entirely satirical or tragic. A few, such as the astonishing *Poem on Seeing the Sword Pantomime Dance,* are both.

For the present discussion only the poems that are more gay than sad are relevant. *To Prefect Chang* sufficiently answers this description. Although something of his moral reservations may be assumed behind the picture of the revelry by the Meandering River, with its loud festivities lasting deep into the night, not until the very last phrases is there any literal or unmistakable sign of them. All appears gay, even to excess. At the end he warns his friend, the Prefect, that on his return by the river he should take no example from the amorous ducks that swim in pairs but should remember his wife, who awaits him anxiously at home. The sudden, wholly unexpected burst of moralizing, even if it is to be taken with a degree of irony, has an unmistakably humorous effect. Without it the poem could not be placed in the category of poems of humor. With it the contrary becomes true. It should further be noted here that Tu Fu, the supercraftsman, gave great attention to the last lines of his poems. They were the rudders by which he steered his course. A bantering tone is, in fact, maintained throughout the entire poem. It is betrayed, for example, in the mention of the coquettish eyes of the courtesans, that not only bear witness to the pride of youth but betray young men. May they not betray the poet's friend, the Prefect Chang!

> Eminent guests dismounting from their horses
> Are welcomed by fair women near the stream.
> Broad fans are mirrored in the water-courses,
> Loud songs re-echo as bright costumes gleam.

Robes sweep widely as they dance and whirl;
Wine pots refract each shimmering sunbeam.
Just note the face of each sweet-smiling girl,
Each bright glance glowing in keen competition,
Each coquettish eye betraying youth's ambition!

With song and dance the shining sun is downed;
Still loud flute-tones pierce the darkening sky;
Gleaming eyebrows move to choric sound;
Each headdress to its neighbor makes reply.
Horses are standing back to back in file.
At dusk far hills glow as the night is nigh;
Perfumed boats drift homeward mile on mile.—
My friend, you have a wife who waits and wakes;
Don't take a wrong example from wild ducks and drakes!

The analysis of the mood of the foregoing poems concludes this evidence of the strong undercurrent of humor giving such distinction to so much of Tu Fu's art and good evidence of an important phase of Chinese poetry, maintained throughout its classical period. A poem typical of humor in his brief, epigrammatic pieces shows humor in another vein. In the epigrammatic form almost to the same degree as in his odes or more truly lyric pieces Tu Fu shows his tendency to take himself humorously, to deal in humorous hyperbole and celebrate the irrational. His Taoistic praise of drunkenness and wine has been seen in several of his well-known poems. But his intoxication may also arise from other sources, producing humorous effects so commonly associated with inebriation. He holds that he can be drunk even on flowers and fancifully implores the blossoms to show him some mercy.

Flowers in confusion by the river shine;
Awed, I likewise stagger as I can;
I can subsist on poetry and wine;
But try not to undo a white-haired man!

The foregoing quatrain suggests one of Tu Fu's most brilliant pieces with a strong humorous flavor, *Eight Immortals of the Wine Cup*, where the irrational moods created by wine itself are the basic theme. This poem has always been one of its author's most popular works. Contrary to the type of humor commonly found in Tu Fu's poems, the vein here is extravagant and even exuberant. Eight scholar-courtiers of the imperial establishment are celebrated not for their contributions to good government but for their superiority in deep drinking and for the sensational effects that wine has upon them. If the outlook were not so clearly hilarious, the poem might even be seen as satire. But the unmistakable inference is that the poet himself would be only too happy to join these brilliant revelers in their potations. He places himself on the side of intoxication. Drink, it seems, brings about the most varied states of mind but all are essentially blissful. One drinker enjoys a luxurious sense of relaxation, another an illusion of possessing divine powers, another a conviction that he has attained supreme wisdom, one exalts in the experience of pure beauty, a sixth finds that wine enhances the relish that he derives from delicately prepared food, a seventh discovers that under its influence he gains incredible powers as calligrapher and poet, the eighth that he becomes master of profuse and spontaneous eloquence. As the testimony of this octet of drinkers draws to its close the testimonials, interestingly enough, turn increasingly to the realm of verbal creation, which is obviously that of the poet himself and his production. The entire work may be described as a bacchic litany, a sequence of beatitudes, a chant in praise of the twin factors of irrationality and joy which are themselves the chief ingredients of humor itself. There are, of course, countless bacchanalian hymns, in the East as well as in the West, as certain Indian chants in praise of the vision-inducing soma and the Japanese songs in honor of the joy-producing sake. Beside Tu Fu's poem all others seem pale abstractions. The personal and historical interest here, the allusions to real individuals, leading figures in a single environment, each sharply distinguished from the others, gives the poem peculiar force. Behind it lies the hint of parody that in no way diminishes the power of the poem itself. Chinese history and legend tell of several groups of worthies denominated "immortals"; hence Tu Fu's allusions to well-known contemporaries gain a religious aura. The worthies in question are equally erring men and demi-deities.

Ho Chih-chang rides his horse like a sailor sculling a sluggish boat,
Half asleep and yet willing to fall in a well, sink or float.
Ju-yang drank three gallons, then going to Court and seeing a brewer's cart,
Declared: "To be Lord of the Wine Spring I'd give the rich blood of my heart."
Our Minister spends ten thousand a day which he gulps down like a whale,
Then explains: "I love things philosophic and whole, where severance may not prevail."
Ts'ui Tsung-chih is a handsome young man with bland, blue eyes;
A jade-tree sparkling in wind, he lifts his cup to the azure skies.
At prayer at a Buddha's shrine, Su Chin is a vowed vegetarian,
But how he enjoys his lapses when turned a mad bacchanalian!
Li writes a hundred poems to a gallon, then sleeps at a vintner's shop.
When the Emperor bids him mount a barge, he cries: "No, sir; I'm God of the Cup!"
Give Calligrapher Chang but three cupfuls, he dances crazy capers
Before the worthies themselves, making clouds ascend from his papers.
Chiao Sui will need five gallons to keep in a conscious state,
Amazing huge crowds by his eloquence in discussion and fierce debate.

One might permit a discussion of Tu Fu's humorous work to rest with an examination of this but the analysis might still fall short of paying full tribute to his extraordinary scope and versatility. Many shades of humor diversify his pages and spring from different aspects of the Chinese mind. In conclusion, one phase of the subject not as yet mentioned may at least suggest from how many sides Tu Fu's achievement as humorist may be commended. Although on the whole a realist and proponent of moral and ethical responsibility, he was by no means so confirmed a representative of what might be called the Chinese "Enlightenment" as to turn aside from the superstitions of the people and the popular love among all classes of his countrymen for the strange and miraculous. This free play of imagination, so alluring to the poetic impulse, is reflected with special force in a number of his pieces. They accept the prevailing view in his country, which was neither to accept wholly nor to reject wholly the claims of the miraculous but in any case to take keen pleasure in the fertile imagination sustaining it.

*Song of the Peach-Bamboo Sticks* belongs in this category. Tu Fu relates that on the eve of his launching upon a journey the Prefect of Tzu-chou presented him with two sticks or canes of a special variety of bamboo. These came from plants growing in the midst of running streams. Legend records that they have magic power to repel river-ghosts and dragons. They would therefore be of service to the poet on his travels, though he would no doubt have to guard against the threat of envious and angry water-spirits to snatch them from his hands. The poem is singularly rich in imagination, reminding us of the incomparable images of river-dragons in Chinese painting. It is a remarkable piece by any account but not the least because of a somewhat unexpected humorous element. Most treatments of dragons and especially of dragons residing in tempestuous water are eminently serious. Here there is clearly a humorous touch. To be sure, the poet receives the poles with sincere and courteous thanks. He does not presume to question their magic powers. He is sure that they will prove useful on his travels by water and by land whether or not they effect miracles. But the poet prefers to assume their supernatural properties. In addition to the poem's brilliant imagery, it has a jaunty tone.

The miraculous in medieval Europe commonly induced a sentiment of piety, that in China often evoked a delight intimately allied to humor. All Asians of earlier generations rejoiced in magicians who were known to fool their audiences but were none the less popular because the audiences were pleased to be fooled. The attitude is seen most often in prose tales, in connection with which it will be considered later in this book. Tu Fu happily struck this vein of magic gold that provided ornaments to his poetry and was destined later to be explored by countless romantic story-tellers. China became the supreme center for the circulation of strange and supernatural legends, many with a delightfully humorous temper springing from the ambivalence of their conceptions. They achieved an intensity of aesthetic conviction, often inducing shudders of the nerves and flesh, at the same time that in the back sections of the mind those who most enjoyed them doubted their literal truth. Such writing succeeds in flourishing in two worlds and by virtue of this ambivalence flourishes with an incontestable sense of humor. Restraints of reason are happily removed but those of at least a species of reality are retained. The result induces a singularly relaxed and happy smile. No better instance can be found than Tu Fu's poem. Some of his dragons are taken far more seriously than these. An instance would be the monster inhabiting the pool within a deep ravine described in Tu Fu's powerful poem, *The Abysmal Pool*. In other instances the dragons introduced seem entirely frivolous creations of fancy. Supernaturalism in this poem achieves a particularly refined variety of humor where conviction and nonconviction meet in harmony, a realm that may be described in William Blake's words as the land where opposites become true.

> The peach-bamboo grows only in midstream,
> Only in blue waves is it tall and fit.

The stem is purple jade in the sunbeam.
When peeled and cut, no goddess can keep it.

The Prefect of Tzu-chou displays a group
Of sticks before his guests, a marveling crowd;
Then, because I'm elderly and droop,
He gives me two that, struck, resound aloud.

They give metallic echoes when I whack them.
Since I am going East, I can't afford
That river-ghosts or dragons should attack them
Where I may have to guard them with my sword.

Let me tell you, sticks, each in its station
Grows sheer and straight; you are my best resort.
Beware of water and the grim temptation
To become dragons, you, my one support!

Ah, you would seal my doom and kill me then
If you should play any such knavish tricks!
Where wind and dust and tigers prey on men,
What would I do if I should lose these sticks?

Humor in one major poet will never be quite like that in another, though when two masters are fellow countrymen it may be supposed that they will share at least some qualities in common. Such is the case when Po Chü-i, Tu Fu's most famous successor, is considered as standing beside the older man. Po Chü-i is probably the more easily approachable to Western readers although he is almost certainly in final estimate the less inspired and brilliantly artful. In almost all respects he is the less elusive, as the acknowledged difficulties encountered by Tu Fu's translators attest. He is relatively straightforward in his expression of emotion, lucid in his descriptions, clear in his intentions, less idiosyncratic and more essentially orthodox than his rivals. No one, I think, would venture to summarize Tu Fu's religious convictions. Moreover, his spirit often hovers between the secular and the religious, the human and the cosmological. When, on the contrary, Po Chü-i writes a poem dedicated to Buddhism it generally follows familiar highways of that religion.

Tu Fu lived a stormy life, now up and now down, at one time a captive in the hands of the barbarians, at another a counselor close to the ear of the Emperor. Much of his life was a struggle with poverty, at times also with ill health. His spirits alternately rose to heights and sank to the depths. Although in some respects a good Confucian, he was no strict follower of the sage's doctrine of the mean. His last poems have a tragic quality, though he apparently never succumbed to despair nor lost his essential dignity.

Po Chü-i's life presents quite another picture. He rose to a fairly secure place in public office, in his last years living comfortably on his country estate. Given these conditions, Tu Fu's humor is more complex and less predictable than that of Po Chü-i, who is more notable for his poise and moderation. Tame it is not, for Po Chü-i is a truly great poet and an incisive reader of human nature. But his work comes closer to being social verse in the Western sense of the term. It fulfills all its intentions, is trifling or merely playful where these qualities are desired and often warm and enthusiastic where warmth and enthusiasm are consistent with the sense of humor. Po Chü-i possesses a highly refined comic sense; his smile is singularly winning, his laughter resonant and clear. One treasures his verse but somehow does not, I think, accord it the very highest laurels. His humor is singularly pure humor, rarely blended with the neighboring but still alien qualities of wit or satire.

Of course all humor and all humorists abhor dogmatism and decline to surrender to it. The purity and thoroughly Chinese quality of Po Chü-i's humor may even be clarified from his own pages by reference to what it is not. Virtually at the end of the hundred or so pages of his poems translated by his foremost apologist and advocate, Arthur Waley, appear two very brief poems, in fact, witty epigrams. Since such wit depends on clear, semantic elements and not on the nuances of a mature poetry, these pieces need not be quoted word for word. The first consists of a simple jest amounting virtually to a stroke in logic. The piece is entitled, *Lao Tzu*. It presumes to catch the philosopher on the hook of a fault in reasoning. The great mystic is quoted as saying that those who speak know nothing, those who know are silent. Then why, asks the poet, did the mystic himself write a book of five thousand words? This is clearly a neat, pleasing epigram but not in the sense of the word employed in this study a work of humor. It admirably exemplifies productions of wit.

The second epigram is a witty assertion of the point of view of common sense in opposition to that of the mystics. The philosopher Chuang Tzu is termed a monist and monism is described as a doctrine that reduces all things to equality. But, objects the poet and spokesman for the common man, a phoenix does seem superior to a reptile! This is wit. It is, of course, the leading feature of much comic writing and theatre in the West. At its roots in the West is the discipline of logic, which insofar as history records arose in ancient Greece and has since never been forgotten. A classical instance is afforded by the witticism that operates to the detriment of a certain man who observed that all Cretans are liars. But the man was himself a Cretan. Hence he was a liar. This is a form of verbal or mental agility. It neither claims nor possesses the spiritual quality regarded as humor—not to mention poetry. Logic is not art.

In any culture, especially if advanced to a high degree of civilization, manifestations of wit will be found. They are allied to a still more distinctly verbal form of comic expression, the pun, found with a diverting effect in all languages. But James Joyce and even Shakespeare notwithstanding, the pun is not the highest form of comedy, indeed, it is not to be supposed that either Joyce or Shakespeare would have held the play on words to be the essence of their superb sense of humor. Nor does wit in itself qualify as humor. It is often an incident in humor but never the core. Thus Aristophanes employs both wit and puns but his humor goes far deeper than this. The literature of the East exhibits much more humor than wit and vastly less wit than that found in the West. The masters examined in these pages are all masters of humor, not of wit. Their humanity and their poetic or imaginative powers are so much the more noteworthy on this account.

In some of the pieces inspired by a scorn of the dull affairs and pompous ceremonies of court and political life Po Chü-i is a follower of the long tradition of quietists, aided by the teachings of Lao Tzu and best exemplified in verse by the much revered T'ao Ch'ien. But Po Chü-i is actually a much more amusing writer than T'ao Ch'ien or most of the figures in this school. There was not a drop of sourness in his system. He could be deeply moving and even tragic but the bitterness of satire was not his. His temperament was in these respects uncommonly favorable to expressions of true humor. In many completely delightful poems he smiles at the stupidity of public manners. His poems are never arrogant, are sometimes even directed against himself. He was himself a scholar and an examiner. But pedantic regimentation and pretentious display were alien to his better nature. Here is one of his typical pieces in which in the end one finds, perhaps, even more to love than to admire. Po Chü-i seems almost too good, virtuous, and reasonable, too singularly blest with charm. The strict aesthetic formality in his writing has, incidentally, induced me to transfer it in translation into the sonnet form.

#### Escorting the Candidates to the Examination Hall

What a to-do about these doctors of art!
Even before the eastern sky is gray
I see your ceremonial pageant start
As horses and coaches throng the public way.
Torches bob; far too many drums resound;
Dust and confusion trouble the city street.
At sunrise these children of earth are up with a bound
Hot on their struggle and strife with frantic feet.
I pity you all as you ride to your early levee,
Scholars and courtiers striving far too soon

For profit and fame while nothing troubles me
As I rise in peace from my cozy bed at noon.
Now that spring is here and my term of office spent
I dream of my hillside farm with new content.

Many of his poems, though in general similar in their humorous spirit to the foregoing, make clearer one of the most familiar features in the work of Chinese humorous writers, smiles directed against themselves. Po wonders why on earth he endures the inconveniences and trials of Court life! He ruminates on the distinction between living at Court and in the country. While, paradoxically, he suffers from the hardships of the one, his friend Ch'en enjoys the luxuries of the other. In the hands of a less amusing writer the theme could, of course, be developed in an entirely serious spirit. Not so with Po Chü-i, who draws an obviously ludicrous picture of the traffic jam at the approaches to the Court and the nipping frost covering the earth at the opening of the morning ceremonies.

In the great capital a foot of snow;
The audience scheduled for the break of day,
Its ceremonial purpose to bestow
Congratulations in the regal way.—
On the high causeway at my setting forth
My horse slipped on the ice and by like fate
My lantern failed me. Facing to the north
I waited hours at the Imperial Gate.
My hair and beard were frozen stiff and through.
Suddenly I remembered my friend Ch'en
In the quiet valley of Hsien-yu.
Blest with warm bed-socks in his bed he lies
Dozing, while the sun ascends the skies.

Po Chü-i, experiencing a more merciful old age than Tu Fu, wrote of it with a more genial comic spirit. Both poets have much to say of baldness. Po Chü-i's poem explicitly on this subject is unusually light-hearted and emphatically humorous. This is certainly not a high form of comedy but the piece serves its purpose well. It may be recalled that men's baldness has elicited humorous expression at many times and in many places. It provided considerable ribald jesting on the commedia dell'arte stage and in the great Elizabethan playhouses. Baldness in the sixteenth century provided a favorite subject for jocose debates at drinking parties. At that time the attribution of loss of hair to veneral disease added a certain piquancy to these rhetorical flights of fancy. One champion would defend baldness, another revile it. Po Chü-i is not as exuberant in spirit as the bravos of the European Renaissance. Nevertheless, for graceful statement and clipped speech on this universal theme few have at any time equaled him. This is his panegyric:

### ON HIS BALDNESS

At dawn I sighed to see my white hair go;
At dusk I sighed, noting how fast hairs fall,
A foolish fear of baldness moved me so:
Now all are gone, I do not mind at all!
I have done with washing and with rubbing dry;
The tiresome labors of my comb are sped;
Best of all, under a rainy sky
Or blistering sun, no burden tops my head.
I have no tasseled hat or massive crown;
Within a blesséd silver urn I store
Water that on my pate goes trickling down
Like baptism in Buddha's holy lore.
Now I know why old priests, sedate and grave,
Free heart and head by virtue of a shave!

The Taoists when in a serious vein lauded quietism, when in a comic vein mere idleness or laziness with the favorite inward-looking view of the subjectivists among the poets. The theme as shown in *Lazy Man's Song*, is clearly a considerable step upward for Po Chü-i from the fantasy on baldness. It is more reflective, more imaginative, and more poetic and all the more humorous when one realizes what a casual opinion this poem must have expressed in the life of the writer. Po Chü-i possessed an extremely strong sense of moral responsibility. The sheer diligence with which he compiled book after book of verse shows him to have worked with seriousness and zeal. In his actual experience idleness was apparently a helpful relaxation for leisure hours. The praise of it as an entire way of life is clearly facetious. Yet how deftly it is done!

### LAZY MAN'S SONG

I could have work but am too lazy for it;
I have got land but I am loth to farm;
My house-roof leaks but idly I deplore it;
My clothes are rent, yet I take no alarm.
I have got wine but through the live-long day
I shun the trouble filling glasses brings;
I have a lute but am too lazy to play
So it is just as if it had no strings.
It's too much pain to eat and as for writing
Or reading, both are trouble. From friend and brother
Long letters come written with their inditing
But opening envelopes is too much bother.
Chi Shu-yeh would play his lute and ply
His forge; even he was not as lazy as I.

The Chinese genius can virtually brew something out of nothing. This alchemy, which is highly self-conscious, takes on at least a gently humorous spirit not because an inflated rhetoric is used but from a mock-heroic manner and the subtlety of the exercise itself. Life is envisaged as humorous because of its contradictions, its incongruities; its happiest moments may be to all appearances those of the least account. Po Chü-i wrote an encomium on one of the commonest of Chinese foods, bamboo shoots, especially praising those in early spring, when soft and pliant. The opening lines and, indeed, the larger number of the lines as the poem progresses, seem almost distastefully slight or even flat. But Po Chü-i is in fact a shrewd artist. His style exemplifies his theme. By the midpoint he feels that he has refuted vulgar opinion; description rises to a delicacy the equivalent of Renoir's astonishing painting of a bowl-ful of softly tinted onions. In the crescendo at the end the tone totally changes. Po affects a violent distaste for elaborate dishes served at banquets and festivals. With the simple, early bamboo shoots passing down his throat he experiences all the freshness of cool, delicious spring weather. The humor, which undeniably is of a quiet nature, lies in the unexpectedly dramatic turn, the affected anger at elaborately prepared dishes and the clearly excessive praise, winged with a poetic imagination, of plain bamboo. A few readers may find no humor in the poem at all. In my own judgment such a view would overlook some of the happiest nuances of Chinese humor.

### Eating Bamboo Shoots

This Province is a land for bamboo groves
Whose spring shoots cover all the hills and dales.
The mountain woodsmen flock to town in droves
With armfuls for the early morning sales.
Things are cheap as they are easily got;
Two farthings for a bundle is the price.
I put the shoots in a large earthen pot
And cook them up along with boiling rice.
The purple skins outside are old brocades,
The inner skins are pearls, glossy and white.
My appetite for other viands fades,
I eat them ravenously, day and night.
Elsewhere we famish on some vile ragout
But here each south breeze makes a fresh bamboo.

No one knowing Po Chü-i's work will deny him versatility. Although hardly as sensitive a poet as Tu Fu, he has his moments of considerable enthusiasm. There is at times a humorous undertone even in these outbursts of genuinely strong emotion. He smiles at himself even when seized by a poetic madness. Moreover, as a profoundly social being, he does not wish to be detected when caught up in an enthusiastic mood that in its very nature is unsocial. His humor is his guide, shrewdly saving him from embarrassment. Under these circumstances he is willing to confess that his passion for poetry is itself a weakness. In general he considers himself a reasonable social being, plagued with only one unsocial habit, his fanatical addiction to poetry. (How pleasantly unlike so many twentieth-century poets, from Yeats to Dylan Thomas, who profess poetry to be virtually their religion!) Thus to escape the just charge of madness and shun the crowd of reasonable men, he climbs a mountain, attains its summit, and madly sings, discovering a gratified audience only among birds and monkeys. It is a refinement and an amusing contradiction as he declares midway in his poem that not only good landscapes but good friends are the incitements to his singing. The song itself is for the silent places in the hills. Again, the imagery alone would admit a thoroughly serious or even depressing connotation. It is abundantly clear, however, that the Chinese poet intends his piece to be not only ironic but amusing.

### Madly Singing in the Mountains

There is no man without some special fault;
My special failing is composing verse.
From countless ties I've managed to revolt
But this infirmity grows worse and worse.
On meeting with good landscapes and good friends,
I raise my voice in some ecstatic song,
Then climb a mountain where the pathway ends
And madly chant my verses, loud and long.
I pull a cassia branch about my head,
Leaning my body on a naked stone;
Monkeys and birds there flock to me instead
Of men to hear me singing all alone.
Fearing rude laughter, I'm content that then
My place is safe, unvisited by men.

How inveterate is his habit of smiling, though with a genial humor, at himself is further suggested by a poem showing his advanced years and susceptible heart in a humorous light. In this poem he describes himself as "an aging mountaineer." He was, in fact, about sixty-five when writing. The subject is a humorous, inconsequential affair of the heart taking place while he was on a trip to a mountain—quite possibly a religious pilgrimage, for these were common where the ascent of a mountain occurred. The excursion, if such was the case, seems to have borne at least some resemblance to the trip of other pilgrims taken to Canterbury. However the occasion may have shaped itself, the feature developed in the poem is the relation between the aging poet and a girl of fifteen. The first lines state, with calculated eccentricity, that the girl was half thirty, her hair still in the topknots of a child. The two climb trees together and disport themselves more or less innocently. The girl has the rapid movements and grace of a trained dancer. Her serious look shows that at least some longing has been aroused. But in the last line the poet beseeches her not to tempt the heart of an old traveler. The humor is as slight as the subject but is humor nevertheless. Some minor liberties have been taken in the translation chiefly to fit the poem into the sonnet form.

### Going to the Mountain with a Dancing Girl, Aged Fifteen

Two topknots not yet plaited into one—
You would be thirty years if twice your age.
Sprig of a girl with ventures just begun,
If stationed in some courtly equipage
First among women in a social whirl,
Yet I am come, an aging mountaineer,
While you are present as a dancing girl
And fate's caprice brings us together here.
In mountain brooks and springs we sport and play;
We climb tall trees; we sport among the leaves.
Your cheeks grow rosy as your dance grows gay,
Paced by mad gestures of your flying sleeves.
And yet your brows grow sad when the tune's slow.—
Tempt not the heart of an old traveler so!

With the slow movements of time that have generally characterized cultural changes in China until the close of the last century, the tendency in Chinese verse was to lose much of its vividness and energy and, in particular, much of its humorous verve. As the modern reader is likely to interpret this evolution, themes were repeated with considerable monotony. Even in Chinese eyes the brilliance of older poets appeared to elude the art of their successors. Li Ho, Po Chü-i's most accomplished contemporary, born later than he but dying before him, possessed a singularly tense nature and a macabre and dark imagination. He contributed little or nothing to the expression of humor. The comparatively minor poet, Wei Chuang, had at his command much of the charm of light verse but little of the force of major poetry. Li Ch'ing-chao possessed an even lighter touch and finer elegance but even less animated humor. The soldier-statesman, Hsin Ch'i-chi, expressed his roistering spirits in verse of considerable energy but with a relatively coarse type of humor. The truly great poet Lu Yu, active in the twelfth century, possessed a robust humor animated with a warming contact with the folk spirit. Typical of this phase of his art is his brief poem, *The Old Apothecary*. The poet praises a disreputable character who sells drugs to incite sexual vigor in order to buy wine and, when drunk, encourages his neighbors, young and old, in singing. The poet declares that he would gladly write a biography of the man but, unhappily, cannot discover his name!

Poets of the Yüan period wrote many exquisite lyrics, where the music ranked about equally in value with the words. Such poems show much refined art but prefer elegance to vigor of imagination and sentimental or melancholy moods to humor. When humor is indeed present, the old themes are likely to be reworked with relatively little fresh or truly creative art. A favorable specimen of a Yüan song with an attractive but still derivative type of humor may conclude the survey in this section of our investigation. The poem is by the thirteenth-century poet, Chang Yang-hao.

Who is it understands Ch'ü Yüan's poem,
"Encountering Sorrow"? Truly, there is none
Who comprehends it, yet its meaning lies
Firmly written on the moon and sun.
His sorrow lingers but the man is gone
We know not where unless, lost in his dream,
He floats among the fish and crabs and shrimps
Happily where he plunged in Hsiang's stream.
Truly, he misbehaved. He should have chosen
Green hills and shaded valleys as his friend.—
Let us drink madly and sing lustily!
May our frantic pleasure never end.

3

———

## HUMOR IN

## DRAMA

✳

Aɴʏ ɪɴǫᴜɪʀʏ ɪɴᴛᴏ ʜᴜᴍᴏʀ ɪɴ ᴅʀᴀᴍᴀ ᴄᴀʟʟs ꜰᴏʀ sᴏᴍᴇ preliminary observations. On the one hand, the theatre and its literature offer particularly auspicious ground for such investigation. In its primary meaning "comedy" signifies a type of drama which, as time has passed, appears one of the major species of theatrical art. Humor, which, of course, pertains to comedy, seems especially at home on the stage. Nowhere does it flourish more lustily than in its form of presentational art. On the other hand, the definition of comedy as a variety of drama is singularly elusive. That the world of comedy is in general sunny and that of tragedy dark, that an Elizabethan stage was commonly hung with yellow for the former and with black for the latter, carries an inquiry only a short way to an understanding of the two forms. A farce may keep its audience roaring with laughter throughout; a comedy of manners or a tragicomedy may for most of its scenes preserve a sober tone. The terms commonly used in the West for dramatic criticism derive for the most part from the Greco-Roman world and in their most negotiable definitions flourish only there and in Western drama during those times, now long past, when classical tradition prevailed on the stage. For most comedies it is best said that humor is merely an element occasionally dominating the scene. The play is humorous sporadically, not continuously. Whereas a short poem or short story may well be humorous throughout, the comic spirit in comedies, which are likely to be works of considerable length, is prone to come and go. Though it may be a leading factor, it is to be remembered that cordial laughter and smiles are normally sporadic; a fixed smile is likely to be considered a grimace, a deformity. In the poetry hitherto considered only relatively brief works have been cited; the assumption has generally been that these are humorous throughout. Pure farces are likely to be short. By far the larger number of plays rewarding attention in respect to the philosophy of humor are more substantial works each of which exhibits a variegated surface.

These observations have special relevance to the Chinese masterpiece, *The West Chamber*, written approximately in 1300 by Wang Shih-fu. At the commencement of a study of humor in Chinese plays it is well to examine this work partly because it is commonly thought one of the finest, indeed possibly the very best of them. Moreover, its humor is clearly representative of Chinese humor at its best. This humor is neither epigrammatic nor savage and satirical. It is manifested by an amused laugh at human errors where good humor and even kindliness prevail, while serious rebuke remains virtually out of the question. This is a sophisticated flower of high comedy, in fact, one of the chief flowers of Chinese civilization. It touches upon some of the deepest emotions and firmly held values in life. Although the general attitude is much more diverting than censorious, the grounds upon which the humor grows are of much consequence. These in *The West Chamber*, to mention two, are erotic love and mystical religion. The playwright's point of view is by no means narrowly limited or doctrinaire. For example, the humor at the expense of Buddhist practices may be taken to infer gibes against Taoists as well, while Confucian ways of thought and practice, if not anywhere roundly condemned, are viewed with several grains of salt. Common sense, as most clearly embodied in an illiterate but shrewd serving-girl, is the germ of the play's considerable wisdom. For the most part its ethics are of a singularly engaging character and the humor is especially fresh and ingratiating. The play is eminently a classic, a work of especially pure humanism. It has long maintained outstanding popularity.

It is by no means an hilarious comedy. In one version a conventional happy ending is supplied, which was, indeed, the usual ending for Chinese plays. But in more ways than one *The West Chamber* is unorthodox according to prevailing standards on the Yüan stage. Scholarship still debates many matters regarding it, leaving answers to questions that are raised so inconclusive that positive assertions are unwise. Fortunately, the arguments as a rule have little or no value in the interpretation of the play. As the text is most often printed the first and longest section comprises almost all that is of poetic, literary, or dramatic merit. This ends in a scene far from distinguished for humor, grave and not gay, with chords by no means resolved to the harmony of the dominant. At least in the judgment of the present writer, this episode constitutes a brilliant and an aesthetically gratifying finale. The remaining scenes in the longer version are certainly far inferior; as the first and longest part of the play reveals Chinese drama at its best, the second and shorter section shows it at its worst, with scenes of the most atrocious melodrama and sensational contrivance. A vulgar audience might possibly gloat over its violent and improbable action but no one could detect in it so much as a trace of the poetic quality or sophisticated humor found in the main part. Whether Wang Shih-fu, the presumed author of the earlier acts, wrote all the sequel, a part of it, or none, the sequel need not be mentioned in more than the preliminary discussion of the drama. It is here mentioned merely because it is well to make clear precisely what is to be discussed and because the glaring contrast between the two parts is actually instructive, revealing the best and worst that the Chinese theatre affords.

The work in its expanded form may even be regarded as five plays instead of one. The usual Yüan drama as performed on the stage consists of four acts. Frequently, however, plays were written in cycles. Thus *The West Chamber* may plausibly be regarded as being originally a cycle of four four-act plays, to which an inferior hand added a continuation in four acts. A cogent argument for this view is given by C. T. Hsia in a recent reprinting (1968) of an English translation by S. I. Hsiung (1936).[14]

Although humor in the earliest period of Chinese literature known to us is often or even very generally refined and sophisticated, the humor during the long period now envisaged as the age of the classics shows an unmistakable increase in urbanity. The civilization acquired in the course of centuries with some strenuous effort became a natural birthright, its ways of thought and action seeming almost instinctive and pursued without effort. After the remarkable synthesis of the philosophical and religious systems under the Sung dynasty, a somewhat complacent attitude existed creating a climate of serenity and relaxation in which humor readily flourished At least something of this evolution where humor is concerned may even be traced in the history of the story on which *The West Chamber* is based.

This story was first told by Yüan Chen approximately in 800 A.D., its title being *The Story of Ying-ying*. Some literary historians have credited the view that its author, with merely a change of names, related an adventure of his own younger years, doing so partly as self-vindication and partly to clear his conscience of dubious conduct. Reduced to its simplest terms the narrative, which is brief, describes an ardent courtship that came to fulfillment, although the progress of the affair was complicated by the timidity of each of the lovers. Circumstances largely of an official nature in time drew the man, named Chang, apart from the woman. The suffering was almost entirely hers. In the end each married a person who was encountered considerably later than the period of the youthful affair. Some dry but unquestioned humor occurs in the narrative, especially in the passages relating the ironic and conflicting tides in the courtship, where the psychological observation is especially acute. But on the whole humor plays distinctly a minor part. The tale is related chiefly from the point of view of a stern Confucian morality. Business should come before pleasure; the duties of manhood are more to be followed than the passions of youth. The author is impelled by a desire to report the emotional life accurately. His story has more harsh realism than genuine humor. A third character, Ying-ying's maid, acts as go-between but wit and humor are barely present in her delineation. The work adds up to a sober and an instructive story.

In approximately 1200 A.D. Tung Chieh-yuan composed a long narrative poem, with alternating passages of verse and prose, entitled *The Romance of the West Chamber*. It followed the general lines of the long-popular short story by Yüan Chen but naturally introduced much that was new. The role of the maid, Hung Niang, was greatly enlarged and developed with considerable humor. In the end the lovers were happily united. This work was commonly regarded as the best long poem centered on the theme of love to be written in Chinese. Its fame made it virtually inevitable that it would later be used as the basis for a play. Apparently Wang Shih-fu was satisfied to dramatize the larger part of the romantic poem but, finding his chief interest, quite naturally, in the earlier episodes, declined to pursue the theme to the conventional happy ending. An inferior playwright carried the story forward to its sentimental conclusion.

Wang Shih-fu clearly possessed an ironic and humorous mind. These qualities he could exercise abundantly in the scenes covering the major part of the story. He was simply not interested in proceeding to a popular, humorless, and optimistic ending.

Of the three versions of the famous love story, successively the short story, the long poem, and the long play, the first is the most consistently serious, the second the richest in episodes, but the last by far the most richly endowed with humor. This humor, as already observed, is of a singularly refined and sophisticated character. The maid, Hung Niang, the arch-proponent of humor, has risen in importance equal to the two lovers; indeed, as Professor Hsia reminds us, the version of the story as seen on the Peking stage in the present century was entitled, "Hung Niang," the leading actor appearing in this role.[15] It is she who understands only too well the unreasonableness of the lovers, which elicits her wry smile, and she who most vigorously condemns the mother's mendacity. At least once the oblique conduct of her mistress for a short time pulls the wool over her eyes but for the most part the outlook of the playwright and audience is virtually her own. She best understands the basic incongruities within the souls of the four characters who share the chief scenes with her, namely Chang, the lover, Ying-ying, the beloved, the straitlaced mother, and the abbot of questionable devotion, who controls the monastery which provides the scene of the action. The playwright was a master-humorist, which cannot be said of the author of the powerful short story concerning Ying-ying nor even of the gifted poet who rendered her misadventures in his brilliant verse narrative.

It should be acknowledged that the over-all impression made by the play is serious. Although we frequently find ourselves smiling at the leading characters and even laughing at the lesser figures, all their errors, follies and self-deception notwith-standing, we also find ourselves sympathetic with them and their vicissitudes, their joys and sufferings. The play's finest music is the poetry of the emotions. One easily recognizes that the lyrical, or sung, passages, which are in fact the heart of the play, have great warmth of feeling and passionate conviction. Much of the time we are unconscious of the current of humor which nevertheless runs through so much of the play. It is part of the miracle of the playwriting that the serious and comic moods can be so united. Perhaps the entire work may be thought of as such a marriage, the serious and on the whole the more vocal element represented by the man, the humorous and more elusive, by the woman.

For English readers, however, this union need present no obstacle. The play may be roughly and succinctly described as a Chinese *Romeo and Juliet,* favored with a more or less happy ending, for even if Wang Shih-fu declined to terminate his play with the conventionally happy marriage, it will be pre-sumed by almost any audience or reader that after passing his examination Chang will return to Ying-ying and make their union, which has already been consummated, regularized, as the mother promises, by officially sanctioned matrimony. (Chi-nese heroes seldom fail in their examinations.) In Shake-speare's play Romeo and Juliet present the serious view of love while Mercutio embodies the humorous view. The two views are harmonized, though Mercutio dies far too soon. At least in a broad and general sense, the same ambivalence gives fasci-nation and vitality to the Chinese masterpiece. The outlook in the English play, however, is simpler than that in the Chi-nese, Romeo and Juliet so clearly representing the romantic sublimation of love, Mercutio love as lusty adventure in sensu-ality. The Chinese lovers, on the contrary, are both seen as em-bodiments of the fundamental incongruities and irrationalities of passion. Humor in the Elizabethan play tends, accordingly, to be on the side of the physical, expressed with vigorous and imaginative bawdiness, whereas in the Chinese play humor is maintained on a higher level of psychological observation, with more inference and urbanity and, I think, it may safely be said, with less strenuousness and more relaxed charm. The Chinese play seems more feminine.

One glaring contrast exists between Elizabethan and Chinese. The messenger or go-between for the lovers is in one very close to being a bawd, indeed Juliet's nurse is as close to the greatest figure on the Spanish stage, the old bawd Celestina, as English manners would allow, whereas the go-between in the Chinese play is a young woman in character both witty and refined. Of course, no generalization regarding East and West can possibly be made from these isolated instances. The Celestina image, that is, the garrulous old bawd, is brilliantly portrayed in Chinese fiction, as in the popular novels, *All Men Are Brothers* and *Lotus*, while the witty maid who serves the lovers and gains the full affection of the Western audience is perfected in the art of Molière and above all in that of Mozart. The subject and the comparison are raised here in general to stress the refinement of which the Eastern mind is capable and in particular to illustrate the elegant and sophisticated vein of humor animating Wang Shih-fu's dramatic masterpiece.

Only one course is possible in the elucidation of Wang's humor; it requires a fairly close inspection of individual scenes and lines. It becomes necessary to examine details. To this end one may begin with the minor or less important figures. Apart from one or two seldom-seen servants, there are ten speaking parts. Of these only two are conventional and humorless figures. These are the two military men, each having only the briefest speaking roles—the loyal general, friend of the hero, and the bandit chief, who, being a bad bandit, is ordered killed by the good general. The brief scenes in which they appear, except for advancing the plot, contribute little more than physical brilliance to the stage decor. The prevailing good humor, however, is exhibited in the confrontation between the two men. Although the virtuous general does decree the instant death of the villain, the bandit chief, he pardons all other members of his rabble. The play's hero humorously and graciously observes that he will pray for the soul of the bandit since he has, indirectly, been the means for his union with his beloved.

All the other lesser figures contribute rather more than their share to the humor of the play, although their contributions are, naturally, upon a lower level than those of the major parts. There is undoubtedly humor in the role of the child, who is an adopted son in Ying-ying's family. Children are forever seeing more than they should and blurting out embarrassing remarks on what they see. This is an old device of comic playwrights. The same humorous observation is made, for example, in the chief comedy of India's leading dramatist, Kalidasa.[16]

Three figures are holy men in the monastery, all more or less absurd. Although the abbot may appear at first a venerable and sincere priest, he is soon discovered in ludicrous positions. He makes sexual advances to Hung Niang. During the memorial service for the soul of the dead statesman he beats on the bald head of his assistant priest, mistaking it for a drum. There is a plausible hint of homosexuality. He invites Chang to share his cell, an invitation that the hero, whose amorous propensities are destined to turn elsewhere, promptly declines. The assistant priest is drawn as a humble creature, almost a parody of religious humility. In his brief interview with Chang he serves to magnify the hero's stature by the contrast between them.

The Buddhists are jocosely treated in most of the passages where they are mentioned or have a part. Chang unctuously proposes to honor the memory of his father by a memorial mass, although he makes it abundantly clear that he does so only to win an opportunity to see Ying-ying. The ceremony itself is presented with much humor. Its chief feature appears to be a thunderous banging of percussion instruments. As this is presented, one infers that the dramatist finds such performances offensive. Buddhism is treated even more cavalierly than Confucianism. It is, in fact, made a major butt of the humor. This, incidentally, does not mean that Wang Shih-fu was himself in the least antagonistic to Buddhism but only that monks often fare badly on the Chinese stage and become a means for exploiting scenes of comedy.

The chief episode dealing freely with Buddhist asceticism is that introducing the only broadly farcical figure in the play, the horrendous braggart, Hui Ming. This fellow, though indeed a monk, is represented as a Gargantuan clown, the antithesis of all that a monk should be. He claims prodigious powers with his weapons, thirsts for the blood of his enemies, has an inexhaustible capacity for food and drink, and harbors hatred of all learning, religious exercises, disciplines, and penances. A creature of insatiable vanity, he demands a splendid retinue to accompany him on his journey as messenger to the camp of the loyal general. In person he resembles the drunken guardsman in *The Abduction from the Seraglio*. The scenes in which he appears clearly stand outside the main current of the play, as they look beyond the walls of the monastery. He provides comic relief, strangely like that provided by certain messengers in Greek tragedy. Here the humor is timely and effective. It further confirms the play's prevailing outlook, which is anti-religious and anti-bureaucratic. The monk is a humorous figure such as the reader frequently meets in popular military romances, of which that best known to English readers as *All Men Are Brothers* is the chief. The long, refined play in four parts might become a bit monotonous if it were not for this single interlude of relatively low comedy.

Although the drawing of the mother is in general harsh and austere, some rather dry humor occurs. Any straitlaced conservative and unyielding guardian of the moral code is likely to appear distorted when seen through the eyes of one peculiarly endowed with humor, as Wang unquestionably was. Yet the character is by no means wholly unsympathetic, as would be the case in strict satire. With an almost disarming observation, she declares in the play's last moments that she has done her best as a parent to whom the guardianship of a daughter is assigned. The role could, doubtless, have been played, even in Yüan China, in different ways. Actually, she says few words. Her intention is always to be serious. Yet the very fact that she is unbending renders her a trifle absurd in the eyes of high comedy. A good indication of this may be seen in the dry comment of her daughter: "You can't imagine her frugality."

Nine-tenths of the play belongs to its three leading figures, Chang, Ying-ying, and Hung Niang. Their importance is emphasized in that they alone have singing parts. The two lovers, though drawn with extraordinary deftness, are essentially conventional figures on the Chinese stage, the young scholar and the supersensitive young woman. Only Hung Niang was substantially a new conception among Chinese playwrights and even she, as we have seen, had appeared in comparatively shadowy form in fiction and narrative verse. Insofar as an alignment exists in the play's humor, it moves between delineation of masculine vanity and feminine volatility. These are venerable themes but seldom developed as discerningly as here or with benefit of such delicate touches of comedy. Much of the delicacy is owing to the kindliness. The young people are lovable almost to the measure in which they are fallible and conceived through the insight of a singularly humane humor.

Chang presents a most remarkable blending of the admirable and the laughable, noble and ridiculous. A more ambivalent hero can scarcely be found. He is the brilliant scholar, the ardent lover, courteous on all occasions, a paragon of social graces, the glass of fashion and the mold of form. Obviously with promise of becoming a high official, as his father has been before him, he commands admiration and respect. As far as concerns intellect, imagination, sensitivity he represents the ideal as Chinese traditional thinking conceived it. He is entirely willing in the end to place public duty before personal involvement; the interests of the individual and the family must, according to the Confucian code, be for the scholar and member of the governing class strictly subordinate to the demands of the state. All this is approved and taken for granted. It is also taken entirely seriously. But for some reason by no means altogether clear, the most popular type of hero on the Chinese stage is not the all-perfect man but instead the young scholar, in time to become a statesman, who in his early manhood is susceptible to any number of venal weaknesses. His justifiable pride of place in the social structure becomes occasion for an absorbing vanity. His extreme sensibility leads to marked traces of effeminacy, his absence of aggressiveness to timidity. As a man of peace and paragon of civilization and urbanity, he has absolutely no capacity as a soldier. Whatever fortitude he possesses is completely destroyed at the touch of a romantic passion. Love overthrows all serenity and assurance, leading him to a temporary state of desperation. These weaknesses indeed seem incongruous beside his undeniable virtues. The incongruity accounts for much of the play's humor. More than any other figure in *The West Chamber*, the hero is smiled at. The audience takes pleasure, it seems, in eavesdropping, catching the hero in his peculiarly unheroic moments.

Perhaps no class of society has exhibited more arrogance and complacency than the Chinese bureaucracy. But happier features have intervened to moderate and ameliorate these traits, saving the scholar-gentleman from his march to fatal hubris and banal heroics. The entire Chinese audience, aristocracy, merchants, and the common people, laughed at the weaknesses of the young scholar-hero of stage tradition. Just how far the figure faithfully and literally represented an actual type may well be questioned. That the virtues depicted were at least sought in reality and the weaknesses present to some degree can hardly be doubted. A social historian, however, might well question the naturalism in the figure-drawing, inquiring whether such a perfection of gentility and such a depth of vanity and self-delusion are strictly credible in a single person. Literal reality, it seems, has been distorted in the interests of a supremely effective type of art and exposition. The qualities are real; it is merely their arrangement, their extravagance and exaggeration, that are artificial, and in so many ways the source of humor.

Chang is clearly pedantic in his fastidious speech and manners. He frankly admits that he is chickenhearted. To save the monastery and its distinguished guests he depends entirely on the services of "his older brother," the loyal general. He boasts inordinately of his irresistible powers as a lover but is pitifully overthrown when the girl whom he romantically adores becomes only for a moment difficult to woo. When fortune appears to favor him, he becomes so conceited and vain that he bows ceremoniously to his own shadow. When he appears at night in the monastery garden dressed in the scholar's black gown, wearing his fantastic scholar's hat at an oblique angle, Hung Niang pretends to mistake him for a crow. In the same scene by an absurd error he embraces the maid, whom he supposes to be the mistress—much the same error in a midnight garden setting enlivens the last act of Mozart's *Marriage of Figaro*. When the maid holds the upper hand she requires the great scholar to kneel before her. On this occasion it is she who quotes Confucius; as American slang pleasantly expresses it, she throws the book at him. Truly, Chang is the most ridiculous figure!

Yet in the end he fully justifies himself, both as young lover and potential statesman. He is and he is not a butt of comedy. Idealism is the base, absurdity the decoration in this character portrait. When he is first seen, he launches upon a detailed and most faithful description of the Great River that shows him basically to possess a keen, clear, highly capable mind. The final scene in Wang's play reveals both his heart and his ethical probity to be of the highest. All this is to be taken seriously. But his love affair, the play's central theme, shows him alarmingly fallible, making him a theme for the most delectable humor. The basic incongruity in humor itself is enhanced by the ironic incongruities of mature dramatic art. Few scenes in any dramatic literature are as tender and emotionally convincing as the chief episodes in this drama, few scenes of pure humor more delightful. The formula stands fully revealed in the treatment of the leading figure. Neither of the preceding versions of the story, the short story or the long poem, equals it as a work of art or exhibits the comic spirit in so masterly a fashion.

If Chang represents the comedy of manners and ideas, Yingying represents that of the heart. She is what the Jacobean playwright, John Fletcher, called "a very woman." It should be added that she is very young. She vacillates between her still-retained girlishness, with dependence upon her mother, and her instinctive movements to personal independence and devotion to her lover. These contradictions themselves have the most serious import for her as a person but nevertheless are the basis for the experience of humor which the part creates for audience and reader. On her first appearance on the stage her only words are spoken to her maid: "Dear Hung Niang, I wish to see my mother." Her last words, drawn from the depth of her heart, witness her devotion to her husband-to-be. Between these expressions of divergent emotions she swings back and forth, now with timidity, now with courage, with artful reluctance or ardent acceptance. All her attitudes seem instinctive yet in many cases she is remarkably shrewd. Her very shrewdness seems natural. A scene of great humorous vigor shows her superiority in strategy and wit even over her clever maid, who is half servant and half guardian. The witty maid becomes the tool of the still wittier heroine. To the maid she hands a letter addressed to Chang which she pretends to be written in anger and which is so presumed to be by Hung Niang. It is, in fact, an announcement that she will come of her own free will to his chamber that very night. This episode is presumably the most delightfully humorous in the play. It is, of course, by no means wanting in refined humor. This is seldom merely verbal, being the humor of discernment and situation.

A well-established convention in the Yüan theatre led to one of the most amusing achievements in Wang's playwriting. This convention (not, to be sure, always meticulously observed) provided that only one person should sing in a single act or scene. The play's two central episodes are the obviously contrasted visits exchanged between the lovers, the first, Chang's visit to Ying-ying's room, when her coquetry completely discourages her chickenhearted lover, and second, her visit to his room, where their mutual passions are gratified. In the first scene the girl sings and speaks eloquently, while the too-easily discouraged lover is reduced virtually to silence; in the second the lover becomes even more eloquent and loquacious than ever while the girl is completely still. Both scenes are, of course, charged with high emotions, yet especially in context they cannot be rightly experienced by the audience without awareness of their strong humorous connotations. Here, again, appears a well-established formula for high comedy: the view of characters on the stage differs widely from the view of their action or predicament as experienced by the audience. The audience may sit below the physical level of the stage but, spiritually speaking, sits far above it, in a higher realm of amused contemplation.

Hung Niang is from one point of view a choral figure whose privilege and distinction are to stand close to the lovers yet above them, well aware of the humorous distortions of vision which arise from emotional excitement. She enjoys, so to speak, the best seat in the theatre. It is primarily through this critical phase of her part that she becomes the dominant factor in the play's humor. She herself, however, is the only important figure who is not conspicuously humor's victim. To be sure, one episode, already mentioned, has been artfully arranged to prove her not all-knowing but, on the contrary, deficient even in the detection of feminine indirections. All the more human for this, she wholly mistakes the intention of Ying-ying's poem-message to Chang. This helps to save the part from becoming coolly didactic, the aesthetic fault in most so-called choric figures. This unhappy condition never threatens the liveliest of the dramatist's character-portraits. He feels sympathy and affection for Hung Niang at least equal in warmth to his sentiment for the lovers. Clearly, the maid is no puppet. She flirts with the abbot, confesses that she is drawn emotionally to Chang, though to all appearances she successfully disciplines herself in this respect; she suffers from the cold as, in her flimsy dress and frail slippers, she stands outside Chang's window; she is completely devoted to her "little mistress"; she is the only person who can stand up to the rigid, all-powerful mother. She bravely endures a thrashing. In the strictest meaning of the word, she is the most heroic figure of all. Yet she is clearly the focal point of the humor. She can quote Confucian maxims in either a diverting or a most serious sense. Clearly speaking in humorous terms, in her first interview with Chang she throws the Master in the young scholar's face:

> Don't you remember what Confucius said?
> 'Never utter an improper word
> Nor make a single move without propriety.'

Her harangue to the tyrannical mother which condenses the play's morality commences with the weighty observation:

> Good faith is basic in all human dealings.
> A faithless man is of no human worth.

Few characters have better claims to citizenship in the world of high comedy.

It has been said that the humor throughout by no means lies in verbal acrobatics or a play of wit. Wang has few such mannerisms. The play and its style are all the more profoundly humorous on this account. About half the lines are in lyric verse and in performance are, of course, sung. Almost any of these passages could be quoted to demonstrate Wang's poetic force. Even many of the prose passages have poetic power. For example, Chang's soliloquy at the end of the scene immediately before the play's climax comes astonishingly close in imagery and strength to Juliet's remarkable lines as she impatiently abuses the sun, watching its slow descent to the horizon before the night so eagerly awaited. This is, indeed, a world-wide theme in poetic expression that is serious and imaginative but not humorous. Shakespeare and other Elizabethans presumably derived the image from Ovid. What lines shall, however, be quoted to exhibit the quality of Wang's humor? A passage from Hung Niang's part, the humorous chorus of the play, suggests itself as most clearly representative of the humorous content and its particular chemistry. Her admonishment to Chang immediately before the climax carries the play's message in language where under the guidance of humor the two contrary forces, humor and common sense, come happily together. Lovers, she holds, must have the courage of their convictions. This is universal comedy. Molière confirms it, as do Shakespeare and Shaw.

Chang, speaking less objectively than the ideal literary critic, says that Ying-ying's poem reporting her forthcoming visit cannot compare with some sentimental verses that she has sent him earlier. Hung Niang bows her head reflectively and says:

> No indeed! Ah, now I see it all!
> My mistress has a magical prescription.

Then she sings:

> When the cassia moon-flower casts its shade
> At midnight scholars should retire to rest.
> You hide within the shadow of a rock,
> Following the fortune that rewards you best.
>
> You may take this potion more than once,
> Again and yet again, yet should reflect
> The all-seeing mother may be still awake
> Or I play false. Therefore be circumspect.
>
> You truly are a pedant if you pore
> Over this note to cure your cold despair.
> The secret of your health resides in you,
> Not in the verses that you ponder there.
>
> When yesterday you saw your heavenly girl
> From sheer embarrassment you missed your cue;

How natural is it that my youthful mistress
Should show this base ingratitude to you!

You sleep beneath a flimsy coverlet
And for a pillow use your long-necked lute.
How can you find the room for her to sleep?
How keep her warm, if so irresolute?

Take courage! Recollect that in the garden
Beside the swing, when night was almost spent
And all was dark, you failed her! Had you not,
Her poem today need never have been sent.

We have silk pillows handsomely embroidered
With mandarin ducks affectionately paired.
We have rich coverlets of turquoise blue.
But to what end are gorgeous beds prepared?

If you do not undress, what does it matter?
Better then not to have come at all.
But if your love is joyfully fulfilled
Happiness shall be yours, beyond recall.

She speaks:

> Master Chang, I ask you to be frank
> Concerning your relations with my mistress!

She resumes singing:

> Her eyebrows are the lines of distant hills;
> Her eyes are pure and dark as autumn ponds;
> Her silken skin is whiter than whitest milk;
> Her waist, like slim and pliant willow fronds.
> Lovely her freshness, lovelier her heart.
> She has no need for elegance of dress;
> She has no need to give you magic potions;
> Only herself can save you from distress.
> She is your god of mercy, loved Kuan-yin.
> With her your cure for sickness must begin.

Then she whispers in prose:

> And yet, however that is, I still have doubts.

Refinement and elegance in the style of *The West Chamber* indicate that the author wrote from the point of view of the scholar class and on the whole with an upper-class audience in mind, even though much of the humor seems directed against the ossification of orthodoxy in religious and political institutions, in morals and in manners. The relative security on which these institutions stood assisted the humorist in subjecting them at least to good-humored criticism. Chinese drama, though it may have begun at an early date as diversion for the aristocracy, at virtually the earliest time from which texts have survived reflected thought from various segments of society. In the leisurely flow of centuries the upper class lost much of its potency; theatres were established to serve the pleasures of an increasingly popular audience. So conservative was the climate of Chinese thought that many elements in the earlier plays persisted in the later. Nevertheless, considerable changes became apparent. A shift occurred from more literary to more strictly theatrical values. Some of the earliest surviving plays, as the celebrated and wholly serious *Sorrows of Han*, appear more poetic than theatrical. Although it would be false to hold that works of this orientation wholly disappeared from the attention either of readers or audiences, their general appeal diminished, a racier and more colloquial drama gaining ground.

This evolution appears strikingly when such a play as *The West Chamber* is contrasted with an exceptionally creditable work of the so-called "Peking Opera," a play *Ch'i Shuang Hui*, which has been brilliantly translated by Yao Hsin-nung under the title *Madame Cassia*. When the two are placed side by side several contrasts and comparisons are suggested. Not even six centuries brought about a revolution in cultural affairs. There can be no denying that the humorous portrait of the young scholar presented as the leading male figure has remained basically the same. Of this figure in *Madame Cassia* the translator writes: "Magistrate Chao belongs to the conventional 'young scholar' type—moody, obstinate, femininely handsome, and so much 'book-poisoned' that he is hopelessly stupid and dumbfounded when confused or faced with unexpected difficulties but unusually sensitive and even witty when untroubled and happy." [17] This description clearly applies in large part to Chang in *The West Chamber*. It would be superfluous to trace here the relation of all elements in *Madame Cassia* to features of the Yüan drama of six centuries past. Suffice it to say that the timorous but shrewd and witty heroine, the brutal jailer, the wicked stepmother, the foolish old man, all type figures appearing in *Madame Cassia*, are directly in keeping with type characters long familiar on the stage. Humor in the earliest plays bears many strong resemblances to humor in the latest. Yet differences are equally evident. There has been a shift from a higher to a lower form of comedy. Humor in *The West Chamber* invites a smiling audience, that in *Madame Cassia*, a laughing audience. There is less dignity and more outright mirth. The figures are less sympathetic and, in fact, well on the way to becoming caricatures. They are less of flesh and blood and more like highly stylized puppets. The plot contains more improbabilities. The mood is more relaxed. Humor that was once insinuating has become hilarious.

The story and the sequence of scenes in *Madame Cassia* at once indicate a comic intention. A rapid summary of the action may be helpful. In a prologue in heaven the planet Venus, conceived as a beneficent deity, on looking down from heaven perceives the brutal wrong done to an old man, Li Ch'i. He is seen as an impoverished prisoner falsely accused of murder, tortured by a fiendish jailer who attempts to extract a bribe. Li Ch'i has had two children, a boy and girl, whom he has not seen in years. The children have lost each other and are ignorant whether their father is still alive, while he knows nothing of them. The daughter, Li Kuei-chih, has married a pompous but timid young man, proud, vain, and refined to a degree of absurdity. Through the divine intervention of the planet Venus the daughter learns of her father's plight. She takes it upon herself to mitigate her father's position. Meanwhile her brother, who has rapidly risen in the scholarly class, comes to the city in all the dignity of a visiting judge. Women, it is presumed, may not plead in court, so the husband induces his wife to disguise herself as a man and request a retrial for her father. She is gravely embarrassed; her disguise, chiefly the man's hat which she wears, falls from her in her excitement but the revelation promptly shows the judge that she is his sister. The pretensions of her timid husband are completely taken down. The villain responsible for her father's sufferings is summoned to trial. Despairing of his case, as well he might, he commits suicide in a singularly undignified manner. The miraculous reunion of brother and sister is occasion for celebration and unlimited mirth. Every incident in the play is conceived in a humorous light. A plot that might well have been used to induce pathos is used almost exclusively to produce mirth.

*Madame Cassia* represents the later stages of a national tradition in the theatre where conventions in stage business are carried to such extremes that to a foreign eye the artificiality may even appear naive and childish. Time and space are elided in the most cavalier fashion. The elaborate ritual of a courtroom trial is suggested by a few gestures and a minimum of furniture. This in itself may have to the foreigner a diverting look actually unknown to persons brought up on these theatrical conventions and symbols, or, in other words, to the manner born. But in final analysis of the play's spirit and in particular of its comic spirit all these considerations are palpably superficial. The humor lies not in chairs and tables but in the human breast. The timidity and vanity of Magistrate Chao, Seventh Class, becomes hilariously amusing, as may also be said of the feigned timidity and actual shrewdness of his wife. Their scene together in the second act proves in this respect truly a comic masterpiece. Madame Cassia's disguise as a man in the following scene is carried off with rare theatrical gusto; her husband's jealousy is presented in the spirit of the gayest farce. The broadly humorous elements are artfully and boldly painted against the background of a solemn, ceremonious, and pompous court of law that in itself is ridiculous. The rapid, almost instantaneous transitions between public and domestic scenes add still another feature to the delightfully complicated comic organism.

All proceeds on the lightness of dancing feet. Action is brisk and continuous, speech reduced almost to a minimum. Yet even with full acknowledgment of the play's strongly choreographic and pantomimic character, it must be recognized as truly poetic. The key to this condition is given by the forescene in heaven, that constitutes a prologue as surprising as it is effectual. Clearly, the body of the play deals with episodes altogether too familiar in daily life of the Chinese people. *Madame Cassia* resembles scores of celebrated Chinese plays, among which *The Chalk Circle* and *Snow in Midsummer* may be mentioned as outstanding, in which trial scenes, with torture, are conspicuous. The theatrical figures, even though caricatures, are only too clearly caricatures drawn from direct observation. Yet extreme artificiality appears at virtually every moment. The scene, then, both is and is not naturalistic. Insofar as it is fanciful, it belongs virtually to fairyland. Hence a mythology far closer in spirit to the traditional Western view of fairies than to the Western view of gods or angels provides material for the forescene of this eminently social comedy. The scene in heaven is obviously designed to be amusing rather than sublime. The episode is both intrinsically delightful and organically a part of the play's essential proposition, which is, to put it simply, that all things turn out happily in the end. Naturally, it should be understood that no one in China ever seriously believed this proposition. It is an assumption of man's incurably romantic mind, the key to the happy ending in fiction and comic drama, an illusion of pure fantasy, forever contradicted in the world of fact. The Chinese are nothing if not a sophisticated people. They do not and cannot at any time have accepted the doctrine literally, yet have consistently played with the idea. Nowhere is it more literally stated than in *Madame Cassia* and nowhere is it clearer that it is viewed entirely in a humorous light.

The forescene declares all's well in heaven and on earth. At the play's conclusion this proposition is advanced by the greatest fool of all, the senile father, and welcomed with unanimity and enthusiasm by all the assembled members of his family. The audience also accepts it for the nonce, patently a legitimate assumption of the theatre. The humor of the episode lies in the recognition of the "credibility gap" between the theatre of fancy and the theatre of the real world. In the great world-theatre the proposition simply does not hold. Only a fool could maintain it. But on the stage itself a fool proposes it and all applaud it. We witness a willing suspension of truth and a patent acceptance of wish-fulfillment. The complete and absolute gaiety of comedy is maintained.

No irony is intended, no reference to theological matters or rationality in any form whatsoever. This theatre unveils a naive and an aesthetic heaven, not one of serious conviction or belief.

Precisely what the psychology of the more sinister episodes in the play may be must remain a mystery beyond the scope of this investigation. Yet it is clear from the beginning that these dark features are not to be taken with realization of their potential emotional force. A degree of masochism may well be found in the torture scenes that abound on the Chinese stage, both in the most serious plays, as *The Chalk Circle*, *Snow in Midsummer*, and *The Little Orphan of the Family of Chao*, and in the most light-hearted, as *Madame Cassia*. In the last mentioned all simulated emotions are seen through a comic lens, whether they be of pain or joy. In the final scene the father is so overwhelmed with joy that in laughing he comes in danger of dislocating his jaw. In the early scene he is subjected to torture before our eyes. But his tormentor, the jailer, is presented as a comic character; more is made of the jailer's cupidity and veniality than of his brutality. The torture scene is not designed to achieve tragic depth. For one reason, the heavenly provision that the victim's cries shall by magic be carried through thick stone walls to the ears of his daughter, who by happy accident as yet unknown to the leading figure lives in a house nearby, assures us that in the end all will be rectified. This is stated succinctly and in no uncertain terms by the god of the Planet Venus, who, speaking words that never fail, certifies to the ultimate triumph of mercy and justice among men. His angels—humorous little cupids who ride the clouds—see to that.

A title often given the play as seen on the Peking stage early in the present century, "An Extraordinary Twin Meeting," emphasizes the implausibility of the story when seen from the literal or prosaic point of view. The assumption is that the better the artist the further his creative ingenuity will take him from a literal representation of life. The entire action is deliberately slanted away from mere verisimilitude. Dialogue is curt and clipped to serve the occasion. Far from any attempt to express passion in words, the style presents only an attempt to draw the mere outline of emotions and events, to reveal the course which they take, leaving the actor to use appropriate gestures. But these gestures will also be hints only. The mere reader must fill in all color and detail, all the warmth or shudders which the incident indicates. The dialogue becomes virtually a synopsis of a serious drama that is neither written nor intended. Such a style may appear naive but its simplicity itself is highly artful and ingenious. The incongruity between statement and reference becomes in itself delectable comedy. To this extent the play might even seem farce, travesty, or burlesque. But it is not this nor is it parody except in the sense that it is all these when referred to "real life." In other words, the playwright has no intention to base his work on a spoofing of a serious classic, as did the masters of the *opera bouffe* in the European eighteenth century. It is all the sounder work of art on this account, since it wholly escapes the undignified state of being parasitical. It stands safely upon its own feet, or, one might better say, on its toes, dancing its joyous projection of a vision of the real world seen in a mirror where all features are reversed.

Unreality, at least when reality is viewed prosaically, becomes the essence of much comedy, an art known to some degree throughout the world but brought close to its perfection in China. In *Madame Cassia*, for example, the astonishment of the four members of the family on finding themselves reunited affords a large part of the scene's humor. Astonishment itself constitutes understatement where reason would conclude not with astonishment but with complete incredulity.

Whereas humor in *The West Chamber* is an occasional outcropping, in *Madame Cassia* it is omnipresent, the groundwork of the entire play. When considered as performing art, the humor is even more obvious in gesture than in speech. The climax of Act Two occurs in the last, hilarious moment, when the humble wife points a humorous finger at the incredibly conceited husband and, with the best of spirit in the world, wins a triumph over him. The climax in Act Three occurs when, terrified by violence in the court, she allows her man's cap to fall from her head, so revealing her real sex. The high point in the final act occurs as the father nearly cracks his jaw laughing with unrestrained glee, gloating over the fall of his enemies. Possibly the climax in Act One occurs as the absurd and brutal jailer is forced to place his own cushion under the knees of the pathetic old prisoner whom he has recently tortured. Here the pantomime is highly laugh-provoking. Stuttering, humming and hawing, prolonged hesitation and physical embarrassment, contribute far more to the humor than manifestations of verbal wit. Repeatedly the two chief butts of comedy, the husband and wife, are reduced to speechlessness. Again, prolonged laughter is achieved as the modest woman is reluctant to reveal the name by which she was known as a child in the intimacy of her parents' household. Her action of grinding ink for her husband's writing at the same time that she achieves complete mastery over him is hugely diverting.

It should be further urged that this absence of verbal eloquence and emphasis on action or simple speech do not actually demean the caliber of the play or of its humor. In fact, the presentation of life here is in many respects closer to reality than in such plays as the vastly more literary *West Chamber*. Persons in real life do not talk in verse. Moreover, the speech in *Madame Cassia* does at times become distinctly artificial. On several occasions in the last act, especially in the episode that depicts the apotheosis of the father, who exchanges his prisoner's rags for a cloak of supreme elegance, his family speaks in unison. Of course it is regrettably true that in social life several people at times do talk at once but here we encounter virtually a chorus performing with the speaking voice, all using precisely the same words. Or at times the same remarks are made but, in accordance with the individual speaking, the proper names are different. The usage belongs not to a naturalistic theatre but to a convention frequently encountered in the comic opera of Mozart.

The scope of the playwright's humor is intimated by his effective use of tears and laughter on the stage. When Madame Cassia relates the story of her father's imprisonment, torture, and imminent danger of death as a common criminal, she shows her sensitivity by bursting repeatedly into tears. She simply cannot bear to relate to her husband the sufferings which her father has undergone. With the most magisterial dignity this magistrate forces from her the promise that she will curb her tears. This she undertakes to do but repeatedly fails to comply with the promise. From the standpoint of pathos the entire scene, of course, should be completely serious. But the comic playwright extracts his loudest laughs from the very moments that elsewhere would wring the heart. The humor in such cases is not really cruel; it is instead the art of a highly sophisticated sense for comedy. Again, in the final scene, as previously observed, the younger members of the family express genuine fears that the father will injure himself through his excessive laughter occasioned by his inordinate glee at the news of his enemy's discomfiture. The entire scene is a brilliant contrivance of comic art. Tears and laughter are alike grist to the playwright's mill.

No figure in the play escapes the shafts of comedy and mirth. The least ridiculous character is, obviously, Li Pao-t'ung, Li Chi's son, who has risen to the high station of supreme judge over an entire province. It is he who lords it over the play's hero, Chao-Ch'ung, magistrate of the Seventh Rank and virtual mayor of a small provincial city. Li Pao-t'ung is one whom fortune has showered with favors that are almost embarrassing. Perhaps he is a youthful genius. In any case, he asks the citizens to show him respect in view of his high office and generously to overlook his surprising youth. Even this part, then, is not conceived in a wholly serious manner. His modesty makes the hero's timidity and deference all the more amusing. In one scene we observe the hero lording it over his obsequious wife; in the next we see him trembling at the feet of his lordly but youthful brother-in-law.

Finally, it is not to be supposed that familiarity bred contempt even in matters of Chinese theatrical decor. The villain of the piece, at least insofar as that term is applicable in such facetious playwriting, is Hu, the easily corruptible retired magistrate of the city. When caught in the surprising net of heaven's irresistible judgment, he announces that he will kill himself. Consequently, he is seen on the stage to jump over a chair and thus drown himself in a well. A moment afterward he rises from the floor and in the guise of a ghost stalks off the stage. Perhaps an historian of the theatre, fortified with academic learning and an extremely severe temperament, might suppose this action to be so far a stage convention that to the playwright and his audience it would be received without a smile. I suggest, on the contrary, that such a view would be misleading and that even the Chinese audience was amused by such scenes of extreme artifice. One can only conclude that *Madame Cassia* is one of the most delightful of extravaganzas and moreover admirably representative of a large section of Chinese drama over a period of centuries.

Another chapter in the humor of the Chinese theatre is disclosed in plays based on popular legends taken by the public as historical. These plays are characterized by an infectious gusto. Humor here is relatively rude and obvious when seen beside the lighter touch and more refined and urbane art of such works as *Madame Cassia*. Nevertheless the category contains plays of considerable merit and a strength that has proved singularly enduring. Most of them are based on the most popular book in the entire annals of Chinese fiction, the Yüan novel, *Shui-hu chuan*, called by some translators *The Men of the Marshes*, but best known to English readers through the free translation by Pearl Buck entitled *All Men Are Brothers*. (The latter title, incidentally, translates a memorable phrase in the novel itself.) Many of its pages are rich in a popular variety of humor transported and even augmented in the scenes of the plays. So intimate and important is the relation between the work of fiction and the drama that a few introductory words are called for regarding the former. The examination of typical plays based on this material may, therefore, be preceded by comments on the famous novel or narrative, based on pseudo-historical legends.

This work was designed as a popular, entertaining narration, not primarily humorous but including strong comic elements. It was extremely episodic, with many exciting stories eminently fit for dramatic treatment. Its contribution to the theatre is easily explained on many grounds; there is violent action; there are vivid characterizations, together with sensationalism and enthusiasm. A large part of the book literally stands half-way to the theatre, being in lively dialogue. Moreover, it originally served even more as a prompt-book for professional reciters addressing an illiterate audience than as an item for a library. Only with gradually changing times was it admitted without hesitation onto the scholar's bookshelf. It was apparently compiled in the Yüan period, synchronously with the sensational rise of the Chinese theatre. Frequently it is remarked that this tale of generous, great-hearted bandits came into being as a secret protest to inspire Chinese resistance to the conquerors. Since it was the unhappy destiny of the people to be for a matter of centuries beneath foreign rule, such veiled protests against authority are easily understandable. The book constituted something of a prose epic, though in many respects deficient as epic literature, partly because it fell short of voicing the culture of an entire people and because it lacks epic seriousness and a background in religion or mythology. The philosophy—if the word is admissible regarding so popular a work—had more of a Taoist than a Confucian complexion. The rigidity of the Confucian system is viewed much askance; the traditional love of scholarship and decorum is largely renounced. In place of Confucian morality is the license encouraged by Taoism, a cheerful sense of freedom from the prevailing moral code and a spontaneous acceptance of miracle, magic, and fantasy. Clearly, the book was unique, being neither epic, novel, poetry, nor chronicle but a blend of all these and much besides. In this free-moving content much humor inevitably found its place. The quality generally understood by the word bravado describes the mood best. There is little wit or refined humor in the sense that these are found in other Chinese classics. But for humorous gusto the book is truly incomparable. Its hardy spirit was readily transferred with much success to the popular stage. Two examples of this contribution to dramatic literature will suffice for examination, the Yüan drama, *Li K'uei Carries Thorns,* ascribed to K'ang Chin-chih, and the traditional drama, *The Fisherman's Revenge,* said to have originally been a Shensi opera. It was later taken over by the Peking musical theatre. It has, incidentally, appeared under several titles, among them being *A Fisherman Kills a Family* and *The Lucky Pearl.*

Li K'uei, the chief character in the first play, is a clownish figure prominent in the popular prose novel. He is essentially humorous, impetuous, violent, irrational, vulgar, and equally extreme in brutality and kindness—the very antithesis of the Confucian scholar-gentleman. At one moment he commits what would according to conventional ethics be held an atrocious crime, in the next he sincerely repents his action. Repeatedly he embarrasses his comrades by the uncomfortable position in which he places them, yet they always forgive him. In one respect he does indeed follow the Confucian ideal for he is not only completely loyal to his friends but feels for them the most sincere affection. His language is profane, his manners are uncouth, his temper is incorrigible. Without his superhuman strength, energy, and valor, however, the robber band could scarcely maintain itself against the forces of law and order. Li K'uei is certainly one of the most brilliant creations of the Chinese imagination. He above all others must compensate for the long centuries of Confucian rigidity. He is scarcely less a part of the image of China than the seers themselves. The humor from which he springs is clearly a lower type of humor than that attained by such scholar-poets as the author of *The West Chamber* or the amazingly suave courtly painters who decorated the unforgettable tiles now in the Boston Museum of Fine Arts. Yet the popular humor may stand only a short way below the sophisticated in China's legacy to the world.

By a stroke of extraordinary good fortune that American scholarship perhaps scarcely deserves, readers of English possess a brilliant, racy translation of this play which in itself constitutes by far the best commentary. This is the work of Professor James I. Crump. Non-Chinese readers are referred to this for any consideration of the details and the texture of the play. Much can be said of the type of humor which it reveals.

Only one character in the drama can be viewed "straight." All others are clownish in some degree, the hero most of all. This "straight" character is Sung Chiang, leader of the band of humanitarian robbers. At his side is commonly seen

"Brother Lu," a priest who has become a bandit and who to a surprising degree resembles Friar Tuck in the medieval Robin Hood cycle of English popular ballads.

Like most Yüan dramas, *Li K'uei* is comparatively short as well as succinct in the treatment of its subject. Only a minimum of speaking parts suffices to suggest a whole horde of land pirates. Outside these inhabitants of the mountain lair are four figures of less importance but nevertheless by no means of small interest. All are burlesque. Most conspicuous is Wang Lin, the keeper of a rustic tavern located in a valley beneath the mountain, affording a favorite haunt for the robbers. He is almost blind, extremely awkward and stupid, but well-meaning and, as befits a tavern-keeper, convivial and devoted to wine. Typical of his blundering actions is the embrace which he gives Li K'uei, mistaking him for his lost daughter. This girl, unmarried, age eighteen, is abducted for three days of uninterrupted sexual delights by two notorious rascals who pretend to be the leaders of the noble robbers, a deception successful less by virtue of their disguise than because of the father's bad eyesight. The girl apparently enjoys her experience. Small trouble ensues since in the last scene her father promises to find for her a respectable husband. The two inferior robbers are obviously comic impostors, on a lower level from the glorious mountaineers.

The plot is as preposterous as the characterization and by its own nature contributes to the play's broad humor. The robber chief honors in particular two holiday seasons, on one of which the action of the comedy takes place. This joyful occasion is celebrated by a vacation of three days for all the robbers, who may, if they will, go out into the world, visit the graves of their ancestors, and enjoy drinking, feasting, and all sensual pleasures. Whoever after his holiday returns late will lose his head. Since the mountain lair bears too much the appearance of a mountain monastery, the relief of such a vacation is readily imagined.

Li K'uei chooses to visit Wang's tavern. It so happens that

shortly before he arrives the two impostors have visited the place and taken away the girl. They pretend to be the robber chief and the robber priest. Their plot is unconsciously aided by Wang Lin's stupidity in calling forth his daughter from the inner room of his establishment to give more gracious service to the thirsty and hungry men. Li K'uei is righteously indignant. Accepting the story of the innkeeper, he hastens back to the mountain to accuse the chief and the priest of the girl's abduction. The chief, of course, denies the charge as absurd. He lays his head as a wager against Li K'uei's head that the innkeeper will absolve him. When the robbers visit the inn the poor old host, half blind though he is, still perceives that these are not the culprits. So the too credulous Li K'uei has lost his wager and forfeited his life. But he does not wish to die. Consequently he returns to the lair bearing a load of wicked-looking thorns on his back. He begs the chief to spare his life and instead of the death sentence to thrash him with the thorns. The device proves futile. The hero, even though repentant, is about to be beheaded. But meanwhile the two abductors have returned, as they had promised, with the girl in hand. The innkeeper, who, though stupid, is not altogether a fool, contrives to get the men dead drunk and then hastens to the mountain to save his generous friend, Li K'uei. His arrival is in the nick of time. Li K'uei now for a second time visits the inn, captures the rascals, who are still too drunk to offer resistance, and returns in triumph to the lair. The villains are killed with torture while the entire robber band rejoices that all has turned out for the best.

From first to last the play is consistently comic, though there is perhaps a moment of apprehension when Li K'uei's head hangs in the balance. Unlike a work of high comedy, as *The West Chamber*, or of middle comedy, as *Madame Cassia*, this is beyond doubt low comedy. Yet it is almost as artful as the more ambitious works. An imaginative style appropriate to such a piece is brilliantly sustained with the highest gusto and bravura.

Although a few snatches of racy songs occur, there is little to compete with the lyrical verse commonly used in more or less sober Chinese plays. Style aims at briskness. All moves swiftly. Speakers shift from verse to prose over a hundred and twenty times. The soliloquy that opens Li K'uei's participation in the play alone contains fourteen such transitions and several other passages assigned to him move back and forth from speech to song to speech again almost as lightly. It is, of course, of still more importance for the comic spirit that the manner alternates between passages deliberately rich in romantic and even sentimental poeticisms and others enlivened by racy colloquialisms. When one considers the play in the general light of Chinese literary history, it almost seems a parody of some epic now lost, though of course this is by no means the case. Undoubtedly it is the better in its poetry and humor for being altogether spontaneous and in no way ridiculing other works of drama or fiction. It stands firmly upon its own feet from the very first words, in which the robber chief introduces himself as "Herald of Justice," to the last verses, as the hero rejoices not in his own escape from death but in the justice done by his master and their gang as servants of "the Will of Heaven," manifest still further in Wang Lin's safe recovery of his abducted daughter. That the play was destined to success is almost assured by Li K'uei's first words: "Drinking without getting drunk is worse than being sober."

Knowledge of Li K'uei's appearance is decidedly helpful in appreciating this role and, indeed, the play as a whole. He is of the type of black-faced clown, deformed in features and humorously terrible to behold. Much is made of his uncouth gestures and appearance even in the play's dialogue. Thus in the course of his first flight into verse he plucks a flower, gazes at it sentimentally, and, noting the incongruity between the tinted blossom and his black, coarse finger, with a guttural laugh and a kind word for the flower tosses it back where he found it. He can at will be rough as a bear or lyrical as an oriole. He knows what he believes to be right but his appetite keeps him from the right or prudent action. Realizing the danger of excessive drink, he makes a genuine effort to pass by the wine-shop but the temptation is too great for him. He is supersensitive to the claims of justice, this being the only ideal that he prizes above friendship, but rash and without the slightest trace of discretion. When he believes his master guilty of a crime, he casts the claim of friendship instantly aside but when his master refuses to grant him punishment by a thorn-thrashing as substitute for a head solemnly set up in a wager, he accepts the judgment completely, addressing his master only in terms of complete affection and loyalty.

It is virtually impossible to condemn a man of so many engaging qualities, no matter what his faults. From the point of view of ethics generally accepted by society he is an incurable criminal. From the viewpoint of the average man he is equally provocative of affection and mirth. The play stands well above the level which we are accustomed to assign to uproarious farce; it is, indeed, a humorous poem of high distinction. There are few productions in the West of this quality. Aristophanes also harmonizes poetic idealism and low comedy, exquisite lyric verse and the commonest talk of street and field, but the singular conjunction of rudeness and tenderness, moral idealism and complete freedom from moral responsibility, remains for the illogical Chinese. The result is exhilarating comedy, a poetic bravado and an unsurpassed example of the essential incongruity within the human soul.

Would that Professor Crump would give the public the formula for the elixir that inspired this typical passage in his translation! The scene gives Li K'uei's account of the maudlin sorrows of the inebriated innkeeper. Needless to say, Li, as always, is drunk.

Li K'uei (sings). Sometimes the old man weakly weeps in his
    thatched shop;
    (speaks) He looks toward our mountain, crying his hatred
    for Sung Chiang.
    (sings) He restlessly rises to his feet

Then whimpers with wrath outside his wicker door,
(*speaks*) Crying, "Oh, Man-t'ang Ch'iao;"
(*sings*) And sighingly sobs his suffering.

*Sung Chiang.* What does he do with his sorrow?

*Li K'uei* (*sings*). He then gloomily looms by his wine vats,
(*speaks*) Picks up a dipper, takes the straw lid from the crock,
Dips up cold wine and drinks it in gulps;
(*sings*) Then dully, dizzily drunk
Clutching his scrap of matting
He listlessly lays it out on his brick bed.
(*speaks*) He goes outside again to look; sees no sign of her, and then,
(*sings*) He sadly sinks to his bed
And snuffles and whines to sleep.
This will not do, brother,
This will not do.

*Sung Chiang.* What does he mean now? [18]

According to a formula for comic effects known in virtually all quarters of the world, the humor in *The Fisherman's Revenge* is the antithesis of that in *Li K'uei Carries Thorns.* In the latter case the hero is a sophisticated man who speaks boisterously, in the former a valiant man who speaks gently. The two conceptions, even though in themselves antithetical, are alike romantic and alike humorous, inasmuch as humor resides in violent incongruity regardless of how or where it may be found.

*The Fisherman's Revenge* is a shorter and simpler work with a perspicuous moral that has long made it popular, from a time lost to conclusive knowledge until the period of modern Communist China. According to one account, this was the last "Peking opera" to be performed before Peking's theatres, only a short time ago, ceased to stage traditional type plays. Although hardly a literary masterpiece, it has considerable merit as a work of imagination, especially from the theatrical point of view, and well illustrates how humor and propaganda may accord. In substance it is a humorous political cartoon with the effect of inspiring one's own party with confidence in its strength and of making the adversary appear weak and ridiculous. It represents folk humor close to its best.

The central figure, Hsiao En, derives in spirit though not in a literal sense from the same folk romances that inspired *Li K'uei Carries Thorns*. He is much addicted to the wine cup. He combines prodigious strength, the impulse for using it, and a passion for justice accompanied by tenderness and poetic idealism. In accord with the tradition of fishermen known throughout the world, he is a quiet, almost a silent man, loving the gentler aspects of nature, shrinking from the madness of the turbulent world. Yet, contrary to such an idyllic image, when aroused he proves ruthless, powerful, and indomitable. One imagines that his favorite reading included the poems of T'ao Ch'ien and *The Men of the Marshes*. In the first scene he appears as a poor old man on the verge of retirement, who stubbornly pursues his fishing as means for sustaining his quiet, frugal way of life. His wife has been dead for some time, leaving in his care a young daughter of marriageable age. She is depicted as a quiet girl, in this respect much like her father. Her first instinct is to shrink from violence. Yet in the end her devotion to her father leads her into the most aggressive action. She changes from the timorous woman, the type most often presented on the Chinese stage, to that other feminine type well known in the so-called "military plays," the fearless and indomitable female warrior. Both with daughter and father much of the humor springs from the surprising transition from the pacific to the militant mode. The very implausibility of the change makes it comic. This may well seem to signify a low form of humor but anyone who still recalls Mei Lan-fang in the role of the daughter must realize that such a part affords an astonishingly good vehicle for the comic actor. In its initial form, as indicated only by the words, the humor is elementary. Nevertheless it gives almost limitless possibilities for the inspired actor.

Among its varied aspects the plot provides considerable opportunities for a type of entertainment long popular on the Chinese stage and by no means unrelated to the comic spirit, the introduction of much purely acrobatic action. Two acrobatic scenes stand as high points in the presentation. The first is the confrontation between Hsiao and the Boxing Master, which is accompanied by only a few words; the second is the general melee in which the landlord and all his household are killed and where language itself fades out completely. Of course in scenes of so conventional a nature a few words, presumably expletives, may be improvised by the actors. The present study, however, deals exclusively with the literature of humor; what remains unwritten cannot be seriously taken into account.

Almost all the play's features are familiar but all show deft handling. The prevailingly gay temper, so typical of most of the Peking theatre, is set by the first episode, a lively drinking party. Two members of a robber band such as that to which Li K'uei belonged pay Hsiao a call on his boat moored to the river bank. These are in substance choral figures or may be viewed as interlocutors necessary in revealing Hsiao's character. One subject of their talk is the forthcoming marriage of Hsiao's daughter. During the party the bailiff of the arrogant landlord who lives nearby on the opposite shore of the river peeks into the boat's cabin to catch a glimpse of the girl. Shortly afterward the landlord's steward arrives demanding that Hsiao pay the landlord a fishing tax. Hsiao declares that the water in the river has been low and consequently he lacks money. An altercation follows between one of the visiting bravos and the steward. The chief significance of this episode in developing the play's comic spirit lies in the wholly deceptive attitude assumed by Hsiao. He is seen as a pacifier, doing his utmost to restrain the bravo and to pour cool water over the angry contestants. At the end of the scene the steward shows himself both shrewd and cowardly. He escapes unhurt. Of special note in the play's lyrical spirit is an exchange of words between bravo and steward concerning the legality of the tax. Question and answer are snapped out like themes in a humorous duet. This passage is, for the sake of emphasis, several times repeated in the course of the play. It contributes an important feature to the play's construction.

The next episode in the artful unfolding of the story is an enlargement and intensification of what has gone before. On this occasion the landlord sends a gang of thugs who may with only slight license be called "company police." Their leader is the Boxing Master. From the first they show, nevertheless, that they are complete cowards and wholly ineffectual. The entire scene is conceived as broad farce, the Boxing Master being the most timid of all the gang. At first he is so afraid of meeting Hsiao that on seeing his cottage he pretends that infallible signs show no one at home. Much nonsense follows in the course of knocking on the door and the inevitable exchange of polite greetings. Again Hsiao declines to pay the tax, whereupon the Boxer proposes to arrest the fisherman, first putting him in chains. By a feat of dexterity Hsiao in counterattack puts the chains around the Boxer. The latter manages to get out of his confinement and, relying on the force of numbers, even commences an out-and-out fight with Hsiao. The engagement is, of course, pure farce but is extremely well contrived to produce its effect. Hsiao first sends the Boxing Master's aides packing. Finally, left alone with the chief, he makes the man wholly ridiculous. Once more the action assumes choreographic form. The Boxer boasts that he can overcome Hsiao simply by butting him with his head. The fisherman accepts the challenge. Three times the Boxer thrusts his heavy head at Hsiao's stomach with no discomfort in the least to the impassive defendant. Next the Boxer boasts that like the sages and mystics he possesses supernatural potency through control of his breath. He asserts that when he holds in a deep breath he becomes invincible. The test proves the contrary; as Hsiao touches him with a finger he collapses. The scene ends with a beating, Hsiao's daughter entering the fray with a bamboo stick to administer the final thrashing.

The daughter, like her father, is compounded of ambiguity. When she first hears her father's intention of launching on his course of desperate violence, her filial devotion and her own intrepid nature inspire her to say that she will accompany him. After a moment's hesitation her father agrees to have her at his side. When, however, the boat that ferries them across the river reaches midstream, her girlish nature gains the upper hand. Momentarily terrified, she declares that she will turn the skiff around and return to the cottage. Her vacillation provides the dramatic value as well as the humor of the episode. Her hesitation proves to be only a passing cloud. She soon plucks up her spirits. The journey continues.

Shrewdness may be allied to humor but it must be acknowledged a rather distant cousin. Hsiao is in possession of a magic pearl that insures success to the wearer. This he has given his daughter before they set sail on their desperate adventure. On reaching the mansion Hsiao pretends that he has a precious gem which in sign of contrition he intends to bestow upon the landlord. To make this transfer the safer he requests that all attendants leave the room. After their departure Hsiao and his daughter easily kill the landlord.

The two diverting plays just examined are characterized by qualities long established in tales of imaginary heroes who live beyond the law and in their own eyes, as well as in the minds of the audience, justify themselves in their violent actions. These they consider to be in the interests of humanity and of the people, validated by "the Way of Heaven," though not by officially proclaimed laws of state. All such plays are overshadowed, historically speaking, by the great Yüan novel to which allusion has already been made. A distinction, though possibly not drastic, exists between such works as these and plays based on at least semihistorical material. In the public eye in ancient China the distinction between history and legend certainly was not great, yet something of the sort did exist. The writing of history and chronicles had, of course, been firmly established at least by the time of Confucius and had long comprised one of the most highly esteemed forms of Chinese literature, the work of the most responsible scholars. It unquestionably established a point of view. The Chinese themselves made qualitative distinctions, for example, between a Li K'uei or a Hsiao En on the one hand and a Ts'ao Ts'ao or a Chu-ko Liang on the other.

It is of considerable interest that the plays based on this historical or semihistorical material tend to be both less humorous and less fanciful than those founded on folktales or folk literature. Yet they, too, are designed to be entertaining. One presumes that their authors had a less serious desire to dispense patriotic instruction in history than did Shakespeare on writing his plays based on the British dynastic wars. The Chinese "military plays," to use the conventional terminology, abound in gay and colorful spectacle, battles that are in fact dances, with much indulgence in pomp and circumstance. On the whole they are clearly more sensational and melodramatic than comic or humorous. Yet they, also, contain strong humorous elements.

In them is a pronounced tendency to present certain figures illumined by flashes of a distinctly comic spirit. The Chinese, like other peoples, tended to view public events as created by persons. This materially aided the creation of *dramatis personae*. There were even a few such persons who broke the closely woven net of theatrical conventions and wore unique costumes and employed gestures appertaining to them alone. The urge, as a rule so much more potent in the West than in the East, emerged to create "characterization." Such figures on the Chinese stage are Ts'ao Ts'ao and Chu-ko Liang, the former a past master of military and political strategy, the latter virtually a magician with a more than mortal intellect. Both, then, are strategists, but Ts'ao Ts'ao instead of supporting virtue and good government is a usurper, a sensualist, and altogether a villain. Chu-ko Liang differs from the majority of the political and martial figures represented on the stage in that he is a man of ideas, an elder statesman who is not himself an active warrior. Ts'ao Ts'ao is no hero at all but a villain, yet one of those ambivalent stage villains who possess uncanny fascination for their audiences and who are, perhaps unconsciously, envied and admired—in short, analogous to Milton's Satan as the foul fiend is envisaged by modern psychology.

Two anonymous plays in which Chu-kuo Liang stands in the center of the field may be selected to illustrate the famous strategist as a humorous figure in the mode of high comedy. This most revered hero of the Chinese people is, of course, never made ridiculous. It is he who makes others ridiculous. He is himself the arch-humorist, secure in the knowledge of his own invincibility. The first play to be considered, *Stealing the Arrows*, deals with one of the most celebrated episodes in Chinese history, the Battle of the Red Cliff. It depicts the defeat of Ts'ao Ts'ao's greatly superior force by Chu-ko Liang's superior generalship. The army loyal to the Emperor, aided by Chu-ko Liang, lacks both men and ammunition. The generals, being in despair, turn to Chu-ko Liang to rescue them from their predicament. He assures them that he will provide ammunition, consisting of a hundred thousand arrows, and also completely destroy the power of the enemy. To effect this he gives the surprising advice that they should fill certain old boats with hay and float them by night down the river. Although this appears absurd to the young generals, they know well enough not to resist the sage's counsel.

Chu-ko Liang meanwhile divides his time between feasting and retirement in his study, wholly unconcerned with the excitement and terror surrounding him on every side. The fatal night of the experiment is foggy; the boats are released; Ts'ao Ts'ao, believing that an expeditionary force is sent against him in the night, orders his men to shoot their arrows at the dimly seen vessels, expecting to destroy the enemy even before they can land. A hundred and twenty thousand arrows are shot, firmly landing in the hay. The wind shifts; the boats come back to the loyal army; Chu-ko Liang has realized all his promises! When the astonished and delighted generals ask the sage how he has known that at a particular moment the wind would shift and that a fog would veil the boats, with supercilious scorn he replies to the young men: "A general who is ignorant of astronomy and geography will never rise above mediocrity." This, if I may be allowed a personal confession, is in my experience the most amusing line in Chinese drama. The scene and all that it contained was cherished in the minds of native audiences. Chu-ko Liang has plausibly been called the favorite figure on the Chinese stage. The line just quoted marks his moment of supreme triumph.

A fairly similar play, *Yellow Crane Tower*, may be cited to illustrate another of Chu-ko Liang's weird successes. Here, as in the incident of the Battle of the Red Cliff, his strategy seems in an equal degree to defy reality but no skepticism troubled the original audiences. With extraordinary faith in their strategic advisor, the leaders of the loyal army go to a banquet offered them by the treacherous Ts'ao Ts'ao, where their betrayal appears inevitable. But they are supplied with a small bamboo case which, it is promised them, will insure their safety. No need here to disclose the secret. They are saved after having enjoyed the feast at their enemies' expense. Such plots are viewed in themselves as humorous and all such plays as this have in the nature of the case a comic aspect.

The noteworthy conjunction of humor and such characterization as the conventions of Chinese drama allow are well shown in another popular military play, *The Battle of Ch'ang-Pan P'o*, where Ts'ao Ts'ao is prominent and Chu-ko Liang is absent. The two chief figures to be humorously drawn are Ts'ao Ts'ao, who is the fascinating figure always revealed when appearing in the theatre, sly, unprincipled, formidable but vulnerable, and the no less pushing and enterprising character, a woman, Tsou Shih, whose lust and ambition lead her to a brief, fatal liaison with Ts'ao Ts'ao. Characterization is, of course, in swift and bold strokes but none the less effective, a style that might be likened to the manner of Franz Hals. Strong exaggeration and high gusto in the delineation largely account for the unmistakably comic effect of the scenes in which the two appear. Viewed as a whole, the play cannot properly be called comic or humorous. It descends at times to commonplace melodrama. But the two leading roles are masterly achievements of the comic spirit.

Still another play with a largely military setting, *Pearly Screen Castle,* presents neither Ts'ao Ts'ao, Chu-ko Liang, nor any figures recently mentioned, but is much more conspicuously marked by hilarious and lusty humor. It seems almost a parody of other military plays. Some of the low but lively comedy shown here may owe its presence to the general setting, which is not in China proper but in Mongolia. The plot concerns military and diplomatic relations between the two countries. The humor lies in the extremely broad caricatures of the leaders in the Mongolian court, where the public functions of the sexes are completely reversed. Chief of the ridiculous characters are an aging king shown as a henpecked husband, and his first and second queen. The first queen is of Chinese extraction, the second of Mongolian. They are alike Amazons but, as might be supposed, the second is more formidable and ferocious. These royal viragoes are drawn in the broadest burlesque, with small trace of naturalism. The second queen is more than a Britomart, the king more senile than Polonius. The playwright, whoever he may have been, shows peculiar craftsmanship as a humorist. No fixed image, as he well knows, can remain long on the stage without becoming monotonous. Throughout most of his scenes the king is pitifully and mercilessly ridiculed, squirming under the heels of his terrifying wives. But in the end it is this fool and coward who with a sudden manifestation of craft and wit overcomes all obstacles and resolves a political crisis "according to the Will of Heaven." As befits Chinese ethics, a man essentially a civilian accomplishes what the military cannot accomplish. This is low comedy but such comedy close to its best. The Chinese theatre in almost all periods as yet documented and especially as the centuries progressed was in part folk theatre, just as much of Chinese poetry, fiction, and music expressed the moral and aesthetic consciousness of the masses. Resulting from this condition are phases of humor ranging in drama from the highly inspired *Li K'ui Carries Thorns* to such works of true but by no means transcendent merit as *Pearly Screen Castle*.

Most plays thus far mentioned are anonymous, although much of the Yüan drama that has been sturdy enough to survive has at least been assigned to known authors. As a rule there seems small advantage in attempting to create portraits of the dramatists, since in most cases little or nothing personal is known of them. One cannot describe the peculiar spirit or humor of this playwright or that with the confidence with which one can draw the literary portraits of Li Po, Tu Fu, and Po Chü-i. Nevertheless, one playwright does to some degree emerge as a fairly distinct figure, Kuan Han-ch'ing, who flourished in the second half of the thirteenth century. Eighteen of his plays are said to survive. They are lively productions, although in no case equal to a few masterpieces by other playwrights who are unhappily known by fewer works. Kuan evidently gave actors and audiences precisely what they wished. His contribution is considerable, yet it cannot be said that without him Chinese drama would offer a materially different image to the world. His popularity seems owing even more to the happily representative and theatrically brilliant quality of his work than to any marked originality or outstanding imaginative power. Kuan Han-ch'ing is highly proficient, a master craftsman, a professional to his fingertips, but hardly in the fullest sense of the words deeply inspired. For the present purposes his work has considerable interest in that a light and pleasing humor characterizes the larger number of his plays. To be sure, in some of them, among which *Snow in Midsum-*

*mer* may be regarded as the chief, little or no humor appears, a seriousness not far from tragedy prevailing. In a recent selection consisting of eight works translated into English by Yang Hsien-yi and Gladys Yang, *Snow in Midsummer* is rightly given the first place and the surprising tragic drama, *Death of the Winged-Tiger General*, the last. Between them is found a series of plays of a decidedly lighter weight, four of which may profitably be commented upon as regards their humorous content. These are *The Butterfly Dream*, *Rescued by a Coquette*, *The Riverside Pavilion*, and *The Jade Mirror-Stand*.

Kuan's *Butterfly Dream*, incidentally, must not be confused with a celebrated Peking opera of the same name, to be commented upon at the close of this chapter. That work is on the whole too tart, ironic, and satirical to be regarded as essentially humorous. The later *Butterfly Dream* would have come close to tragedy if the author had not preferred to view his story for the most part with a satirical spirit and considerable application of salt. Kuan's play, on an entirely different theme, relates the misadventures of a family. In one sense the play is the precise reverse of conventional tragedy, since death and disaster strike hardest in the first act, not in the last. The father of the Wang family is murdered. Angry to the verge of madness, the three sons kill the murderer. But the murderer was a man of influence. Consequently the sons are all arrested and tried. According to law, a single death must be paid for by a single death. Which of the three sons shall be executed? The play depicts the dire straits of the youths and their final release. They show extreme gallantry, each urging his own death as payment for the alleged crime. A certain amount of almost scholastic wit is thrown about in the insistence that three men, or boys, are too high a fine to pay for the death of one. Episodes balance episodes, as stanzas in a popular ballad. The youths are devoted Confucian scholars, true to every letter of the law, their natural feelings under an unbelievably firm control. In the end the law is gratified by a ruse well known to the theatre. The youngest son is taken from jail in wrappings that are supposed to contain the corpse of a common murderer. After the boy's mother has mourned profusely over the supposed body of her son the boy leaps forth and all is well. Superficially the play might be taken for a burlesque of a tragic emotion. It is a curious but remarkably consistent affair, a tragicomedy in which in fact the comedy far exceeds the tragedy. A few scenes in Western drama offer analogies, yet it would be hard indeed to find in the West such consistent tragicomic buffoonery. No direct parody is, of course, intended. The Chinese have pursued the incongruity present in all humor to its ultimate source. To some eyes this, like other ideals carried to their extremes, may seem more extravagant than profitable. Be this as it may, Kuan's work is an achievement intrinsically interesting and emphatically Chinese.

Two Kuan Han-ch'ing comedies, *The Riverside Pavilion* and *Rescued by a Coquette*, are complements to each other, both showing humor achieved more through lightness of touch than through its more robust or strenuous assertion. This is the comedy of situation, providing an enviable role for the leading actor. In *The Riverside Pavilion* a lecherous lord attempts to secure the wife of a magistrate as his concubine. In pursuit of this goal he intends to have the husband beheaded on a false accusation. The faithful wife, however, manages affairs to her own liking. The lord enters into the revels of a day of carnival. Disguised as a fishwife, the woman plays the coquette with him at his drinking party. After he and his companions have drunk to a state of stupefaction, she steals his insignia of office. This places him in such an embarrassing situation that she easily bargains with him to leave both herself and her husband unmolested. The woman's part is clearly central in the play, the ribald humor of the scene of coquetry its heart. This incident with a magistrate's wife who, in her earlier years, had actually been a pious young lady in a convent, not only has humorous overtones; it is of the essence of humor peculiarly effective for realization in the theatre.

The second of Kuan's comedies mentioned here with a witty

woman as its leading figure, *Rescued by a Coquette,* presents the story of two singsong girls who are devoted friends. One makes the mistake of marrying a profligate. In a short time the marriage proves intolerable to her. Her dear friend, the second singsong girl, easily tempts the husband and so far fascinates him that he completely drops his wife. In the end the libertine is left without either wife or mistress and the two girls are contented, one of them married to a promising young scholar. A scene of coquetry, which gives the play its name, is again the centerpiece. The wiles of the intriguing woman are not only clever but humorous, setting the play in a purely comic mode. Both these comedies give admirable parts for the leading performer.

A subtler form of humor and one more distinctively Chinese animates *The Jade Mirror-Stand.* The uncommonly compact and simple story unfolded in this deftly composed and well written little play in itself indicates its light, comic spirit. A pedantic scholar, member of the august Hanlin Academy, pays a formal call on his cousin, a shy, unmarried girl. Her mother secures him as the girl's tutor in calligraphy and music. Although the scholar is middle-aged, he at once falls in love with the girl. He employs a matchmaker to arrange the marriage. The girl violently rejects him. The conclusion should be taken with more than a grain of ironic salt. A prefect succeeds in reconciling the aging groom and young bride by forcing the academician to pass a test as an impromptu composer of verse. The girl is so impressed by his triumph in this over-conventionalized art that she no longer finds him repulsive. Under highly implausible circumstances the two are reconciled and, at least insofar as appearances go, are united.

The play's essence, however, lies, as is to be expected, not in the plot but in the characterization, admirably drawn by means of both incident and gesture. The play's title refers to the mirror in which the principal figure and chief butt of the playwright's humor delights in viewing himself. The man is of the conceited scholar type so often met in comic scenes in the Chinese theatre, yet differs considerably from such figures as the conceited husband in *Madame Cassia* and those in the majority of plays in question in that he is in his declining years though, blinded by insatiable vanity, he still regards himself as a dashing young lover. Kuan's humor has some psychological depth. It also has remarkable lightness of touch, providing the beguiling charm and vernal atmosphere peculiarly delightful in the gayer passages of Chinese drama.

An outstanding quality of the Chinese people has long been their suavity. This is also an outstanding quality in the lighter plays ascribed to Kuan Han-ch'ing, several of which, like *The Wife Snatcher* and *Lord Kuan Goes to the Feast*, are better described as dramatic romances than as true comedies. If any Western playwright in this regard rivals this most famous of the Yüan dramatists it is possibly the most celebrated master of dramatic poetry in Spain, Calderón de la Barca.

In concluding this review of humor in Chinese plays three other works may give slightly new insights. They are, or at least were, found in the repertory of the Peking musical theatre in the present century but in origin date from much earlier years. All are anonymous. They have been reserved for the last part of this inquiry because for differing reasons they are by no means creations of pure humor throughout but none the less contain certain striking humorous elements. The first to be noted is the Peking play, *The Butterfly Dream*. Interestingly enough, the play is admittedly more humorous and less satirical and ironic than its ultimate source, the admirable Ming story, *The Inconstancy of Madame Chuang*.

*The Butterfly Dream* is, in fact, based upon a story known for many centuries and in many lands, having been especially popular in the West during the Hellenistic period. It admits many varieties of interpretation, ranging from cynical to hilarious. Briefly summarized, it tells of a husband who determines to test the fidelity of his wife, who has overprotested the firmness of her affection. He pretends to be dead, whereupon she almost immediately violates her pledge of faithfulness to his memory. In the Chinese version the husband is a magician. After he is supposed dead and deposited in his coffin, he reappears to his wife as a young scholar. This handsome young man suddenly contracts a grave illness. A master of magic declares that his disease can be cured only by a medicine taken from the brain of a man recently dead. Since the only corpse readily available is her husband's, the wife herself breaks open the coffin. Thereupon her husband arises from his grave to confront her with her heinous misdeeds. Terrified by what seems to her an apparition and mortified by her guilt, she hangs herself. The play's title has a bearing upon the work as a whole, although it gives no clear key to its interpretation. According to an extremely well-known story, of considerable import in the course of Chinese thought, the cynical philosopher, Chuang Tzu, dreamed that he was a butterfly and on waking found it impossible to determine whether he really was a man dreaming that he was a butterfly or a butterfly dreaming that he was a man. The gist of the fable is, of course, that life is a dream, reality an illusion. It is inevitable that to some minds the story will signify comic relief, to others bitter disillusionment. Even the tale itself has the germ of ambivalence.

The Ming prose version is decidedly serious, a dignified and almost tragic statement of a black view of life and morals. The modern version performed less than a generation ago as a Peking opera is of another complexion. The chief explanation is that the cheerful frivolity and general optimism prevailing in this form of entertainment precluded the traditionally austere, satirical, and pessimistic outlook. Peking opera was furthermore in most of its productions highly sentimental. But the sentimentality and orthodoxy of the modern Chinese musical stage in this instance equally discouraged a humorous interpretation. As a result the play is neither in the black of tragedy nor the gay colors of pure comedy. It turns out to be in a neutral gray. The larger part of Peking opera is of minor or less than minor literary value. Materials for comedy, or, for that matter, for tragedy, are present but no notable achievement in poetic drama is obtained.

These conditions, it must be admitted, militate more strongly to the disadvantage of the play as literature than as theatre. It is one of the basic contentions of this study that, contrary to widely voiced opinion, Chinese drama possesses strongly potential attraction as world literature, notably, of course, if artful translations are available. It seems unlikely that the classical plays will often be performed in the West or in the near future even in China itself. Still, a considerable number may well be read with much pleasure and satisfaction. But *The Butterfly Dream* is scarcely one of these. Especially is it deficient and ambivalent in humor. The potential for humor is present but the achievement remains inadequate. It neither stirs the audience to anger, as satire would, nor evokes hearty laughter or even amused smiles, as would comedy.

Professor A. C. Scott's recent translation, with admirable and extensive stage directions of his own, attests to these conditions. He is certainly correct in holding that this is a play to be seen and not read. His version is presented not as offering aesthetic pleasure to its readers but as affording a helpful prompt-book for possible productions. The translator states that his commentary springs not only from his wide observation of Chinese stage practices, a field in which his acumen surpasses, I believe, that of any other Westerner today, but from his actual participation in a production in the United States. The stage directions are in reality more alive than the dialogue but can hardly be taken as dramatic literature. A Bernard Shaw can write directions as inspired as a brilliant dramatic text. So did Yao Hsin-nung in his translation of *Madame Cassia*, already discussed in these pages. His translation has comments in moderation. The stage directions in no way smother the text. In Professor Scott's method, on the contrary, the directions are drawn to far greater length than the dialogue. From an historical point of view his treatment provides an account of productions in both China and America. From a literary point of view the work is actually more his own than that of the anonymous Chinese playwright. This condition contributes further to the alienation of the play from spontaneous and effectual humor. *The Butterfly Dream,* whether as a production or as a printed text in any form, is a fascinating and curious work. Rather surprisingly, all things considered, it is not aesthetically successful from the standpoint of comedy.

An instructive variant of this case appears in another Chinese play based on a story of long and world-wide currency, *The White Snake.* This presents, with considerable imagination, sympathy, and tenderness, the tale of a snake who becomes a woman and a devoted wife. As might be presumed, complications arise. In all the early versions of the story appearing on the Chinese stage the end is—contrary to some overfacile statements on Asian drama—tragic. In the version recently seen on the stage in Communist China and translated into English, the end is happy. Comedy is of necessity good-natured. When shadows pass over a comic scene, the comedy itself vanishes and out of its defunct body is born another species of art, quite likely to be satire, even possibly tragedy. The happy ending leads in this instance to romantic sentiment, not to comedy.

In the recent version the ending is entirely choreographic. A dramatic dance is performed by supernatural beings, divided into two groups, the good and the malign. The discomfiture of the evil spirits is certainly intended to be understood not alone as joyful but also to some degree as humorous. The evil angels are outwitted, outsmarted, fooled. The audience may even experience glee at the spectacle. This implies humor of a sort but not a fully developed humor. It represents rather good humor, which is quite another matter than the spirit of true comedy, mirth taking humor's place. Besides, the last scene in *The White Snake* lies completely outside the domain of poetry or dramatic dialogue. Whatever is conveyed to the reader is likely to be pale, since verbal description is generally

feeble in translating the meaning of a dance or at least successful only when a major poet writes at his best. Joy is not humor
although humor in the strict and most viable sense of the word
springs from some measure of well-being and happiness.

Chinese no less than Western drama, then, raises delicate
questions concerning the nature of humor or comedy. The
proposition cannot, of course, be considered without definite
reference and such reference here is provided by the highly
successful play, *Beating the Drum and Cursing Ts'ao Ts'ao*.
This is a truly fascinating work that once enjoyed considerable
popularity in stage production. As already noted, like all three
of the works discussed at the close of this chapter, it is anonymous. The familiar figure of Ts'ao Ts'ao is conspicuous but
the most important and central figure is a pedantic scholar,
Mi Heng. Only in respect to pedantry does he recall the many
members of the scholar class represented as leading stage characters. He is, or at least thinks he is, champion of free speech
and truth-telling. The frankest and harshest of critics confronts
Ts'ao Ts'ao, the most redoubtable of tyrants. The result as
shown in the play is inconclusive, although Mi Heng is clearly
doomed to a swift fall and death to occur shortly after the
action of the play has closed. The play may well have stood in
a cycle of works which included the final episode, Mi's death,
but no such piece, at least to my knowledge, exists today. The
generally optimistic Chinese theatre was, of course, far more
disposed to the happy than the tragic ending. Besides, the
scholar class was to some degree sacrosanct. It is in keeping
with the traditional and partly humorous delineation of Ts'ao
Ts'ao that he should act slyly rather than impetuously. Fortunately for the satisfaction of the audience, he gives Mi Heng
the opportunity to speak his mind freely. Credulity is strained
somewhat in this instance but both the image of Ts'ao Ts'ao
and that of the angry scholar are served by the scene as it
stands.

The story is so striking and also simple that a brief account
of it is serviceable. Mi has been chosen as a member of Ts'ao's

Court. On his first appearance before the great minister he breaks forth in a long harangue pronouncing Ts'ao a common rascal and all his generals and ministers of state mere fools. Ts'ao listens with repressed rage. In the end as a device to place Mi in the most ignominious position possible he orders him on the following day, which is a feast day, to serve as drummer. It is understood that this would put Mi in the very lowest possible station in the Court. With a counter-scheme of his own in mind, Mi accepts the insult. He believes that he can turn the penalty itself into a grave embarrassment to Ts'ao and his contemptible associates. When on the following day he stands before the Court as a drummer, he strips himself of his clothes, appearing stark naked in the midst of the gorgeous ceremony. Verbal abuse is again exchanged. Finally, Ts'ao Ts'ao orders Mi to carry a diplomatic message to a neighboring principality. Mi accepts. In a typical, cynical aside Ts'ao whispers to his ministers that Mi need not expect to remain long alive. The inescapable inference is that some trap will be laid for him either during his journey or immediately afterward. Mi, courageous as ever, indicates no suspicion or fear. The play is actually no more than a highly effective episode. There is no plot, only a vivid character portrait and a serious problem posed in the field of ethics and behavior.

Mi Heng is a Confucian scholar—if one credits his own words, the greatest of such scholars. There is no doubt that he is a man of learning nor is there a question that much of his abuse of the evil minister and his aides is just. But Confucian teachings were at least presumed by the Master and his followers to be practical and workable. One of the chief books ascribed to the Master is on the doctrine of the mean. Clearly, Mi is depicted as imprudent in his exclamations and excessive in his denunciations. Distortions of wisdom refute wisdom. The distorted figure becomes grotesque and ridiculous. Some humor is inferred, some comedy inevitable. As *The Book of Songs* declares, "too much is much too much."

Yet what is the quality of this comedy? Can it be that moral sentiment has overpowered the sense of humor? It is a moot question. Much the same doubt has often been raised concerning Molière's masterpiece, *Le Misanthrope*, which declines to fall into categories commonly used by historians and critics of drama. Satire appears to gain the upper hand. The idealism avouched by the leading figure turns against him through its excess. So much is evident. But shall the fault be thought laughable or simply deplorable? No final answer is available. Yet it seems clear that if laughter, the laugh is qualified, while if the episode is moralized, the voicing of morality is embarrassed by suspicion of humor. A play cannot, of course, be judged a failure simply because it fails to comply with categories smugly maintained by critical theory. All that need be inferred is that a comparatively unfamiliar type of expression has been used. *Le Misanthrope* is certainly a very great play; *Beating the Drum and Cursing Ts'ao Ts'ao* is assuredly a very good one. But as a work of humor it must be admitted to fall short of fulfillment. To consider it in relation to pure humor is instructive and valuable for interpretation of the play itself, of what should be considered pure humor and what should be held foreign to it.

*Beating the Drum and Cursing Ts'ao Ts'ao* also is instructive by indirection in the appraisal of the spirit of Chinese drama as a whole. It is most unusual in that it impinges on the problem play. It demands of any intelligent audience some consideration of ethical problems. The Chinese have, of course, long been among the people most eager to engage in ethical speculation. Yet this is hardly to be inferred from typical Chinese plays. On the contrary, their imaginative view of life is in general neither speculative nor in a strict sense intellectual. In a typical Chinese play ethical values are stated dogmatically and presumed to be fully and finally established to the satisfaction of all. Humor in the plays flourishes to much advantage on this secure basis, as garden plants flourish when undisturbed by high winds. Accordingly, when considered in terms of comparative literature *Beating the Drum and Cursing*

*Ts'ao Ts'ao* is a window in the Chinese temple opening toward the West. Theatrically the play is a marked success. Conflict on the stage is brilliant, psychology in the delineation of both Ts'ao and Mi is illuminating. The traditional occupation of the Chinese mind with ethical subject matter is admirably shown. But speculation leads to wit and not to humor, opening the road to a satirical drama highly developed in the West, barely initiated in the East. With consideration of this distinctly exceptional play an examination of humor in Chinese drama may, then, come logically to an end.

# 4

---

## HUMOR IN

## NARRATIVES

\*

I<small>T WOULD BE PRESUMING FAR TOO MUCH TO HOLD THAT</small> any art comprehensively or faithfully reflects all major aspects of a civilization. Even in their collective whole the arts are partial reflectors while each art presents an image fragmentary and in many respects partial. This view proves to be all the more warranted when the body of work regarded as the classics in any art is considered. Time is a winnower, leaving a simplified image. As indicated in the preceding pages, classical tradition in Chinese poetry favors emotional, moral, or descriptive writing; although much Taoist and some Buddhist influence shines through the centuries, the most potent force here is Confucian. As years passed *The Book of Songs* became the most powerful spring-head for Chinese verse. Though its qualities were not precisely what later poets desired, since Chinese culture became riper and richer with the passing of centuries, it became clear that the main directions had been set early. Such Taoist elements as persisted did not greatly affect the development of verse or drama. The humanistic tradition prevailed.

Similarly, in the theatre of live actors conditions were hospitable to reflections of social and ethical aspects of life. Fanciful and artificial as the Chinese theatre may appear, at heart it remains in accord with the prevailing outlooks of history, manners, and social relations. Only a few plays deal with mythology. The supernatural is secondary to the terrestrial scene; the proper study of drama, it seems, is man in relation to his fellow men as observed from the standpoint of the family, the marketplace and the city. The few ghosts that appear behave much as though they were known persons who simply had not died but merely remained for the most part hidden from human eyes.

In this respect there is good evidence that the so-called live theatre differed materially from the long popular puppet stage. Strangely enough, this stage offered a scope and freedom denied the living actors. A puppet can perform acts entirely beyond the range of the human actor. Puppets may also represent birds and beasts much more readily than actors of flesh and blood. Limitations of scale that weigh upon the live theatre have no significance for the puppet theatre. Puppets attained early and held long the enthusiastic devotion of audiences in China as well as through virtually all Southeast Asia, India, and the Malay archipelago. In a large proportion of puppet-shows fancy ran riot; they blithely represented deities and demons, the leading figures of folklore and mythology. Puppetry became one of the most fertile media to exploit the boundless license of the imagination. It was also, as it ever has been, a medium to express not only the marvelous and miraculous but the grotesque and the laughable. It is hardly too much to say that throughout Asia puppetry proved the ideal medium for folk humor. Unfortunately, just what words the puppet-masters of Asia may have spoken is lost virtually beyond recall; indeed, the plays, very seldom put into writing, almost completely escape us. Only in Japan did puppetry incontestably produce a great literature to last through the ages. This is one of the many unique features of Japanese culture. Unhappily, China has left no such legacy.

Despite this default, China affords an unsurpassed or even unequaled medium of expression, at times sharing the freedom of the puppet stage and capable of carrying much of high value for the romantic phase of Chinese civilization—the prose narrative. The Chinese are singularly happy in story-telling of all sorts. Although admirable Chinese narrative poems exist, such as *The Romance of the West Chamber*, chief source for the play of the same name, the genre of the long verse narrative failed to win the popularity in China which it attained in the Near East and in the West. Prose became the favorite medium for the story-teller. In very early times the short story was raised to a high degree of refinement, chiefly created by oral story-tellers before their tales were collected and circulated, first in manuscript and subsequently in print. So enthusiastically was the short story cultivated that when long prose narratives began to appear they inclined to a strong episodic structure. Lengthy books thought to justify designation as novels are, of course, extremely well known and in a few instances possess almost the organic structure of the chief works of fiction in the West. Yet the short story remains the most representative form of Chinese narration and many of the most celebrated long tales prove, when their form is analyzed, to be collections of brief tales strung more or less loosely together. Many books are literally travelogues, by their very nature episodic.

Most Chinese long stories fall into the category of naturalistic fiction. Although in view of the nature of Chinese culture no such story can be entirely divorced from the supernaturalism deeply entrenched in the popular mind, these books stand as a rule close to the general tenor of the stage. They stand quite apart from the main current of classical poetry, partly because the larger number of true novels are erotic whereas eroticism was expressed in verse chiefly in popular lyric verse, firmly wedded to music. Many of the most famous Chinese novels, as *The Dream of the Red Chamber* and *Lotus* (*Hung-lou meng* and *Chin p'ing mei*) are tales both emotional and realistic with only slight infusions of humor. As already noted, very considerable humorous elements enliven the famous folk novel with a semihistorical setting, the *Shui-hu chuan*, translated by Pearl S. Buck as *All Men Are Brothers*, providing materials for countless plays lusty in humor. Some humor, though by no means in such an abundant stream, flows through the episodic and more historically grounded book, *The Romance of the Three Kingdoms*. To examine the humor of these works could only lead to considerable repetition, since the finest essence of this humor is distilled in plays considered in the preceding chapter.

The two veins of humor that at present invite critical attention are, first, that proceeding from the fantastic, the exuberant, and the unfettered imagination, often lifted into supernatural realms or to a complete dreamlike release from all sober naturalism, and, second, virtually the antithesis of the foregoing, the humor derived from intimation, inference, and insinuation, in turn springing from a sophisticated outlook on manners and morals. It is hardly extravagant to hold that in both these areas Chinese literature is unsurpassed. Fantasy attains its most amazing heights in Chinese story-telling; Chinese civilization further attains the sharpest edge of social refinement. Humor finds itself at home in each domain. That humor is a biforked being is widely recognized, if on no other grounds than the elementary distinction between its physical manifestations, the reactions upon the human face in laughter and smiles. On the whole, Chinese story-tellers, especially in the classical age, are more fertile and fluent in the exuberant than in the reticent forms of humor, although many celebrated specimens in each category might be cited.

For purposes of the present inquiry, though several works may be mentioned in passing, two famous examples of the humor of released fancy will be reviewed, the long, episodic tale, *Hsi-yu chi, The Journey to the West,* first known to English readers through Arthur Waley's delightful translation as *Monkey,* and the famous collection of short stories by P'u Sung-ling, translated by Herbert A. Giles as *Strange Stories from a Chinese Studio.* Incidentally, no complete English translation of either of these books exists. Waley rendered less than half of his original text, omitting the majority of the episodes. A second translation into English, entitled *The Monkey King,* by George Theiner, closely parallels over a third of Waley's work but renders a considerable number of the tales omitted by his predecessor. Yet it falls equally short of the full length of the Chinese book and the tales first translated by Theiner are on the whole of less interest than those which Waley's rendering includes and his successor omits. Although Giles also omits many stories in P'u Sung-ling's lengthy book, even so, he is generous in the number of tales that he offers.

Although neither of the Chinese masterpieces, then, has as yet been fully rendered into English, both are available to English readers in versions that may be considered representative of the whole and virtually as faithful to their originals as the limitations of translation inevitably admit. There are some omissions of passages which the average English reader might interpret as indecent or salacious, yet these omissions, even if thought regrettable, are not seriously injurious. The book here chosen to represent the arch and insinuating humor grounded upon a relatively sober observation of the manners and morals of Chinese society is *The Scholars (Ju-lin wai shih)* by Wu Ching-tzu, which has been rendered into English by Yang Hsien-yi and Gladys Yang.

*Monkey,* as Wu Ch'eng-en's book will henceforth be called, has been categorized in various ways as, for example, a "folk-novel" or a "picaresque novel." In the end it must be admitted that it complies with no category in Western literature and is virtually unique even in the East. It certainly does not resemble the novel considered as a literary form. As already indicated, it has something in common with most long narrative books in Chinese in that it is distinctly episodic. Its theme places it among books of travel, but to say this is to say little, for the *Odyssey* complies as well with this description but in no serious way resembles *Monkey*. When examined more critically in terms of its essential qualities it proves to be a veritable chimera or zoological monstrosity, since it combines the spirit of many species, like a Chinese dragon, where beast, bird, and fish unite in one organism. It is in part history, romantic entertainment, religious meditation, philosophical lucubration, ecclesiastical satire, and, in very large part, hilarious humor. Only the last of these constituent features is, of course, of primary concern here, but some further scrutiny is required to segregate this element from the bewilderingly rich complex in which it stands with so much brilliance, like lustrous stones embedded in heterogeneous materials of sober hues.

The humor is all the more delightful because of its unexpected setting, which instead of overwhelming it sets it off in a massive frame. Although the statement that all in the book which is not humor exists merely to show forth the humor to greatest advantage would doubtless be an exaggeration, one is almost tempted to risk it. Were we to attempt to underline passages indisputably humorous we should, to be sure, find that only a minor part of the book had been so marked. But quantity and mass seldom prove vital considerations in art's appraisal. Quality outdoes quantity. Conditions in the arts are closer to chemistry than to arithmetic. A few grains of an intrinsically potent infusion may actually give the whole its essential color and flavor.

The entire conception of the story is obviously absurd and its telling is all the more ludicrous because it is so often executed with a straight face. The world has applauded *Monkey* as a remarkably humorous and vastly entertaining book. Most of it, if read in a sober mood, will seem to be a record of wonders, a recounting of strange and often miraculous adventures. The narrative has something in common with the fanciful wonderbook popular shortly afterward in Europe, *The Travels of Sir John Mandeville,* describing a journey to Jerusalem and the Near East.

Yet *Monkey* is clearly a travel book of wonders and much more. It recounts a long and painful pilgrimage, a mission half human and half animal, to secure the most compendious collection of the Buddhist scriptures. With the complete success of this religious and heroic venture the story ends. Comparatively few of its readers, however, have taken this pious achievement as the author's chief object. He is clearly a humorist who takes much greater interest in the amusing idiosyncracies of his characters than in the contents of the holy scriptures, which, incidentally, only one of the band of devoted pilgrims could read, all but this single, almost colorless individual being profoundly illiterate. Who can imagine Monkey, Pigsy, Sandy, or the White Horse reading a book!

It should at least be clear that *Monkey* is the best of all animal fables. It is stored with all the imaginative riches which this universally cultivated type of literature and popular legend admits at the same time that it happily dispenses with the dubious moral which became puritanically attached to the species ever since it took fixed form in the Sanskrit of the *Panchatantra.* Read from one point of view, it glorifies the Buddhist faith; read from another, it glorifies animals. The two heroes with whom the reader clearly sympathizes most and who chiefly capture his imagination are animals, namely, Monkey and Pigsy. In precisely what sense they are animals is a question initially to be considered, since much of the story's humor hangs on the calculated ambiguity of their condition.

Are these characters to be thought of as animals with certain human properties or humans with animal properties? Or just what are they? The answer first of all must be that the reader is not expected to insist upon an answer but to believe in them as he finds them. The only thoroughly dull and melancholy major figure in the book is the only priest, the all-too-human Tripitaka, an historical figure, leader of the expedition to secure the sacred texts. All the others have commenced their lives as supernatural creatures. Monkey has drunk the elixir of immortality. His immediate comrades in Tripitaka's service are all indestructible and have at one time or another been in heaven, although only Monkey's career in the celestial spheres is related at any length. Pigsy and Sandy have been monsters. Through the intercession of the deity of mercy, Kuan-yin, they have been converted, the first into a chimerical being with a pig's head and a body half-way between pig and man. Sandy's appearance is left vague though he may well be thought of as having to some extent a serpent's head. Monkey, of course, has a monkey face and body, though dressed as a man. All speak and think as men, though each is sharply characterized in relation to the animal he represents. Monkey is clever and virtually all-powerful not so much by means of his physical strength as through his mental agility. He possesses by far the greatest assortment of magic tricks and has twice as many incarnations at his command as any of his comrades. These transformations are said to number seventy-two but, of course, the author avoids stating precisely what is meant. For example, is his power to appear as a man considered one incarnation or does the initial statement include the number of individual persons whom he represents? The former supposition is the more plausible, since he impersonates humans so prodigally.

Behind this type of literary imagination stands the representation of animals in art and on the stage by live actors or puppets. As already stated, the last medium is the most effective because of the extraordinary liberties which it permits. So far as known, the truly dramatic theatre of China, unlike that of Japan, made comparatively little use of masks, though make-up was employed in the most extravagant manner. The imaginative reader is invited to experience the fantastic world evoked by the story under consideration as a carnival of figures masked as animals. An interesting refinement is mentioned in Monkey's case. According to the rules—and all, even in wonderland, proceeds by rule—whenever he attempts to deceive people by pretending to be a person his head changes completely. But under his garments he remains a hairy monkey. When stripped of his clothes, he is revealed for what he truly is.

At least half the figures in the main part of the book, that recording the pilgrimage to India, at one time or another are not what they seem to be. In other words, they possess the power to project their souls into other bodies than their own. This conception, so convenient for an author addicted to humor and the flights of fantasy, harmonizes, of course, with the serious religious doctrine of the transmigration of souls. Humans become animals and animals humans. Such transformations are natural as breathing. Probably the most popular pathway for supernatural commerce of this kind was between foxes and humans. The present story makes use of this belief in folklore, although this particular transformation by no means holds the dominant position which it occupied in the brilliant cycle of animal tales in the West, *Reynard the Fox*. In the Orient a woman might only too readily be a fox or a fox a woman. Who could say? Only a magician could know. Life is imagined everywhere as a scene characterized by an infinite number of metamorphoses.

This observation raises questions pertaining equally to humor, to myth, and to religion. Where the priest possesses the powers of a magician he is held by his followers to be a true priest, whereas in alien eyes he appears as a magician. So in the Christian Middle Ages the saints performed miracles through their relationship to God (or God performed them through the medium of his saints), whereas in Christian eyes the Mohammedans who performed wonders by aid of the devil were obviously not saints but magicians! The performance of secular miracles constitutes magic, which, rightly understood, is reserved for the intervention of saints, angels, and God, violently altering the usual course of nature. The Taoists made, in fact, no such sharp distinction, although especially in the eyes of the Buddhists, incredulous of Taoist performances, these frequently appeared the illusions of black magic. They were considered performances that would not bear the test of reality; the figures so conjured were illusions and not, in Hamlet's words, true and honest ghosts. The pious reader of *Monkey* interprets the supernatural proceedings as true miracles, the humorous reader presumably sees them as works of magic. But all the ancient inhabitants of Asia delighted in magic and magicians and were highly susceptible to believing in them. Their sentiments in this regard were aesthetic rather than religious. Even when knowing themselves fooled, they delighted in being fooled. That the sleight of hand was invisible was enough. The praise was for the dexterity of the performer. The more inscrutable the act became, the better.

The humor of *Monkey* lies in large measure in the ambiguity which has just been traced. One can read its story as a pious tale or as riotous entertainment. To be sure, the author specifically avows his piety. He does not announce himself as an entertainer but to have done so would have been to violate the laws of entertainment itself, as he knows so well. The magician must at all cost retain a grave face. Though others laugh at his performances, he does not. He leaves the matter safely at the disposal of young and old, who are only too eager to accept the bait artfully laid for their delectation, just as is the reader who is in quest of humor and fun.

The analysis of humor almost inevitably has its forbidding side, yet a turn of the wrist may to some degree redeem it. Be it remembered that in nine pages out of ten in Wu Ch'eng-en's story one or more persons are in grave trouble or even in mortal danger. It is the extreme of understatement to say that the journey to India is beset with almost continuous peril and that in the prelude to the novel largely devoted to Monkey's life in heaven this mock-hero is continually in deep water. There is, to be sure, a pattern visible everywhere that might according to logic much relieve the seriousness of the situations, yet by the unstated rules of humor's game the reader is forbidden to take it into account. He must presume the danger in each instance to be real, although should he pause to reflect he would know that from each deadly peril the pilgrims are bound to emerge safely. No matter how desperate the danger may seem, Monkey's wit will save the day. So the book, together with most manifestations of humor, is founded upon a contradiction. By its very nature it defies the ways of nature which everyone knows. In real life some incidents are bound to end badly. Monkey's story constitutes the apotheosis of the happy ending following on mortal dangers. This occurs again and yet again. Unconsciously the reader discovers the clue, playing the game according to the rules. With each episode he persuades himself to shudder at the perils into which the pilgrims have fallen. In each instance he laughs with pure delight at the cleverness by which Monkey extracts himself and his fellow travelers.

The book is actually in two parts, brief scenes before the pilgrimage commences and the much longer section, in reality the body of the book, which occupies the pages after Tripitaka leaves the capital of China and acquires the companions who alone make possible the success of his venture. All the preliminary scenes are of high value for the work as a whole. Monkey, not his master, Tripitaka, is certainly the heart of the story. It is with his birth out of stone that all begins. Here Buddhist doctrine is the clearest. The most immobile form is changed into the symbol for all mobility. Only for a few pages, where the scenes become quite realistic and we witness the decision of the Emperor, during a magnificent feast, to send his mission to secure the scriptures, does Monkey fall out of sight. He has been motionless for five hundred years, imprisoned in stone because of his shameless escapades in heaven. The lights of the story are artfully dimmed during the recess when the stage is occupied primarily with the Emperor and his chosen scholar, Tripitaka. For the moment fiction turns to history. The lights go on again only when Monkey is released from his confinement and constituted Tripitaka's guide-in-chief.

Arthur Waley suggests that the scenes in heaven are an allegory of scenes on earth, that Monkey symbolizes "genius" and the hosts of heaven represent the dull, stupid, and tyrannous regime or, in terms of modern popular usage, the corrupt and stupid "establishment" that in governing actually misgoverns.[19] To be sure, much Chinese literature and especially the more imaginative and poetic forms of this literature suggest this view. There is no intention here to deny it some validity. But the main contention here is that the book is both more philosophical and more facetious than Waley's statement suggests. Insofar as there is an allegory, Monkey might better be viewed as wit and intellect but in heaven he is also clearly irresponsible and irrepressible. He is by no means the same after his incarceration and his conversion. Earlier he again and again offends sound morality or at least conventional morality. There seems really no reason to doubt that the author accepts the orthodox view of the Heavenly Way, holding the Emperor in heaven at least essentially just. It is important to note, moreover, that Tripitaka himself does not effect Monkey's conversion. Kuan-yin, the gods, and Monkey himself effect that. Monkey has learned the hard way. Although never ceasing to be something of a playboy and himself a humorist, he does indeed become an instrument of righteousness. He even acquires guardian angels who stand ever at his side. The precise nature of his heavenly guides is nowhere stated, a reticence on the author's part that leads his translators, for example, to designate these supernatural beings at times as "angels" but more often merely as "guardians." The familiar and optimistic thought behind the book's bifurcation seems to be that evil can be turned into good if the innermost heart has at all times been sound. Youth sows its wild oats. Afterward come enlightenment, conversion, and true insight.

Monkey's career sets the key for the other portraits as well. Pigsy, Sandy, and the White Horse, his chief associates in aiding Tripitaka, have all been changed from monsters and menacing creatures. Life, the humorist observes, is essentially inconsistent. Among living beings are millions of transformations and metamorphoses. Most spectacular of all is the repeated transformation whereby evil turns into good. It is indeed a cheerful thought and sound basis for erecting a giddy edifice to house the comic spirit.

There can be no question as to the quality of extravagance conspicuous in the forescenes in heaven. The entire book is a temple dedicated to humor. Humor is the only true god. Monkey continually gets drunk, indulges himself outrageously, robs the Emperor's orchard, gulps down Lao Tzu's elixir of immortality, sleeps when he should watch, and roves mischievously abroad when he should sleep. Although the gods are not bluntly ridiculed, they repeatedly are victimized by the acts of this redoubtable and irrepressible ape, the bad boy of heaven. How any normal child, restive and possibly rebellious in the face of parental authority, must rejoice in this episode in heaven! The most sacred objects of Buddhist and Taoist ritual are presented in a thoroughly absurd light. Decorum, which stands close to the heart of all true Confucianism, is utterly violated. Of course in the end Monkey suffers for his pranks and is converted, or at least half converted. His rebellion notwithstanding, heaven remains secure. The Evil Angel is at first expelled but, with a greater charity than appears in orthodox Christianity, seen in a somewhat minimal conversion. Evil is disappointed but wit, intellect, and, above all, humor remain and even triumph. Waley's limited view in this instance might itself even be taken to reflect the bureaucratic outlook. Perhaps just for once he wrote as a mere Englishman.

The book's temper depends in part on its delightful theogony. While gods and philosophers are not actually ridiculed, as would be the case did the Chinese book resemble the *hilariocomedia* or the Western burlesques of the gods best represented by Lucian, even the gods are denied a reign of unbroken dignity and solemnity. Heaven's Emperor is, perhaps, too remote on his far-away throne to feel the wind of comedy blowing strongly. Actually, the most important deity in the book is Kuan-yin, goddess of mercy, after the great Buddha himself the most often depicted of all members of the Chinese pantheon. She occupies much the position in the humorous epic, *Monkey*, that Pallas Athena holds in the *Odyssey*. One goddess protects the hero, Monkey, the other the hero, Ulysses. Yet Pallas in the Greek poem at all times maintains her dignity and her divine aspect, even when seen in her metamorphosis as an eagle. Kuan-yin is, on the contrary, overseen at times in an undignified condition. Once, for example, when Monkey is forced to go to her serene forest retreat seeking aid, he finds her literally with her hair down, no make-up on her face, and her clothes and ornaments in confusion. She has been absent-mindedly pondering all day on her favorite's perilous plight. Unprepared for social intercourse, just as she is she hurries unceremoniously from her sacred grove to save the stranded pilgrims. The reader is, of course, sympathetic with this all-powerful goddess of sympathy but the humor is inescapable.

As befits a humorist, Wu Ch'eng-en offers no general apology for mankind, though he devoutly believes in the resilient spirit residing in the eminently fallible human race. The burden of his imagery is to remove the gods from unruffled serenity in heaven, since Monkey assails their palaces with his rough-housing, and still more to call human dignity and pretensions to account but, with the essential perversity of all humor, to exalt the animals, especially at the expense of man. Wu's book humorously turns the universe upside down, or rather it is an ape who turns heaven upside down while on earth the semi-animal attendants of Tripitaka far surpass that sage in all useful points of knowledge. They have no personal involvement in the goal of the expedition. The scriptures are the last things on earth to attract them. They have enlisted in the quest out of sheer goodness of heart and the fervent wish to care for and protect the poor human being who has so rashly undertaken it.

It is Tripitaka, the one completely human, historical being in the adventure, who alone is impotent and witless. Despair continually overtakes him. Repeatedly he collapses, breaking down into hopeless tears. He even falls off his horse from fright. Perhaps the greatest understatement in the entire story is Monkey's comment that Tripitaka is somewhat timid. His tears are positively maudlin. Monkey declares, as well he might, that he hates to be preached at by Tripitaka. The latter is utterly earth-bound and prosaic. His inability to make up his mind and the ease with which all persons impose upon him and totally deceive him lead Monkey to remark that his master is pliable as water. In short, he is a perfect fool if ever there were one. From this conclusion only a mind totally divorced from humor could conceivably dissent. Yet Tripitaka is in one sense clearly the moving figure in the story, Monkey, Pigsy, Sandy, and the dragon horse being merely his satellites. The knowledge of the holy scriptures and fervent devotion to them appear to do him no earthly good, nor does the author consent to show that any real consolation or happiness springs from meditations on the divine. Tripitaka is a point of no motion about which revolves a world alive with motion, color, energy, and laughter.

As with virtually all manifestations of humor, the master-key is paradox. The plot of almost any episode might easily be used for a thoroughly serious or even tragic tale. In this regard two of the best-known stories may be cited. One, the story of the Lion Demon in the Kingdom of Cock-Crow, has a plot remarkably close to Shakespeare's *Hamlet*. A villain has murdered a king, usurped his throne and married the murdered king's wife. The ghost of the slain monarch appears to an avenger, who rectifies the situation with a thoroughness, to be sure, even beyond the powers of the noble Prince of Denmark. It is of much moment that the Chinese story ends with a touch of sublimity. It appears that the villain was not really a villain but the lion-vehicle on which the great Bodhisattva, Manjusri, is accustomed to ride. Buddha himself had decreed the entire course of events.

This story, or, in other words, this episode within the book, ends with a scene surprisingly like an apotheosis in a baroque opera. The deity ascends to Heaven riding on the lion-vehicle, leaving all well with the mortals upon earth. All wounds are healed. This story, to repeat, might be told with complete seriousness. But in *Monkey* all actions exist on two levels, the lower marked by gravity, the upper by gaiety. No doubt whatsoever exists as to which receives the greater attention from the average reader or, for that matter, from an enlightened reader. In the course of this episode the chief characters appear in the most ridiculous attitudes. Probably the climax of the comic element occurs when Monkey lets Pigsy down a well, where he will discover the miraculously preserved body of the dead king. By a still greater miracle the king's soul is induced to reenter the body. The good king has suffered because of an inadvertent error that offended the deity. Like most figures in the story who have fallen into error, he is after due penance forgiven and established in his original state of happiness. But who could believe that this sequence of eminently serious events would become the occasion for a veritable whirlwind of comedy?

The second episode chosen to illustrate the book's calculated ambivalence is the equally well-known story, The River That Leads to Heaven and the Great King of Miracles. Here the kernel of the action is a legend known in virtually all quarters of the world reflecting what was originally a sacred rite held in utmost veneration, the sacrifice of one or more children to be devoured by a watery monster as offering for the security of a city. The Chinese story by no means flinches in indicating the pathos implicit in the situation. But soon the tables are turned decisively in the direction of comedy.

The children offered to the monster are, in reality, Monkey and Pigsy, one impersonating the male child, the other the female. As the episode develops it grows increasingly ludicrous. A religious myth becomes an uproarious farce.

Some further remarks on the book's general reception assist at this point in interpretation of its humor. Commentaries, especially from the point of view of esoteric Buddhism, have been lavished upon it. It would be exceedingly captious and supercilious to dismiss such commentary as beside the mark. The book contains much impressive symbolism. It would be equally erroneous to hold that it is primarily satirical or that it lacks satirical or humorous elements. When it first appeared, approximately 1370 A.D., and indeed long after its appearance, it was generally regarded as frivolous, existing quite outside the province of serious or legitimate literature, a book to be shunned by all polished readers. But if its literary value was denied, especially by orthodox Confucians, its value as entertainment of a lower order could not be denied. Hence it was described as a temptation which the right-minded scholar-gentleman should resolutely put aside. But this was clearly puritanical idealism. The book has always been popular among young and old, the innocent reader and the informed. Especially worth noting is its popularity with children or adolescents. Certainly it must often have been read to the young rather than by them, for fluent reading ability in Chinese is only attained, except by children of genius, after childhood. Many anecdotes tell of young people who have reveled in *Monkey*, concealing their enjoyment to avoid the frowns of older and wiser persons. *Monkey* is a book for the normally growing child much as *Pilgrim's Progress* was for the child destined to become an austere Puritan. The book has the maturity of *Gargantua* and the beguiling quality of *Winnie the Pooh*. It is a book singularly beyond time, delightful for young and old, for the old world and for any world as yet imaginable. Its humor is infectious today as always.

Whoever analyzes the book does well to recall that humor

is by its very nature a transitory phenomenon. Only an idiot laughs or smiles continuously. Taking one consideration with another—to quote W. S. Gilbert—a reader would be rash to regard *Monkey* either as a wholehearted apology for Buddhism or a satire upon it. The fundamentally humorous aspect so pervasive throughout precludes any entirely consistent or logical interpretation. As the author speaking in his own person at one time informs us, "the three religons," namely Buddhism, Taoism, and Confucianism, are all to be honored for the three are really one. Also, none is to be revered so far as to exclude its advocates from the swift shafts of humor. There is no conclusion, only an ending. Thus the visit to the long-sought temple of the Supreme Buddha in India by no means brings the pilgrimage to a thoroughly solemn termination. On the contrary, the monks, annoyed for no sufficient cause, at first fill the pilgrims' baskets with scrolls having no writing on them whatsoever. On casually unrolling these shortly after the pilgrims have begun their homeward journey, they discover that they have been tricked. With a bland rather than an angry temper they return, modestly requesting to have the sorry state of affairs remedied. This is done by placing genuine scrolls in the pilgrims' hands so that they again proceed on their homeward way.

The episode must assuredly be an anticlimax in any thoroughly pious view of the story, though it may well be a parable in mysticism. Yet during the first major part of the story, the episode of Monkey in heaven, an incident occurs much to Buddha's glory and much to the boastful ape's consternation. Buddha declares that if Monkey alights on his hand he cannot escape from it. Monkey interprets Buddha's remark as a challenge, takes a mighty leap through space and preens himself with the belief that he has come to the end of the universe, where stand five massive red pillars. When he recovers from his illusion, regaining his right senses, he finds that he is still in the hand of Buddha, whose fingers do in truth comprise the pillars guarding the universe. This is a typical though decidedly eloquent religious fable, carrying conviction to any devout and susceptible mind. The comment may follow that the author believes in the theological doctrines of Buddhism but perceives greed and evil in the priesthood. This supposition would be to impose a logical view upon him which his persistent sense of humor will not tolerate. His book is not overt propaganda. Clearly, the right course is to accept him with all his inconsistencies upon his head and to find in humor the chief key to the riddle of interpretation.

The religious name which Monkey wins in heaven contributes considerably to the book's meaning. This name signifies "Aware of Vacuity." It implies a mystic outlook shared by Buddhist and Taoist alike. Here vacuity signifies the conception of a universe where coherent meaning for the whole is impossible for man to attain. Within vacuity, then, the winds of caprice blow as they will. The irrational alone is magnified. Humor above all other elements in man's spiritual being thrives in this atmosphere. In China a metaphysical humor belonged more to the Taoists than to the Buddhists, while Confucianism nourished a fundamentally different kind of humor. With much aesthetic justification, the initial section of the narrative, which might be called "Monkey in Heaven," prepares the ground on which the most prominent species of humor in the work flourishes most readily.

The book's humor is, incidentally, elucidated by the comparison, seldom if ever made, between the symbol of the monkey here and the attitude toward monkeys in the *Ramayana*. Did Wu Ch'eng-en know the Sanskrit poem? Possibly he did not, though it is by no means impossible that in one form or another he did know it or at least felt its influence indirectly through stories of monkeys popular in all parts of Asia. Hanuman, king of monkeys, has been even more endearing to the Hindus than the chief character in Wu Ch'eng-en's book has been to the Chinese. It is true that in the episode relating his secret entrance into the harem of the demon Ravana in the city of Lanka, and in his interviews there with Queen Sita in captivity some traces of humor can be found. Yet on the whole Hanuman is regarded not only as being a king but virtually as a god, while he and the other noble monkeys in Rama's army of liberation are conceived throughout the epic in serious and heroic terms. Glints of humor almost inevitably occur in the picturing of the monkey world—how could it be otherwise?—but in the *Ramayana* gravity and even pathos prevail. Rama is seldom seen to laugh. He even takes his relation with the army of monkeys with special seriousness. How different, then, is all this from the vastly more amusing conception of the monkey king in the Chinese masterpiece! A reader at any time tempted to view the Chinese tale as primarily serious and grave does well to place it beside the other great monkey legend of the East. The contrast should cast some light upon the true character of Wu Ch'eng-en's whole work.

Just as the completely incongruous juxtaposition of the animal figures on one hand and Tripitaka on the other produces an exquisitely humorous effect, so does the juxtaposition of the equally sympathetic characters, the clever, quick-witted Monkey and the slow-moving, stupid, and sensual Pigsy. Here once more their creator obviously loves both his children and plays no favorites. He is extremely kind to Pigsy, especially in view of Pigsy's ludicrous form and still more absurd mentality. The formula underlying the book, in keeping with the principles underlying the purest forms of humor, rests in the incongruous conjunction of raillery and friendship, envy and loyalty, existing between the two chief animal figures. Few passages in their story rival those which depict their repeated quarrels and reconciliations. Among these passages, to mention but two, is, first, the account of Monkey frightening Pigsy out of his wits by pretending to be a demon-messenger from hell and, second, the episode depicting Monkey's transformation into a hoglouse to pester Pigsy by nipping him in the ear. Again, the contrast is perfected in the contrasted caricatures. Monkey, being by nature restless, makes a miserable failure in his effort to simulate meditation, whereas Pigsy repeatedly falls asleep when important action is demanded.

The book, its composite form notwithstanding, keeps admirably to its subject, yet scope as well as harmony becomes a leading feature. Many tales possess a perverse species of dignity. Tripitaka, for example, resembles Don Quixote in Cervantes' more ambitious passages, where pathos and even nobility obtrude upon a largely risible narrative. Yet at other times the humor stoops to that of the picaresque story so popular in the Renaissance or even to the *Commedia dell' arte.* "The Cart-Slow Kingdom," one of the most quoted episodes, begins to all appearances seriously. A large group of Buddhist monks is subjected to brutal labor by a misguided monarch who falls beneath the influence of some false Taoists. (Be it noted that these magicians are explicitly stated to be impostors and not true Taoists.) The pilgrims are arrested at this corrupt Court. They are forced to undergo a series of competitions in magic with three pretenders, who in the end are shown to be a tiger spirit, a deer spirit, and a ram spirit, all three being malign. The tests in magic involving transformations which the little company of heroes endures are entirely in the temper of performances by magicians before a breathless public audience. So clearly do they also constitute ideal materials for puppet performances that it is really hard to believe that these were not consciously in the author's mind when composing his scenes.

As noted above, the book has been called by some Westerners commenting on it a picaresque story. This obviously implies a likeness between Monkey and the heroes of these humorous tales in which the chief character is at once a sympathetic figure and very much of a rogue, a scamp for whom accepted principles of morality have no binding force. He is usually afflicted with poverty and born of humble stock. He lives off his wits, practicing deceits upon his betters. Considerable merit and weight must be granted to these tales, which cannot properly be dismissed as trivia or shallow entertainment. Yet how meager they appear when placed beside the far more profound apprehensions of the Chinese masterpiece, behind which lies a commentary on three religions, on an entire metaphysics, on social relationships rationally conceived and on the very roots of the sense of humor! It is no work to be summarized in glib phrases or facile generalizations but is in essence one of the world's major poems, a triumph of imagination made possible only by virtue of the highly sophisticated culture from which it sprang.

It is more a tribute to its excellence than any sign of weakness in its style or texture that quotation from it in order to illustrate its essentially humorous qualities is exceedingly difficult. All its sentences should be taken in context. There are quotable phrases, it is true, with witty proverbs surprisingly like those from Sancho Panza's tongue, but no one or one hundred of them gives the remotest picture of the book's imaginative richness. Characters and concepts are developed structurally, woven like a tapestry or laid stone by stone to constitute a miracle of architecture. Although, properly speaking, the book has no plot, there can be no pulling out a specimen thread or stone to represent the whole.

Yet occasionally action pauses for a moment to present a tableau where the chief characters appear in peculiarly significant aspects and in specially significant postures. Such a passage is the triumphant conclusion of the tale, "The River That Leads to Heaven and the Great King of Miracles." A beneficent spirit in the form of a huge turtle ferries the pilgrims across a river of great width that has during the days immediately preceding this event placed them in mortal jeopardy. The entire company, including the White Horse who has sprung from a dragon, assembles on the turtle's back. The Western reader does well in this instance to recall the many sacred associations which the turtle-image must have evoked. But what an amusing picture these comedians make as they float serenely across "The River That Leads to Heaven" on the back of this strange monster! There is a certain sublimity in the conception but surely Wu Cheng-en was no man to miss the ludicrous aspect of his scene. Arthur Waley, with his accustomed skill, translates the passage as follows:

The white horse was led on to the middle of the turtle's back; Tripitaka stood on the left, and Sandy on the right, while Pigsy stood behind its tail. Monkey placed himself in front of the horse's head, and fearing trouble undid the sash of his tiger-skin apron and tied it to the turtle's nose, holding the other end in one hand, while in the other hand he grasped his iron cudgel. Then with one foot on the creature's head and the other firmly on its carapace, 'Now turtle, go gently, he cried, 'And remember, at the least sign of a wabble, you'll get a crack on the head.' 'I shouldn't dare,' said the turtle, 'I shouldn't dare.' Then while the turtle set off smoothly over the waters, the villagers on the bank burnt incense and kow-towed, murmuring 'Glory be to Buddha, glory be to Buddha!'

In less than a day they had safely traversed the whole eight hundred leagues and arrived with dry hand and dry foot at the further shore. Tripitaka disembarked, and with palms pressed together thanked the turtle, saying, 'It afflicts me deeply that I have nothing to give you in return for all your trouble. I hope that when I come back with the scriptures I shall be able to show you my gratitude.' 'Master,' said the turtle, 'I should not dream of accepting a reward; but there is one thing you can do for me. I have heard that the Buddha of the Western Heaven knows both the past and the future. I have been perfecting myself here for about one thousand years. This is a pretty long span, and I have already been fortunate enough to learn human speech; but I still remain a turtle. I should indeed be very much obliged if you would ask Buddha how long it will be before I achieve human form.' 'I promise to ask,' said Tripitaka. The turtle then disappeared into the depths of the river. Monkey helped Tripitaka on his horse, Pigsy shouldered the luggage and Sandy brought up the rear. They soon found their way back to the main road and set out for the West.[20]

With this passage before us, we may leave the magical and humorous world of a book that combines in one narrative a hundred or more episodes, virtually short stories in themselves, to consider much the same factors in the most famous Chinese collection of such tales, *Strange Stories from a Chinese Studio*, or P'u Sung-ling's *Liao-chai chih-i.* Since many of these stories are short and all self-contained, extended quotation for illustrative purposes becomes entirely feasible. A word should further be said about these translations. The Chinese itself is in prose, interspersed, as is quite customary in Chinese narratives, with verse passages. It has seemed to the present writer that P'u Sung-ling possesses an extremely poetic mind and style and that his tales of strange and miraculous happenings bear a fairly close relation to the narratives of miracle and wonder so popular in the Middle Ages and so often recited in a popular octosyllabic rhymed verse. These are the much less serious but, if possible, even more miraculous and almost certainly more fantastic tales popular both for reading and recitation in the East through several centuries. Although their more sophisticated readers probably at times questioned their historical validity, discounting the gesture of historical documentation which the author almost invariably makes, in most cases the readers presumably believed in their veracity. The word in the Chinese title which the English translator, Herbert A. Giles, renders as "stories" might equally well be translated "reports."

For the present discussion it is, of course, of chief importance that a large number of the tales are humorous, as all are presumed entertaining. But to the Chinese of the seventeenth century, and indeed for long periods before and after, no essential reason existed to divorce humor from reality or reality from humor. The world, claimed the Taoists and the Ch'an Buddhists, was like that—a scene far from abiding beneath the control of any reason apprehensible to man. Hence truth, if one could speak of it at all, was even more likely to appear humorous than prosaic. Popular belief in magic, in fox-men and fox-women, in transmigration, in transformation, and in ghosts prevailed on every hand. Grave scholars, even men like P'u Sung-ling, collected such strange tales, relishing them to the highest degree. It may be recalled that Edgar Allan Poe almost, if not actually, persuaded himself to believe in supernatural manifestations. How much more natural, then, that Chinese scholars three centuries ago should think and feel in this fashion! The highly sophisticated medieval schoolmen believed in miracles and in demonic visitations. Much of the supernatural world of the Chinese imagination appears to Western eyes closer to folklore than to religious faith, yet for the East the Western distinction barely applies. Science was, of course, in part alchemy while alchemy stood midway between science and religion. The freedom actually granted the poetic imagination in all these fields liberated the aesthetic mind from prosaic notions of reality and encouraged the free play of a highly animated sense of humor.

Sometimes the smile is kindly, naive, or both, sometimes distorted by a sense of the grotesque and even combined with shadows of malice. Especially to the Chinese modes of thought, devils and imps are loud in laughter; the underworld resounds with a sinister laughter; demons are even more humorous than men; ghosts delight in humorous trickery or the practical jokes of hell. The mere dexterity of the magician may in itself seem humorous and still more so his thoroughly innocent deception of those before whom he practices his secret arts. Admittedly, not all P'u Sung-ling's tales are humorous or even contain glimpses of humor, but many do so and many of his best stories fall into this category. No well-rounded view of the more powerful and more typical features of Chinese humor becomes possible without a fairly close scrutiny of these altogether fascinating features.

Much as in analysis of the attraction of *Monkey* for those reading or hearing its stories, so in the study of the legends recorded by P'u Sung-ling the fascination of such materials for children is of much importance. In the following tale,

*Theft of a Peach,* the narrator, speaking in his own person, declares that the miracle or magic which he reports he himself witnessed as a child and has never forgotten. He relates his story with several grains of salt. The incident has by no means a serious setting. The performance of a mountebank, it takes place during a carnival. The atmosphere is by no means greatly unlike that of a scene in a square at carnival time say in Venice of the days of Marco Polo. A large public, young and old, has assembled specifically to be amused. The judges of the events make no effort to investigate the circumstances of the miraculous show, the sudden erection of a peach-tree out of season and the harvesting of its fruit. The entire assembly is, it seems, only too happy to be deceived, since in the case of such an agreeable deception conviction is itself a pleasure. The public roots as eagerly on the side of the magician as an American sport crowd cheering for its home team.

The essential innocence or naivete of the scene is further enforced by its *dramatis personae:* the senior magic-maker enjoys as his indispensable aid the services of his young son, who climbs a pole that stands for the tree and plucks the magically ripened fruit. But this is by no means all; the best is yet to come. Parts of the boy's body fall in succession from above and lie on the ground. The father, bathed in tears, places them in his magician's box. Next, with loud cries of grief he collects contributions from the sympathetic crowd to secure the means to give his son's soul a fitting funeral. Everyone in the back of his mind knows well enough the deceit but takes pleasure in it. Finally, the father raps loudly on the box, now presumed to serve as coffin, commanding the lad to come out and bow in appreciation before a generous and madly applauding crowd. The entire story is a masterpiece of humor, a secular miracle, a tribute in words to the entertainment arts of the populace. Actually, all classes, from grave officials who reign over the festivities of the day to the poor enjoying one of their rare holidays, delight in the performance, joining in the communal laughter. Certainly much

of the humor and temper of the people can be discerned from
examination of this tale.

### THEFT OF A PEACH

When that I was a tiny boy
Town-visits were my keenest joy.
Spring was the time of festival,
Feasting, dancing, carnival.
Then as warmer days would come
Merchants flocked with flag and drum
Preceding them, while brilliant flowers
Were thrown about in lavish showers.
Revelers made their chief resort
The pageant at the mayor's court.
I went with friends to share the fun
Of what was said and what was done.
Officials dressed in red were all
Seated by the mayor's hall.
I was much too young to know
Who were these great men, row on row,
But loved the crowd's incessant humming
Plus sounds of singing, shouting, drumming.
Right in the middle of the square
I saw a boy with dangling hair
Led by his father to the mat
Behind which the great statesmen sat.
The fellow with uncanny strength
Carried a pole of monstrous length.
It seemed to me he said some word
That in the din nobody heard.
I only saw the officials smile,
After which, in a little while,
The loud-mouthed herald of the Court
Ordered him to show his sport.
"What shall it be," the man inquired.
"What is the magic most desired?"
After a minute's hesitation
The leaders at the judge's station

Asked the man himself to state
What trick he thought most intricate.
The man declared he could invert
Nature's course and so convert
Spring to fall and fall to spring,
Toppling laws for man and thing.
After a pause the herald bade
The man to prove the words he said,
Bringing to hand before them all
Peaches that ripen in the fall.
The man observed that he could do it
By putting special effort to it
But that he was too sorely tasked
In doing what his masters asked,
For winter frost was barely past
And peaches usually the last
Fruit to ripen; so he held
Himself by such demands compelled
To what no man beneath the sun
At any previous time had done.
Still, he declared that he would try
Even before his master's eye!
He then removed his hat and vest,
Placing them in a wooden chest.
Meanwhile the boy reminded him
That he had wagered life and limb
On what the two of them could do.
Honor called to prove it true!
The man was full of many a guile.
He hedged and grumbled for a while,
Then said: "Peaches will not grow
Here on this ground where recent snow
Has lain, but always grow on high
In the bright garden in the sky.
The mother goddess of the air
Keeps them and we must find them there.
Your greatest masters have collusion
With the goddess of illusion."
"But how get there," the youngster cried,

To which remark the man replied:
"We have the means." At that he drew
A cord out of his box and threw
It up and up, till it was flung
To where the clouds themselves are hung,
To where the lark can scarcely fly
Beyond the reach of human eye.
No man in all the crowd could look
Aloft and see that magic hook!
Next, he called to him his son
Explaining what his art had done
But said the rope declined the freight
Of his own full and manly weight
So that the youngster must ascend
The cable boldly to its end.
The boy himself pretended fright
Calling the cable far too light
And frail ever to carry him
Without grave risk of life and limb.
To this the father loudly said
That they had rather both be dead
Than fail that day to do what both
Had promised with a sacred oath.
Moreover, they could not afford
To lose the promised, rich reward
Which, with precaution laid aside,
At length would win the boy a bride.
At that the youth no more evaded
The project, readily persuaded,
But clasped the cable and ascended
Beyond the point where vision ended,
Clambering like a spider there
Into the dizzy heights of air.
Then, with applause of all the town,
Abruptly a large peach fell down
Out of the clouds. Next, as most fit,
The father proudly handed it
To the high magistrates who took
On this at first a doubtful look

But presently were all agreed
It was a perfect peach indeed!
Just then the rope itself fell flat,
Resounding on the ground, whereat
The man exclaimed: "Some fiend has crossed
My magic here and all is lost!"
Then something from the heavens fell
To earth. Quicker than words can tell
He took it up and, weeping, said:
"This is my son's dissevered head!
The heavenly gardener, no doubt,
Saw the thief and threw him out
Causing my dearest lad to fall
Over the heavenly garden's wall."—
Next, legs, arms, body with the same
Fatal precipitation came
To earth. The father to his breast
Clasped them and placed them in his chest.
"This was my only son," he said,
"Who here so cruelly is dead.
Now I must place him on his pall
And carry him to burial."
He then approached the judges' seat
Casting him down beneath their feet:
"You see," he cried, "what a peach cost
Since I in reaching it have lost
My precious son; therefore I pray
That you who saw my deed this day
Will generously give to me
Money to pay the funeral fee."
The judges, smilingly, believed
The loving father as he grieved
And generously dismissing doubt
Poured their contributions out.
The father next with heavy knocks
Beat upon his magic box
Crying: "My boy, why must you hide
Ignominiously inside
And not come forth, a grateful son,

With thanks for what the judge has done?"
At that a subterranean sound
Was heard; next, with a joyful bound
The boy leapt out and deeply bowed
Before a madly cheering crowd.—
I saw this trick many years past.
I still can hold its image fast.
Men tell me that the same effect
Is used by the White Lily sect,
Who doubtless learned their magic lore
From him I knew long years before.

As a generally cheerful people, unusually successful in mercantile enterprises and, since Confucius set them firmly upon
their path, a people no less practical than imaginative, the
Chinese have cultivated humor arising from what seems even
in their own eyes a curious and amusing conjunction of naturalistic and fantastic elements. Reality lies down beside fantasy. This is precisely the case in a story told by P'u Sung-ling,
*Boon Companion*. A young scholar, fond of drinking, goes to
bed with three bottles of liquor on the shelf beside his head.
In the dead of night he awakes to find to his amazement that
a fox lies at his side and that one of the bottles, full when
he retired, is now empty. The considerate scholar refrains from
disturbing the animal and himself calmly goes to sleep again.
Most foxes in Chinese folklore, to be sure, are evil spirits
and at one time or another appear as beautiful but treacherous
women. Here events prove altogether the contrary. The story
seems written from the fox's point of view. When the student
awakes, he discovers the fox gone but a handsome young man,
fully dressed, at his side. He hails him as a boon drinking
companion. Pleased with this cordial reception, the kindly fox
commences to befriend his companion. He leads him to two
stores of buried treasure, guides him in shrewd investments, is
a loyal and good friend to his wife and proves a general and
comprehensive blessing to the family. In Chinese eyes part of
the story's humor undoubtedly lay in its inebriate optimism.

Such kind services were hardly to be expected from a fox. But then, humor lies in paradox and incongruity and this tale is obviously intended both to entertain and amuse:

### BOON COMPANION

There was once a bright young man
Named Ch'e, whose natural feeling ran
To wine; he had a certain dash
Of humor but too little cash.
He found he hardly slept aright
Without three stoups-full every night.
Commonly as he went to bed
Three bottles stood beside his head.
One night he woke and turning over
Felt something strange beneath the cover.
Thinking that it was only clothes
Slipped off, he turned aside to doze
But stretching out his hand to see
What the obstacle might be,
Found his fingers grasping at
Something silky, like a cat,
Though larger, neither shirt nor sox.
Behold, he saw it was a fox,
Its head upon its silken paw!
Glancing upward, then, he saw
One of the bottles that he had
Beside his bed to make him glad
Was empty, with its cork outside.
"A boon companion!" then, he cried,
But careful never to awake
The creature, out of friendship's sake,
He covered it and laid his arm
Across it, shielding it from harm.
He next arranged the candle's light
Not to disturb the fox's sight
Yet, when it should awake, to see
What transformation there might be.
About midnight the creature stretched

Itself out full. Eyes closed, it fetched
A yawn, then snuggled in Ch'e's lap.
"You've had a comfortable nap,"
The man observed. But as he drew
The bed-clothes back he had in view
No fox but a young scholar dressed
Elegantly in the best
Garments that fresh young students wear.
He bowed and thanked Ch'e for the care
He took of him all night instead
Of rudely cutting off his head
Or giving some resounding curse.
"Oh," replied Ch'e, "I'm not averse
To any liquor when I view it;
In fact I'm much addicted to it.
Let us be bottle-chums together
Through all the turns of chance and weather!"
So they lay down again to sleep,
Ch'e urging his new friend to keep
Firm faith in their companionship,
Letting no chance of meeting slip.
This was agreed, but later on
When Ch'e awoke, the fox was gone.
On the following night Ch'e poured
The best wine that he could afford
Befitting as a special treat
When he and his new friend should meet.
Sure enough, when twilight fell
The fox-man came and all was well.
They drank. The fox told jest on jest,
So that the scholar Ch'e confessed
He had not heard such stories ever
Nor met with anyone so clever;
He added that his heart was sore
Not having met with him before.
The fox said: "How can I repay
Such kindness as you show today
In giving me such warming drink?"
Ch'e replied: "Oh, never think

A thing about it! What's a glass
Of wine? Just let the matter pass!"
"Well," the fox answered, "you have not
Much money; wine's not easily got.
I must try to find a plan
To make you a rich gentleman
Or at least how to accrue
Some good wine-capital for you."
He came next evening with a tale
He promised would in no way fail:
That two miles down the south-east road
He would find a glittering load
Of silver. "It is yours to take;
But start from here before daybreak."
So at next dawn Ch'e went out,
At first attended with some doubt
But found beside the common way
That two large lumps of silver lay
For anyone to take; so he
Took them himself and happily
Expended them on food and wine,
Sure that the fox would come to dine.
The fox next said that in the yard
Behind his house there was a barred
And hidden vault where he would find
Things still more welcome to his mind.
Ch'e did as told and found a treasure
In coins almost too great to measure.
"Now," exclaimed Ch'e, "this wealth of mine
Suffices all our needs for wine!"
"Ah," said the fox, "every one knows
Money not only comes but goes.
I must do something more for you."
Accordingly a day or two
After this he said: "Note how
Buckwheat in the market now
Is selling cheap; but I incline
To favor buying in this line."

Ch'e purchased forty tons, believing
All the advice he was receiving,
Though he incurred much ridicule
And neighbors took him for a fool.
Presently in a dreadful drought
All kinds of grain were rotted out
At which the price of buckwheat went
Upward hundreds of percent.
From this his wealth so much increased,
He purchased a square mile at least
Of the best ground and always grew
The grains the fox-man told him to.
The fox held Ch'e's obsequious wife
A sister of his own for life
And also lovingly befriended
His children till their own lives ended;
Yet after Ch'e had died, he never
Came to their house, vanished forever.

As already noted, much of the humor linked to fantasy becomes in Chinese thought also allied to the religious and philosophical system most cordial to fantasy, humor, incongruity,
and illogicality, Taoism. Magicians were likely to lean toward
Taoism, Taoists were almost certain to have faith in magic
since the pillars on which their world-system reposed were
alchemy and astrology. Matter might be conjured before them
or readily conjured away. Their irresponsibility and unpre-
dictability had a distinct tang of the humorous. Their thought
also had a nocturnal and mysterious quality, as elves hovering
in moonlight. Laughter rang from hidden places in the dark.
A literal-minded person would stand dumbfounded in the
midst of their conjuring. Deception became a profession in the
hands of the unscrupulous. Those who were kindred spirits
with the magicians were befriended. Those who were alien to
their occult ways of thinking and their mysterious behavior
were liable to be discomforted.

Many amusing stories told with a dry humor relate their

arts of mystery or deception. Several charming and truly lyrical tales of this sort are given by P'u Sung-ling, as by countless other popular story tellers. *Spirit of the Hills* is typical.

### SPIRIT OF THE HILLS

Once on a time a man named Li,
Crossing tall mountains, chanced to see
Country-folk sitting on the ground
Passing cheerful cups around.
The group accosted him and vied
To have him lavishly supplied
With drink, forcing upon him there
Trays loaded with the costliest fare.
Together all sat down to dine
On richest food, with sharpest wine.
Such delicacies Li thought strange
To find on that rough mountain range!
Then, as they drank and sung and cheered,
A stranger suddenly appeared
Wearing a jet-black, yard-tall hat
Above a face as long as that!
The revelers were terrified.—
"The god, the mountain god!" they cried.
Not one was brave enough to stay;
They bolted, terrified, away,
Scattering in all directions, blind
With fear, nor dared to look behind.
Li found a hollow in the ground
With roots and boulders circled round,
Hid for a while; but then, at length,
Gathering some timid grains of strength,
Peeped out to see how the land lay.—
The wine and food were swept away;
The forest floor was wholly cleared;
Marks of the feast had disappeared;
Where revelry and fun had reigned
Only some dirty shards remained.
Lizards and efts, in eerie files,
Crawled over stained and broken tiles.

So many humorous and grotesque tales, laughing fantasies of the macabre and the miraculous, use the underworld for their scene that a representative showing encourages quotation of three of them. In the West, to be sure, both princes and common people of the underworld who cast morals and ethics to the wind were during the Middle Ages humorously conceived. Hell is indeed perhaps the only contribution of Christianity to humor. Thus in that eminently devout and religious masterpiece of Middle English poetry, *The Ludus Coventriae*, or *Play of Conventry*, on the whole preeminently serious, the brightest spot of humor is a soliloquy by Satan. To Milton, as a faithful Protestant, Satan had lost his humor and, for better or worse, become heroic. Thought on such matters in the Middle Ages was more relaxed and diverting. Among the peculiarly resilient and cheerful Chinese this tendency appears more advanced still. Whereas Buddhism in India depicted a hell that was seldom taken lightly, in China the doctrine of the underworld, by the medieval period largely Buddhistic, assumed less austere aspects. Especially by the seventeenth century, when P'u Sung-ling collected his tales, humorous pictures of the underworld were distinctly common.

His *Saving Life* affords a typical example of a bizarre and essentially lighthearted view of hell's torments. Quite obviously, it not only lays no claim to orthodoxy or religious conviction, it is told solely to entertain and to amuse by virtue of its macabre images and infernal laughter.

A judge of the common court dies and goes to hell. There he learns that the shades are being prepared for their next incarnations. Most men, being evil, are doomed to become animals and hence are fitted out with animal skins taken down from a huge rack where thousands of hides are hung. This judge is doomed to become a sheep. A sheep's pelt is painfully affixed to him. But suddenly word comes from the Clerk of Hell that while a judge the dead man had done a single deed of mercy in sparing a person unjustly condemned. To his excruciating pain, the sheep's hide is flayed from the judge's limbs. He is dispatched back to earth in the honorable condition of man. Still, he barely escapes; the transformation is imperfect. Throughout his new incarnation in human form he wears the stubby remnant of sheepskin clinging to his shoulder.

### SAVING LIFE

A scholar from Shan Yu believed
He knew impressions he received
In earlier lives and could retail
Adventures from beyond the veil.
He said that in past life he, too,
Had been a scholar, but death blew
Life's candle quickly out and sped
Him to the High Court of the dead.
There in Hell he saw in glory
The Lord High Judge of Purgatory.
Cauldrons stood with burning oil,
With torture engines, coil on coil,
Through which the guilty souls were hurled
Just as we read of in this world.
There by the eastern wall were strung
Huge frames on which the fiends had hung
Skins of sheep, dogs, horses, deer.
All condemned to reappear
On earth in these debased conditions
Found hides fit for their new positions.
A skin is lifted off its rack
And fitted on each sinner's back.
This magistrate of whom I keep
Account was judged to be a sheep.
Fiends had already clothed him in
The livery of a fresh lamb-skin,
When the Clerk of Hell declared
That by him once the life was spared
Of one who in time long gone by
Had been unjustly doomed to die.
Hearing this, the Judge of Hell
Declared since he did one deed well,

Though countless sins decreed his fall,
One life spared redeemed them all.
The devils then tried, limb from limb,
To rend the sheep-skin clothing him
But found the going strangely rough;
No yank or pulling proved enough.
However, after he had been
Tortured both in flesh and skin,
They ultimately came to flay
The man and tore the hide away.
Still their success proved incomplete;
Their flaying was not wholly neat.
One tuft of sheep-skin still betrayed
The man beside his shoulder-blade,
A sign infallibly to tell
That he came recently from hell.

Many stories with scenes in the underworld retain a humorous element blended with a much stronger infusion of the sinister and diabolical. Humor is present but is tart and astringent. Such is the case in a tale developed with considerably more ingenuity than the foregoing and spun out to somewhat greater length, *The Censor in Purgatory*. Here the butt of the humor is again a member of the official class. Having pried too curiously into the affairs of men, this unfortunate bureaucrat decides to investigate hell. Popular report has told of an entrance to the underworld through the mouth of a nearby cavern. Although neighbors struggle to dissuade him from his rash and impious attempt, he is determined to make the effort. At first he is full of confidence in his success. Presently he finds himself in the Court of Hell, before the Judges. Being something of a judge himself, he is invited to sit upon hell's gorgeous throne. But it soon becomes clear that from hell *nulla est redemptio*. Being in, it seems, he cannot get out! Suddenly, however, a messenger comes from heaven announcing the gods' decree that *all* souls shall be released. Though at first elated, the censor soon finds hell's exit extremely hard to locate, a profound darkness covering all. At this point the truly inspired humor of the story becomes manifest. A benign spirit informs him that he will be aided on his way only as he recites passages from the *sutras*. (There is a trace of orthodoxy here but humor is more conspicuous than belief.) The censor has been a poor scholar, his memory retaining only snatches of a single *sutra*. Whenever he recalls a few lines, a light glimmers in hell, enabling him to take a few steps forward. Whenever forgetfulness clouds his mind, darkness returns. Only after long delays and painful stumbling does he finally regain the light of day. The final passage is indeed a divine comedy, Dante's hell lit by the kindlier light of Chinese fanciful humor.

### THE CENSOR IN PURGATORY

According to an ancient story
The entrance into Purgatory
Lies in a cave beyond Feng-tu
Bottomless to human view.
All implements of torture there
Are thrown in total disrepair,
The tools that men have sometimes made
To serve them in their vicious trade.
There are the obscene remains
Of worn-out fetters, gyves and chains
Left at the cavern's dismal head
Until another load instead
Is brought upon another day
And that in turn is hauled away.
Night-working fiends hurry them down,
Charged to the budget of the town.
This sight in the Ming Dynasty
A rich official came to see
Whom some would title an Inspector,
A Censor or a Tax Collector.
He had a boundless inspiration
For personal investigation.
He would not believe the vulgar saw
Told by the common-folks in awe

And only when he had the view
Of things themselves would believe them true.
People labored to dissuade
His dangerous visit yet he paid
No heed to them, but, rashly brave,
Entered the hell-mouth of the cave,
Holding a lighted candle up
Fastened in a common cup.
Two trembling servants at his side
Followed him, their fearless guide.
They had gone some half a mile
Plodding through the deep defile
When suddenly the candle's spark
Flickered a while, then all was dark.
They stumbled down a rocky stair
Hung between terror and despair
Till entering in all their glory
The Ten Great Courts of Purgatory!
Each judge was on his judgment seat,
His robes and tablets all complete.
On the East wall there seemed to be
A throne left as a vacancy.
When the judges saw this man
They all precipitately ran
Down the stairs to clasp his hand
And made him firmly understand
That time had ripened when his grace
Should fill the stately, vacant place.
"So you have come at last," they said.
"We did not know that you were dead!
We trust that you were rich and well
Before death carried you to hell."
Hua asked about the chair
Which they were offering to him there,
As if it were some special treat
Or lofty academic seat.
When he heard this was the Court
Of Purgatory, he stopped short.
Less moved now to rejoice than grieve,

He begged the Court freedom to leave.
"No, no!" they said. "Your seat is there.
Assume your honorable chair!
Isn't it absolutely plain
You can't return to earth again?"
Hua was overwhelmed with fear,
Begging the Court of Hell to clear
Their captive as a special case
Patently deserving grace.
The judges said none could proceed
Against the judgments Fate decreed,
Then bade their servant take a look
At Fate's irrevocable book.
This showed that on a certain date
It was his firm, predestined fate
To enter in his mortal coil
The realm of night and burning oil.
Hua read the words and shook
As though cold water from a brook
Was streaming down his shivering back.
He thought of all things he would lack,
How he would surely see no more
His loving mother of four-score
Or see, while on his sombre throne
In hell, fair children of his own.
Just then a heaven-sent angel came
With golden armor all aflame
Entering hell's dismal mouth
As one who brings cool drink to drought.
In hand he held a document
Which he was eager to present.
Aging, yellow silk portrayed
Whatever message Fate entailed,
All the judges bending low
Before their Master, row on row.
When the instrument was read
This is what the writing said:
"Grant general amnesty to all
Who languish in hell's darkest hall—

And note, you demons, we say *all!*"
Hua might therefore take his way
Back to the brighter realms of day.
The judges gave congratulation
On his more favorable station,
Setting him gently on his road
To his more amiable abode.
But he had scarcely gone a slight
Half mile when he was plunged in night
So thick and sudden that his breath
Was shaken, as he yearned for death.
Then suddenly a god appeared
Before whom thickest darkness cleared,
Red-faced, long-bearded, from whom rays
Of splendor set the dark ablaze.
Hua at once made up to him,
Asking how to escape this dim
And dismal chasm where he lay
And reattain the world of day.
The god succinctly said: "You must
Repeat the *sutras*, child of dust!"
At this he vanished, not a trace
Remaining of his form or face.
Now Hua saw his perilous lot
Since certainly he had forgot
Almost all he ever knew
Of liturgies or legends, too.
However, he recalled a shred
Or two that he had one time read
In the *Diamond Sutra*. Hands in prayer,
He ventured to recite them there.
No sooner spoken, than a spark
Of daylight glimmered through the dark;
Then faded memory broke the chain.
The night-time settled down again.
He labored fiercely to recall
How the next syllable should fall.
Step by step the man would go
Forward by repeating so

Fragments of *sutras* that he knew
Until the cave was traversed through.
Finally, as his memory cleared
Blesséd daylight reappeared.—
What fate overtook the two
Servants no one ever knew.
It would be useless to inquire
How they escaped the infernal fire.

Not only hell itself but the grim monster, Death, may resign his claims to total terror beneath the bizarre fabrications of Chinese humor. Poetic imagination makes sport on Death's doorstep. A good representation of this is afforded by an unusually brief story, *Death by Laughing*. The suggestion that, like the preceding, this may have been a folktale lies in the character of its chief figure and butt of eccentric satire. A rich man is hung by enemy soldiers passing through a town. The soldiers leave him suspended, presuming him dead. But servants come, take the man down and to their surprise discover him still alive. In time he wholly recovers with one exception; a wound remains on his neck. His head fails to sit comfortably on his shoulders. Several years later, once more a prosperous man, while eating and drinking at a feast with boon companions, jokes are told. The man, half drunk, becomes hilarious, laughs vehemently and in the end laughs so uproariously that at the point where his neck is wounded his head falls off, completely severed from his body. The Chinese are unrivaled in this macabre form of humor.

### DEATH BY LAUGHING

Sun, a master of the rules
Governing the local schools,
Tells of a wealthy man cast down
By rebels passing through the town.
First they clubbed the man half-dead,
Then blithely hung him by the head
With such a jerk that from the noose

The dangling trunk suspended loose.
Shortly the rebels left the place.
Next, the man's servants had the grace
To take the body down and found
Their master's windpipe still was sound
And still some feeble signs of breath
Negatived the threat of death.
Bringing him home to his estate,
These servants set his head on straight.
The next day he commenced to moan.
After his blood-stained wound had grown
More bearable, the man, half-dead,
Was mercifully nursed and fed
With a small spoon until at last
His limbs were firm, his head was fast.
Some ten years afterwards he sat
With boon companions in a chat
Where many jokes were told, where jaws
Were strained and ears dinned with applause.
Our hero clapped his hands and rocked
Backward and forward until, shocked
By gales of laughter, seams of red
Appeared between his neck and head.
Then, shortly, he fell truly dead!
At first his father claimed his son
Murdered by the jesting one.
To this the company objected,
So for the common good collected
A sum for which the man suspended
His suit and all proceedings ended.

The three foregoing pieces illustrate something of this sinister type of extravagant fantasy with strong increments of
humor. They suggest the phase of Chinese literature closest to
folklore and to influences from the more imaginative religious
cults. In keeping, however, with one of the most deep-seated
ambiguities in Chinese thinking, another type of humorous
story developed with its witty and somewhat cynical comment
on manners and morals, such stories being guided by a con-

junction of common sense and uncommon intelligence. In their mildly satirical humor they reflect the pronounced worldliness in Chinese thought, its urbanity and sophistication. They constitute humorous critiques of the official class, as the novel presently to be examined, *The Scholars*.

With a penchant for realism quite equal to their love of the marvelous, the story-tellers turned to many phases of social life. Here sex, the favorite theme of much Chinese fiction, is considered refreshingly from a rational point of view, the narrator's sympathy almost invariably with those who keenly enjoy a normal sexual life. The puritanical or repressive forces, as frequently manifested by parental tyranny, are subjected to a highly civilized humor. This attitude has already been seen brilliantly expressed in the celebrated drama, *The West Chamber*. Proud virginity or obstinate widowhood are commonly viewed askance. This becomes the theme in a story equally notable for its common-sense morality, its passing recognition of the supernatural and its tone of restrained, virtually elegant comedy. Its setting is high life; the central figure, a prudish woman, is, however, pilloried by the humorist as decidedly foolish. Her admirer, who is later so absurd as to be her platonic lover, is even more ridiculous, forgoing a wife of flesh and blood to die of devotion to a statue! The wife, a far more sensible person and, unlike this Chinese Pygmalion, made of flesh and blood, slaps the face of the Virgin, who has been elevated as a goddess. The story is respectfully recommended to Christian moralists.

THE MARRIAGE OF THE VIRGIN GODDESS

Before divinity was won
Ma was a lady in Tung-wan;
At Kuei-chi town there stands a shrine
To the Plum Virgin, now divine.
Ma was once betrothed but when
Her lover died she foreswore men,
Believing it divinely plain

Widows should never wed again.
After her death her kinsmen raised
A monument and duly praised
The lady, giving her the name,
"Plum Virgin" to enlarge her fame.
Some years later a profound
Young Confucian scholar found
His way to Kuei-chi and saw
This shrine with reverential awe.
(Kuei-chi was the midway station
En route to his examination.)
That night he dreamed a servant came
With summons in the Goddess' name
To visit her before the shrine.
This he did and the benign
Virgin said: "I thank you, sir,
Since you so graciously confer
A visit on me. To repay
Your courtesy in such a way
As seems befitting, I will be
Your handmaid for eternity."
Mr. Chin bowed his assent
And shortly after as he went
Townward the lady happily
Kept him loving company,
Then said in parting: "When your day
Is come, I'll carry you away."
Waking next morning, Mr. Chin
Was by no means happy in
This dream; but still, that very night
A villager in dreams caught sight
Of the Plum Virgin, who affirmed
The marriage in heaven as confirmed.
She also gave a strict command
That pious citizens should stand
An image of the man beside
Her own, as now a heavenly bride,
An honor possibly too small
Yet better than not wed at all.

The city elders, thinking queer
To have a young man's statue here
Next to their Virgin Goddess' shrine,
At first resisted the design
But since they shortly all fell ill
At last they did the Goddess' will.
Thus today two statues stand,
Virgin and man, on either hand.
Scholar Chin now told his wife
The Virgin Goddess claimed his life,
Put on his hat and robes, defied
All obstacles, and promptly died.
His wife, in rage, went to the shrine
Where the man with the divine
Goddess stood, a hateful place!
And promptly slapped the Goddess' face.—
The lady, in her heavenly life,
Now is called, "Chin's Virgin Wife."

Finally, a humorous tale of an almost wholly intellectual
nature illustrates how deftly the Chinese story-teller can skirt
the edge of satire and yet by virtue of good humor save his
work for the domain of singularly pure comedy. Few countries have created more pedants than China and few have
given the world so many brilliant poems, plays, and stories
ridiculing pedantry. This outlook gave the prose writers their
favorite subject matter. Chinese aesthetics and literary criticism attain remarkable subtlety; thought and style often reach
great suavity; rigid rules are noted only to be rejected in favor
of intuitive and perceptive imagination. A Romantic point of
view which nevertheless is by no means anarchistic is held
superior to the absolutism too often afflicting the orthodox
Confucians. The cogency of the liberal position as against the
conservatives or reactionaries is seldom so well expressed as
in one of the stories, or rather, in an episode of one of the
stories, to which Herbert Giles affixes the appropriate title,
"Smelling Essays." The characters in this dialogue-tale include
a profound, well-seasoned scholar, who is blind, and a voluble

and specious young man who brings his essay to be judged by his senior. Characterization of both men is swift and sure. The blind man is clearly an intuitive judge of literature, a connoisseur endowed with singularly refined taste. He observes that he cannot read an essay, since he is blind. Moreover, the thought of subjecting himself to an oral reading is more than his frail patience can bear. Nevertheless, out of the goodness of his heart he declares that he can tell the merit of an essay by the smell of the paper on which it is written when burnt. The burning of the essay by the young literary fop creates a foul odor in the sage's nostrils. A modest and more promising young scholar submits his essay to the flames, bringing forth a delightful perfume. Later, when the essays are submitted to the board of examiners, the specious essay wins the prize, the fragrant essay is rejected. The victorious student thereupon returns to the sage prepared to jest with him regarding his poor judgment. The man pleasantly replies that he is a good critic, with no pretensions as a prophet, and must not be held responsible for the bad taste and bad judgment prevailing at the time in the official centers of learning. The times, it seems, are out of joint both for good creative writing and sound criticism. A more sharply pointed and imaginative parable would be hard to find or a story or poem with more wisdom and less contamination from prosaic or didactic influence. Chinese critical thought appears here close to its most humorous and to its best.

### Smelling Essays

Two witty scholars, Sung and Wang,
With one less gifted from Yu-hang,
One day decided to resort
To an old ruined temple-court
Where, as their glances roamed around
That sanctified though dingy ground,
Where calm, scholastic learning reigned,
Suddenly scholar Sung exclaimed:

"Look, friends, and see a man of parts,
Master of all learned arts!
Though age has robbed him of his sight
He glows with keenest inner light.
Not the abstrusest composition
Evades his boundless erudition.
The paper that we just discussed
So inconclusively we must
Now hand to him to estimate
Its worth and veritable weight."
So they addressed this blind old man
And this is how their talk began.
Wang was the first to speak. He cried:
"Great doctor!"—Then the priest replied:
"No more of that! But tell me, please
The symptoms of your grave disease."
Then Wang explained: "We do not seek
Your service as men ill or weak
In body but we come to find
Help in matters of the mind.
We hear that while you cannot see
With eyes you see internally
And though denied the outward view
Know profoundly what is true."
The priest replied: "In my condition
How can I judge a composition
Which I can never hope to scan?—
You are an idiotic man!"
Next Wang replied: "Then it appears
You only have to use your ears.
Let me read my essay here
And so its contents will be clear."
"What, man!" the sage said, "don't presume
I shall consign myself to gloom
Hour after hour! I covet leisure,
Not to induce more pain but pleasure.
However, I can judge your prose
Accurately through the nose,
Nor is this the least offense;

In judging art good sense is sense.
Just burn your essay and I'll say
How much your lucubrations weigh.
Burn your papers through and through
And then observe what I can do."
Wang complied and threw a quire
Of paper in the sacred fire.
The old priest snuffed the smoke and said:
"Not so bad! You are well read
And competent to gain a place
In this year's academic race,
Even to win a foremost station
In the State Examination."
The youthful scholar from Yu-hang
Found the blind man's judgment rang
Unconvincingly and said
Aside: "Come, let us burn instead
A classic work that all men hold
A masterpiece, revered of old,
Making this blind fool hold his tongue
By proving his brash judgment wrong."
Readily the men acquired
An essay such as he desired,
The product of a famous name,
And cast it boldly on the flame.
One snuff was all the priest demanded
Until his lungs with joy expanded.
Before the work to ash expired
His tongue declared, "Divine! inspired!
Ah, how truthful, clear, auspicious!"
The savor is indeed delicious!"
The Yu-hang man felt a sharp pain
At this but dared to try again.
He threw an essay of his own
Into the fire. Dense smoke was blown
Into the nostrils of the priest
Who cried: "How dare you spoil my feast
With such a foul and nauseous smell!
May this stink descend to hell!"

At this the young man slunk away,
Hoping for a better day.
Later, when examination
Returns were published to the nation,
The scholar from Yu-hang came first
While Wang was rated with the worst.
In arrogance the former went
To see the priest with full intent
Of mocking him but he replied:
"The examiners you think keen eyed
And so mere vulgar judgment goes.
I see far better through my nose.
Besides, I spoke to you of art,
Which means a judgment from the heart.
Every honest man should see
I speak of art, not destiny.

*The Scholars,* a prose work of considerable length, reflects similar views shown in a much more spacious mirror. This novel by Wu Ching-tzu, written in the mid-eighteenth century, presents many problems of importance in the interpretation and appraisal of Chinese humor. Often described as humorous, it has almost as often been called satire. The theoretical distinction has several times been made and discussed in the course of this study. Answers can never be given wisely if put in dogmatic form, yet the issues crop up insistently, possibly more often in dealing with Chinese literature than in the description of any other. Although it should not be expected, then, that definitions of such elusive terms can be brought to finality, in the course of an argument something of consequence may be observed concerning the spirit and substance of a large number of Chinese masterpieces.

The peculiar difficulty in use of these terms where the Chinese are concerned lies deep within the spirit of Chinese writers themselves. With what may seem to a foreigner a sophistry of the emotions, the Chinese, it appears, can at the same time smile and be angry. This, after all, need not be surprising, since throughout the world experience abounds in such contradictions, as when eyes fill with tears of joy. Again, the Chinese, being to all appearances less romantically sentimental or soft-hearted than Westerners, seem often to find humor in incidents which might even seem to Westerners to evoke pathos. When a work of wit and trenchancy shows moral indignation on one hand or tender sympathy on the other it veers away from pure humor, becoming in the first instance satirical, in the second romantic. Naturally, like any other body of literature, the greater part of Chinese writing is straightforward and direct expression of the emotional life, without fires of indignation or direct expressions of sympathy with either joy or sorrow. It remains more or less objective, a reporting of events whether real or imaginary.

Beyond doubt Chinese tradition has to an unusual degree emphasized the moral sense. The outstanding role of Confucianism has stressed morality. Actions are judged as good or bad, ethically sound or censorable. Modes and manners have been established with remarkable firmness. Deviations from the straight path have thus been readily detected. The principles, strictly formulated, require, owing to the recalcitrancy of human nature, continual restatement and emphasis. The Chinese have, accordingly, exhibited an exceptional appetite for the didactic. All these tendencies have frequently played into the hand of satire and discouraged humor.

With a plasticity often surprising to outsiders, the Chinese have succeeded in developing both sides of a psychological condition; they can be extremely bitter and harsh, even to a degree that seems to others a height of cruelty, and also be particularly blithe, cheerful, and gay. Although a doctrine of the mean was formulated by Confucius and stressed by the earliest scholars following in his tracks, the social history often seems to refute this philosophy. On the one hand emotions grow tense and passions rise almost to a frenzy; on the other hand spirits relax as gaiety, fun, and frivolity win ascendancy. Sanity is achieved not by avoiding extremes but by balancing them.

A large proportion of Chinese fiction, both in short stories and long, maintains a serious tone. Much of the work may be described simply as straightforward accounts of life, without strong bias toward the weighty or the light. There are also many tales with a truly tragic insight. An unusually large number have a moral leaning. Of these, a considerable proportion also are unquestionably satirical. As a rule the satirical pieces are less personal and more moralized from a broad ethical outlook than is the analogous case in other cultures, for example, that of ancient Rome. Evil is drawn black, virtue shines bright. Sheep are segregated from the goats. This outlook has already been noticed in popular Chinese drama. The conception of hero and villain, protagonist and antagonist, has proved exceedingly popular in China and frequently discourages the rise of either the tragic or the comic sense, playing instead into the hands of melodrama.

This strong moral proclivity brings it about that in traditional Chinese fiction skies are often threatening and dark. Tales are sharply bitter; at least the bitterness remains sufficiently strong to repress the quality that Westerners are accustomed to consider humor. But the Chinese can smile more readily at the wry aspects of life than can most Westerners. The tartness of their humor has already been illustrated to some extent in several of the stories from P'u Sung-ling's famous collection. Obviously, the pieces cited here have seemed at least to the present writer governed more by the spirit of humor than of satire. Yet elements of the satirical they certainly possess. As well known, much humor involves someone's discomfiture. The reader or spectator laughs at the man who experiences a fall. The fall is painful to him, ridiculous to the viewer. The clown becomes hero in the literature of pathos. Humor can, indeed, be cruel; at times Chinese humor seems most cruel of all. When bitterness is in excess, a work presumably becomes satirical and not comic. The morality grows dense, the comic spirit becomes attenuated. No matter how the Chinese reader of such harsh scenes may feel or whether or not he laughs, the Westerner neither laughs nor experiences comedy.

Some of the most famous Chinese stories illustrate the character of Chinese satire and its mordant temper. Mention has already been made of the famous story, *The Inconstancy of Madame Chuang*, an anonomyous tale on a virtually legendary theme. The tale, as previously noted, contributed the plot to the popular Peking opera, *The Butterfly Dream*. This, it will be recalled, is the story of the wife who opens what she supposes to be the coffin of her recently deceased husband in order to procure a medicine for her new lover, in reality her husband in disguise. To the Chinese the story, as well as the play based closely upon it, is both satirical and humorous. Yet on the whole to Westerners it is considerably more satirical than comic, more sardonic than amusing. In appraising the mood in which the Chinese public experiences such works the attitude of the sage at the end of the famous story proves revealing. He becomes a misanthrope in general and a woman-hater in particular, ever afterward shunning female company. The Chinese, then, often desire their humor blended with much vinegar and salt. The French prefer another dressing, even for much the same dish.

The problems just considered are strictly relevant for the interpretation of Wu Ching-tzu's brilliant but difficult book, *The Scholars*, which is clearly a bitter exposé of the scholarly or official class as it appeared in the mid-eighteenth century, when the social system, whose roots were in Confucianism, lay heavily upon the entire country. The deposit of centuries had created a preposterously topheavy, ossified, and pedantic academic class which ruled the land, a government, so to speak, by aging professors. There is small doubt of the seriousness of Wu's attack. The entire book is a broadside launched at a single target. Although in its literary form highly episodic, in its moral and political intent it preserves a remarkable unity. The book's fame rests not only on its brilliant writing but upon its unity of purpose and, above all, upon the importance of the subject and the palpable justice of much of the indictment of what would now be termed "the establishment." It is a book in these respects almost without precedent, for few writers have had the courage to say what is said here and no other writer of Chinese prose had at his command such a vigorous style or such relentless force.

How, then, does the book differ in spirit from *The Inconstancy of Madame Chuang* and how can it be seen as humorous? At times, it should probably be admitted, its approach is truly satirical. Nevertheless, it maintains on the whole a remarkable blending of humor and indignation wherein humor as a rule gains much the upper hand. The author appears objective in the sense that he gives small evidence that he himself bears a merely personal grudge against the established system. Clearly endowed with astonishing powers of observation as well as of expression, he stands so far above the scene depicted that he may well afford to find it ludicrous. His art is purer than that of the satirist. Sometimes, too, one feels that he employs humor as insulation against a spectacle that would be unbearably oppressive or painful if viewed without humor and in its naked enormity.

Many angry books, especially in America, miss the mark because of their excesses. Their writers are moved so violently that their blows miss their mark. It is too easily forgotten that the best fighter is the man with the cool head, whose blows are closely calculated. Here beyond a doubt lies one of the best apologies for humor considered from either the psychological or the pragmatic point of view. *The Scholars* is a masterpiece of sanity. Not always did Chinese writers neglect the Confucian doctrine of the mean. In such masterpieces as this an ideal poise is achieved between an earnest moral purpose and a natural desire to afford entertainment. Humor is the salve that keeps the athlete's limbs nimble. The Chinese found a magic formula for this particular elixir.

Unusual, on the whole, as *The Scholars* may be, at least some rough parallels can be drawn outside China that assist in characterizing Wu's book. A broad sanity in the literature of social observation and reform distinguishes what is probably the most effective body of work in Western fiction of the nineteenth century, namely, Russian writing from Gogol to Chekov. There, too, wisdom and sanity were enlisted by writers equally skilled in realism and humor, combatting the dead weight of a decadent and an essentially cruel officialdom. *Dead Souls* is, possibly, the closest parallel in the West to *The Scholars* in the East. At heart the two books present notable similarities. But where there is so firm a base for comparison there is also a fair basis for significant contrast. First of all is the vast gulf between a society that has already achieved a most advanced stage in civilization, with certain of its institutions already showing marks of extreme decadence, and a society that has long suffered a rude and almost barbarous state of manners and which abruptly finds itself in the throes of a brilliant awakening. One civilization is threatened by over-ripeness, the other by the painful unrest of adolescence. Each is ripe for revolution, although their needs and specific conditions show extreme discrepancies.

The consequences for literature of these discrepancies in life are manifested by contrasting points of view in Wu's humor, which falls like sunlight and assists in hastening the growth of the new life as well as the disintegration of the old. The Chinese humor is essentially more complex than the Russian. The latter is more open and masculine, the former subtler and more feminine. In China the bureaucracy was poisoned by book-learning, in Russia it was deficient in it. One body of writing is burly and hearty, the other ironic and insinuating. In this respect, then, Wu Ching-tzu comes even closer to the great French humorists than to the Russian. His work combines the strength and sturdiness of the Russian heart with the suavity and refinement of French artfulness. A famous and often-quoted episode in *The Scholars* depicts a miser on his death-bed who, no longer able to speak, holds up two fingers as means of communication. Only his wife understands the dying man's gesture. He longs to have one of the two wicks in the bedside lamp extinguished, since two mean waste and extravagance. The miser dies true to character. Even in matters of stylistic detail, the scene strongly suggests Molière and such refined comedy as *The Miser*.

Here and there parallels between the Chinese work and masterpieces in the West may be found. Yet no Western writing approximates the total effect of the Eastern. Ingredients of satire and humor, morality and comedy are blended to give another taste and another sparkle. The Chinese wine is by no means identical with the French or Russian. Wu's laughter is at once peculiarly Chinese and profoundly universal. Strength and amusement stand poised in one of the happiest and most meaningful books known in the annals of literature.

No other work examined in these pages bridges the gap between East and West more smoothly or, for that matter, the opposite poles of past and present, ancient and modern. Here the chief cohesive force is a doctrine common, roughly speaking, to East and West, the doctrine of the mean. Moderation in this sense seems part of the saving grace of all civilized mankind. It has saved the humorist from many an outburst of satirical anger. Aristotle taught it from one angle, Confucius from another. In Wu's book the dislike of extremes is almost as conspicuous as the scorn of bureaucracy. Wu is actually no revolutionary. He accepts the basic theories of Confucianism as surely as Wu Ch'eng-en in writing *Monkey* accepts those of Buddhism and Taoism. The faults that Wu Ching-tzu finds with society as he observes it lie almost as much in emotional distortions as in bureaucratic paralysis and spring from the same source. The Confucian system of society is presumed in theory to be essentially sound; the trouble lies in wrong application of the theory and in excessive emphasis, whereas normal, serene living dispenses with stress and strain, avoiding evils of enthusiasm and excess. A passage clearly revealing this appraisal may be cited. An aging man has at last passed the examination granting him his entrance into the official or mandarin class. But he is so overwhelmed with joy that he becomes virtually a madman, rushing about his village, shouting wildly, crying "Passed! Passed!" His derangement threatens to be incurable. At length, however, his neighbors hit upon a therapy surprisingly modern. He must, they decide, be subjected to shock treatment. If he is struck violently on the head by the man he fears most, the evil demon of excess will be exorcised, opening the way for his return to sanity. The formidable villager answering this requirement is a hulk of a man, the town butcher, accustomed to slaughtering large animals at a single blow. The passage that follows has considerable interest from a psychological point of view, showing insights popularly thought peculiar to recent thought in the West though in reality quite in accord with discerning observations of life intuitively made in China more than two centuries ago.

They found the new graduate holding forth before the temple, dishevelled and smeared with mud, clapping and shouting, "Passed! Passed!"

Forbidding as one of the escorting generals in a funeral procession, the butcher went up to him and thundered, "You ne'er-would-die beast! Passed! Passed what?" and gave him a resounding blow in the face. All the neighbors laughed. But the butcher was frightened by what he had done, his hand trembled and he dared not strike again. Nor was a second blow necessary, for the first had felled Fan Chin to the ground. The neighbors hurried up to him, rubbed his chest and pounded his back until they brought him to. The butcher felt a dull pain in his palm and could not bend his hand. He repented his rashness and said, "Indeed a star from Heaven should not be touched. I am being punished for my sin." He brought a plaster from a drugmonger and put it on his hand.

"How did it happen that I am here?" Fan Chin asked.

"Congratulations, Your Honor." the neighbors said. "You have passed, but you were upset a bit by the news. You are well now, so please return home and send off the proclaimers."

"Yes, indeed," Fan Chin said, "I remember now. I won the seventh place." He did up his hair and washed his face in a basin borrowed from the drugmonger. Catching sight of his father-in-law he prepared himself for another scolding but the butcher said to him humbly, "Your Honor my worthy son-in-law, it was not that I was imprudent, but your honored mother wished that I should try to persuade you." [21]

By no means all the book's humor steps so frankly into the open as in the foregoing passage. Indeed, it is of the essence of the studied and deliberate style that one is rarely assured as to precisely the mood or view which its author prefers. A more elusive writer would be hard to find. Only a few generalizations may safely be made. On the one hand, he is presumably conservative, accepting the fundamental teachings of the sages, both of the Confucian and the Taoist schools. On the other hand, he finds that practice betrays theory; society is corrupted not so much by false ideas as by the decadence that has overtaken the old ideas when applied to actuality. The Confucians have become mere pedants, the Taoists mere anarchists. All this may be easily discerned through his amazingly broad canvas of Chinese society. Nevertheless, the picture is painted with such extraordinary objectivity that just what at any moment is in the author's mind proves as hard to discover, to use a ready parallel, as in the case of Shakespeare. One of the obstacles to a forthright statement is that he explores the wide spreading roots of the social ill in the general cupidity, the roots of virtue in the natural goodness in human nature. In each case his thinking is unsystematic although at least orthodox.

The book's terrain may best be charted by turning not to its more puzzling passages but to those where the intention seems most nearly clear. If there is any one hero in the narrative it is Doctor Yu, who presides over the Confucian ritual eloquently described in Chapter Thirty-Seven. This scholar has never passed the higher examinations. Only for a brief period does he serve the state at the capital and while there he clearly is uncomfortable. Most of his career is spent as teacher in an academy in Nanking, where he enjoys a considerable degree of intellectual and personal freedom. Even from this agreeable public position he retires in his later years. He is no innovator of new truths; he champions instead a return to the purity of old truths and old practices, a return to the innocence and ceremony of nobler and better times. Yet it is typical of the author's art and outlook that even Yu is not depicted as faultless. In some of his moral judgments he is clearly shown as over-severe. In the epilogue we are told that the temple over which this good man has presided has been allowed to fall into melancholy ruin.

Yu is the constant north star shining in a sky that has for the most part fallen into dire confusion. The humor arises from malpractices as seen through critical and discerning eyes. All classes are shown not only as fallible but as fallen. Episodic as the work is, it observes an underlying and artful plan. The prologue and epilogue are alike inspired for the most part by the Taoist outlook. The former celebrates an historical figure who flourished in what for the writer himself is time past, the philosopher and eccentric, Wang Ming. Rather than take a government post or a government examination, Wang conceals himself in a hermitage in the Kuaichi Mountain. The epilogue introduces similar thoughts but in a somewhat more humorous spirit. Here are four eccentrics instead of one, all four social bohemians divorced from the contamination of a stupid establishment. One is a calligrapher, another an herb-seller who delights above all in the game of draughts. The third has once kept an unprofitable pawnshop and later a small tea-shop; he delights especially in composing poems and painting pictures. The fourth, by profession a humble tailor, acquires small wealth but is also a true lover of poetry, painting, and wine. All four are seen as whimsical characters, humorous primarily because they are to such a pronounced degree detached from the heat of social and public contention, at heart relaxed and more amused than pained by existence. The author is not merely detached, as is T'ao Yüan-ming; he is a master of social comedy.

Within this frame of prologue and epilogue he paints a canvas with multifarious figures from all walks of life, the learned and the ignorant, monks and tradesmen, rich and poor, civil servants and untamed outlaws. Broadly speaking, he has his reservations regarding all and smiles at all, at the same time that he deplores the universal folly. A rough pattern is discernible. The early pages, from which quotation has recently been made, tend to pictures of villagers and the relatively poor; the later pages, to portraits of the affluent and aristocratic. The farmers are boors, the aristocrats fops; the former have no manners, the latter affected manners. Cupidity and materialism have corrupted all classes. True culture and pure taste have given way among the scholars to dry, pretentious pedantry. The ruling class is the scholar class, whose pride of place is founded on a system of examinations that has fallen into an abyss of stupidity and corruption. Much of the humor derives from the lamentable story of cheating in the examinations and the deplorable and widespread venality by which success is attained through bribes.

The handful of scholars who in some measure escape from the pedantry so pernicious among the Confucians is represented as at least mildly ridiculous because of their romantic moods and extremely perverse eccentricities. This becomes especially clear in one of the book's most brilliant sections, that depicting the effeminate and utterly unpredictable head of a decaying and once enormously wealthy family, the aristocrat Tu Shao-ching. He is a man of infinite eccentricities. His most fantastic characteristics derive from dislocations of the Confucian ideals themselves, for example, family piety. Thus he goes to any extreme of generosity to befriend any person who has in earlier years been in the good graces of his revered father. He is an essentially good, generous, highly intellectual man who, however, has lost his allegiance to the Confucian ideal of the mean. The author is clearly warmed by the spectacle of his lavish liberality, at the same time that he smiles at his total impracticality. So far does he remain free from the reigning vices of the mercantile class that he passes to the contrary extreme, becoming as ridiculous as, in the opposite manner, is the miser who protests the waste of two candles where one will suffice. The vulgar, it seems, worship property and material values in general; the decadent aristocracy simply does not know how to use the wealth in its possession and will consequently in the end become dispossessed. These are the pageants of human folly that *The Scholars* so vividly depicts.

Some generalizations regarding humor in China are, then, possible and a few have been advanced in these pages. But in the end a true statement of the case must be more concluding than conclusive. While unique qualities are discernible in Chinese humor, the sum of the matter is that virtually all types of humor in civilized lands outside China have flourished brilliantly in it, though never with precisely the same features as found elsewhere. Ultimately, all study of literature must be of comparative literature. In the house of humor are many rooms. Envisaging this house as a vast museum, at least a picture from China may rightly be in each gallery. As horizons in the twentieth century expand, pictures hitherto unfamiliar to the world at large are mounted on the walls. This book, to state its aims briefly, has attempted to display masterpieces of Chinese art and literature in these newly opened halls.

Nevertheless, if almost all the familiar types of humor are found among the vast treasures accumulated through some three millennia by Chinese art and literature, certain features may well be thought especially representative. These will in the nature of the case be related to our general conceptions of Chinese taste and imagination. The humor of any people is merely a part of its total culture or civilization, the section, one might say, on which the sun shines with special scintillation. The Chinese take humor seriously. It not only signifies happy surprise but happy intuition, a form of insight above or at least beyond logic. Hence they are indisposed to look down upon humor and condescendingly to admit a category of "light verse." Even in the earliest recorded times the Chinese people, whether in towns or in the countryside, appear both uncommonly humorous and urbane. Naturally, their humor and urbanity join hands. Their language itself abounds in intimations implicit in their written characters and in the halftones of its extraordinary inflections. Hence the incongruity at the root of all humor lies peculiarly at the root and germ of Chinese humor. This is less outspoken or obvious than ours, less dependent on verbal wit and even less conspicuously resting on the surface than humor of the Hindus or the Japanese. The refractions are peculiarly delicate, the emanations singularly subtle. For this very reason the field cannot be too often studied and explored.

There is, quite obviously, no possibility of pinpointing terms in an area of necessity so elusive. Reluctantly as it may be, one turns in the end to Matthew Arnold's device of the touchstone, quotation. The magic of a particle of oriental jade must serve as well as may be to carry a seemingly disproportionate weight of meaning. There is a famous quotation from the poet Ts'ao Chih, which may at the same time indicate the common ground that actually exists between East and West, between their seemingly disparate strains of humor and the peculiar quality of the humorous irony distinctive of China itself. The poem is at once homely and refined, like a common vegetable favored by a hand singularly skilled in cooking. The translation is by a witty poet born in China, at present living in the United States, Shih Shun Liu:

> Beans are boiled with beanstalks as fuel;
> The beans cannot help crying out in the pan:
> "After all, we two spring from the same root.
> Why press so hard with so fierce a flame?"

It is hard, I believe, to imagine this poem as derived from any other literature than the Chinese. It bears the pungency of a perfume perfected in only one land but enjoyable in all. It may, then, serve as a talisman for any inquisitive student of civilization who cares to enter and explore the enchanted world which is the traditional Chinese sense of humor.

# Selected

# Bibliography

### Chapter 1. Humor in Art

d'Argencé, René Yvon Lefebvre, *Chinese Treasures in the Avery Brundage Collection*, New York, 1968.

Bachhofer, Ludwig, *A Short History of Chinese Art*, London, 1946.

Bowie, Theodore, *East-West in Art*, Bloomington, Ind., 1966.

Bunker, Emma C., Bruce Chatwin, and Anna R. Farkas, *Animal Style Art from East to West*, New York, 1970.

Cammann, S., *China's Dragon Robes*, New York, 1952.

Cahill, James, *The Art of Southern Sung China*, New York, 1962.

————, *Chinese Painting*, New York, 1960.

————, *Fantastics and Eccentrics in Chinese Painting*, New York, 1967.

Chiang Yee, *The Chinese Eye*, London, 1960.

Cohn, William, *Chinese Painting*, New York, 1950.

Fry, Roger, ed., *Chinese Art*, New York, 1935.

Gray, Basil, and Sir Leigh Ashton, *Chinese Art*, London, 1952.

Gray, Basil, *Early Chinese Pottery and Porcelain*, London, 1952.

Grousset, René, *Chinese Art and Culture*, New York, 1959.

Gyllensvärd, Bo, and J. A. Pope, *Chinese Art from the Collections of H. M. King Gustaf VI Adolf of Sweden*, New York, 1968.

Hajik, Lubor, *Chinese Art*, London, n. d.

Hansford, S. H., *Chinese Jade Carving*, London, 1950.

Jenyns, Soame, *A Background to Chinese Painting*, London, 1935.

————, *Later Chinese Porcelain*, New York, 1964.

————, *Ming Pottery and Porcelain*, London, 1953.

Lee, Sherman E., *A History of Far Eastern Art*, New York, 1964.

Mizuno, Seiichi, *Bronzes and Jades of Ancient China*, Tokyo, 1959.

Priest, Alan, *Aspects of Chinese Painting*, New York, 1954.

Rowley, George, *Principles of Chinese Painting*, Princeton, 1947.

Sickman, Laurence and Alexander C. Soper, *The Art and Architecture of China*, Baltimore, 1960.

Siren, Osvald, *The Chinese on the Art of Painting*, Peking, 1936.

——, *Chinese Painting: Leading Masters and Principles*, 7 vols., New York, 1956–58.

——, *Chinese Sculpture*, 4 vols., London, 1935.

——, *A History of Early Chinese Painting*, 2 vols., London, 1933.

——, *A History of Later Chinese Painting*, 2 vols., London, 1938.

Speiser, Werner, *The Art of China: Spirit and Society*, New York, 1960.

Sullivan, Michael, *An Introduction to Chinese Art*, London, 1961.

Swann, Peter C., *Chinese Painting*, Paris, 1958.

Sze, Mai-mai, *The Way of Chinese Painting*, New York, 1959.

Taichung National Palace Museum, *Art in China*, 6 vols., Taipei, 1955.

——, *Chinese Cultural Art Treasures*, Taipei, 1965.

Visser, H. F. E., *Asiatic Art*, New York, 1952.

Waley, Arthur, *Introduction to the Study of Chinese Painting*, London, 1924.

Watson, William, *Ancient Chinese Bronzes*, London, 1962.

Willetts, William, *Chinese Art*, 2 vols., London, 1958.


Chapter 2. Humor in Poetry

Birch, Cyril, *Anthology of Chinese Literature*, New York, 1965.

Bynner, Witter, and Kiang Kang-hu, *The Jade Mountain*, New York, 1929, 1964.

Chen, J. C., and Michael Bullock, *Poems of Solitude*, London, 1960.

Frodsham, J. D., and Ch'eng Hsi, *An Anthology of Chinese Verse*, London, 1967.

Graham, A. C., *Poems of the Late T'ang*, Baltimore, 1965.

Hawkes, David, *Ch'u Tz'u, Songs of the South*, London, 1959.

Hightower, James R., *The Poetry of T'ao Ch'ien*, London, 1970.

Hung, William, *Tu Fu: China's Greatest Poet*, Cambridge, 1952.

Karlgren, Bernhard, *The Book of Odes*, Stockholm, 1950.

Lao Tzu, *The Way and Its Power*, tr. by Arthur Waley, London, 1935.

——, *The Way of Lao Tzu*, tr. by Wing-tsit Chan, Indianapolis, 1965.

Li Po, *The Works of Li Po*, tr. by Shigeyoshi Obata, New York, 1922, 1964.

Liu, Hsieh, *The Literary Mind and the Carving of Dragons*, tr. by Vincent Y. C. Shih, New York, 1959.

Liu, James J. Y., *The Art of Chinese Poetry*, Chicago, 1962.

Liu, Shih Shun, *One Hundred and One Chinese Poems*, Hong Kong, 1967.

Liu, Wu-chi, *An Introduction to Chinese Literature*, Bloomington, Ind., 1966.

Payne, Robert, ed., *The White Pony*, New York, 1947.

Rexroth, Kenneth, *One Hundred Poems from the Chinese*, New York, 1959.

Su Tung-p'o, *Poems*, tr. by Burton Watson, New York, 1965.

T'ao Ch'ien, *Poems*, tr. by Pao-hu Chang and Marjorie Sinclair, Honolulu, 1953.

Waley, Arthur, *The Book of Songs*, New York, 1954.

————, *Chinese Poems*, London, 1964.

————, *The Life and Times of Po Chü-i*, London, 1949.

————, *170 Chinese Poems*, London, 1919.

————, *The Poetry and Career of Li Po*, New York, 1950.

————, *The Temple and Other Poems*, London, 1923.

Wang Wei, *Poems by Wang Wei*, tr. by Chang Yin-nan and Lewis C. Walmesley, Rutland, Vt., 1958.

Watson, Burton, *Early Chinese Poetry*, New York, 1962.

Wells, Henry W., *Ancient Poetry from China, Japan and India*, Columbia, S. C., 1968.

Yang, Richard F. S. and Charles P. Metzger, *Fifty Songs from the Yüan*, London, 1967.

## Chapter 3. Humor in Drama

Arlington, J. C., and Harold Acton, *Famous Chinese Plays*, Peking, 1937; New York, 1963.

Birch, Cyril, *Anthology of Chinese Literature*, translations of *Li K'uei fu ching* (*Li K'uei Carries Thorns*) and *Han kung ch'iu* (*Autumn in the Palace of Han*), New York, 1965.

Bowers, Faubion, *Theatre in the East*, New York, 1956.

*Ch'ang-sheng tien* (*The Palace of Eternal Youth*), tr. by Yang Hsien-yi and Gladys Yang, Peking, 1955.

*Chao shih ku-erh* (*A Little Orphan of the Family of Chao*), in Du Halde's *History of China*, 1735, English translations, anon., London, 1736, 1741.

*The Fisherman's Revenge*, anon., tr. by Yang Hsien-yi and Gladys Yang, Peking, 1958.
*Ho han Shan* (*The Compared Tunic*), tr. by J. F. Davis, London, 1849.
*Hui lan chi* (*The Chalk Circle*), tr. by Ethel Van der Veer in Clark, Barrett H., *World Drama*, New York, 1933; also tr. by Frances Hume, Emmaus, Pa., 1954.
Irwin, Vera R., ed., *Four Classical Asian Plays* (containing *The West Chamber*, tr. by H. W. Wells), Baltimore, 1971.
*Kuan Han-ch'ing, Selected Plays*, tr. by Yang Hsien-yi and Gladys Yang, Peking, 1955.
*Lao sheng erh* (*An Heir in His Old Age*), tr. by J. F. Davis, London, 1817.
*Madame Cassia*, anon., tr. by Yao Hsien-nung in *The T'ien Hsia Monthly*, Dec., 1935, pp. 537–584.
Scott, A. C. *The Classical Theatre of China*, New York, 1957.
———, *Traditional Chinese Plays*, I, Madison, Wisc., 1967.
———, *Traditional Chinese Plays*, II, Madison, Wisc., 1969.
Wang Pao-ch'uan, *Lady Precious Stream*, tr. by S. I. Hsiung, London, 1935.
Wang Shih-fu, *The West Chamber*, tr. by H. H. Hart, California, 1936; also by S. I. Hsiung, London, 1936; New York, 1968.
Wells, Henry W., *The Classical Drama of the Orient*, Bombay, 1965.
*The White Snake*, anon., tr. by Yang Hsien-yi and Gladys Yang, Peking, 1958.

## Chapter 4. Humor in Narratives

Birch, Cyril, *Stories from a Ming Collection*, London, 1958; Bloomington, Ind., 1958, New York, 1968.
*Chin p'ing mei, The Golden Lotus*, tr. by Clement Egerton, London, 1939; New York, 1954.
Howell, E. Butts, *The Inconstancy of Madame Chuang and Other Stories*, London, 1924.
*Hsi-yu chi*, translated as *Monkey* by Arthur Waley, London, 1942, and as *The Monkey King* by George Theiner, London, 1964.
*Hung-lou meng* (*Dream of the Red Chamber*), tr. by Chi-chen Wang, New York, 1929, 1958.
*Ju-lin wai-shih* (*The Scholars*), tr. by Yang Hsien-yi and Gladys Yang, Peking, 1957.
Kao, George, ed., *Chinese Wit and Humor*, New York, 1946.

*Lao Ts'an yu-chi* (*The Travels of Lao Ts'an*), tr. by Harold
  Shadick, Ithaca, 1952, 1969.
*Liao-chai chih-i* (*Strange Stories from a Chinese Studio*), tr. by
  Herbert A. Giles, London, 1880, 1908, 1910, 1925.
*San-kuo chih* (*Romance of the Three Kingdoms*), tr. by C. H.
  Brewitt-Taylor, Rutland, Vt., 1959.
*Shui-hu chuan* (*All Men Are Brothers*), tr. by Pearl S. Buck, New
  York, 1933, 1937.
Wang, Chi-chen, *Traditional Chinese Tales*, New York, 1944.

# Notes

1. d'Argencé, René-Yvon Lefebvre, *Chinese Treasures from the Avery Brundage Collection*, New York, 1960, p. 62.

2. Lee, Sherman E., *A History of Far Eastern Art*, New York, 1964, p. 64.

3. d'Argencé, p. 74.

4. Ibid., p. 56.

5. Kao, George, ed., *Chinese Wit and Humor*, New York, 1946, pp. xxix–xxx.

6. d'Argencé, p. 58.

7. Cahill, James, *Fantastics and Eccentrics in Chinese Painting*, New York, 1967, p. 76.

8. Ibid., pp. 76–7.

9. Kao, p. xxxiv.

10. Watson, Burton, *Early Chinese Poetry*, New York, 1962, p. 240.

11. Hawkes, David, *Ch'u Tz'u, Songs of the South*, London, 1959, pp. 105–8.

12. Liu, Shih Shun, *One Hundred and One Chinese Poems*, Hong Kong, 1967, p. 29.

13. Payne, Robert, ed., *The White Pony*, New York, 1947, p. 177.

14. Hsiung. S. I., tr., *The West Chamber*, New York, 1968, p. xxi.

15. Ibid., p. xxiv.

16. Wells, Henry W., *Ancient Poetry from China, Japan and India*, Columbia, S. C., 1968, p. 428.

17. *The T'ien Hsia Monthly*, December 1935, pp. 532–584.

18. Birch, Cyril, *Anthology of Chinese Literature*, New York, 1965, p. 405.

19. Waley, Arthur, tr., *Monkey*, London, 1942, p. 7.

20. Ibid., p. 277.

21. Kao, p. 205. The translation is by Chi-chen Wang.

# Index

"Smelling Essays," 212-6
smile, 4
*Snow in Midsummer*, 131-2, 153-4
"Song of the Peach-Bamboo Sticks," 96
*Songs, The Book of*, 7, 9, 28, 42-67, 162, 165; individual songs: no. 1, 52-3; no. 2, 53-4; no. 20, 54-5; no. 21, 55; no. 39, 55-6; no. 43, 56; no. 52, 63; no. 72, 56; no. 76, 57; no. 87, 58; no. 95, 58-9; no. 96, 59-60; no. 100, 60; no. 101, 60-1; no. 125, 62; no. 129, 62; no. 135, 63; no. 136, 63-4; no. 138, 56; no. 141, 49; no. 184, 68; no. 190, 64; no. 217, 65; no. 225, 66-7
*Sorrows of Han, The*, 128
Southern School, 73
Spenser, Edmund, 31
"Spirit of the Hills, The," 200
squirrel, in art, 28
*Story of Ying-ying, The*, 113-4
*Strange Stories from a Chinese Studio*, 9, 169, 188-216
supernaturalism, 166
Su Tung-p'o, 68, 74, 76


T'ao Ch'ien, 68, 70, 72-77, 145
Taoism, 13, 23, 41, 51, 73, 79, 93, 103, 112, 165, 182-3, 185, 188, 199, 224
T'ao Yuan-ming, *see* T'ao Ch'ien
"Theft of a Peach, The," 190-5
Theiner, George, 169
Thomas, Dylan, 106
"Three Sennin Dancing Around a Toad," 24
"Through Snowy Mountains at Dawn," 21
tiger, in art, 25
"To a Monk on the Tai-Pei Mountain," 79
"To Prefect Chang," 91
toad, in art, 23-4

tragedy, 9
tragicomedy, 111
transformation, 172
*Travels of Sir John Mandeville, The*, 171
Tripitaka, 179
Ts'ao Chih, 228
Ts'ao Ts'ao, 149-52
tsun, 29
Tu Fu, 9, 12, 69, 74, 80-99, 153
Tung chih-yuan, 114
turtle image, 186-7
Tu Shao-ching, 226-7
type figures in drama, 129

understatement, 48, 65

verbal agility, 100
Visser, H. F. W., 19, 25, 32-4

Waley, Arthur, 169, 176, 177
Wang I, 70, 72
Wang Ming, 225
Wang Shih-fu," 111-129
"Wangsun, The," 72
Wang Yen shou, 70, 72
Watson, Burton, 70
Way of Heaven, The, 148
Wei Chuang, 108
*West Chamber, The*, 9, 52, 111-129, 210
*White Snake, The*, 160
*Wife-Snatcher, The*, 157
*Winnie the Pooh*, 181
wish-fulfillment, 132
wit, 4, 47, 99-100, 164
Wordsworth, William, 52
Wu Chen, 13
Wu Ch'eng-en, 169, 178, 183-4, 187
Wu Ching-tzu, 169, 216-27

*yang* and *yin*, 10
Yang, Gladys, 154
Yang, Hsien-yi, 154
"Yang P'u Moving His Family," 40